EXPLORING THEOLOGY

A Guide for Systematic Theology and Apologetics

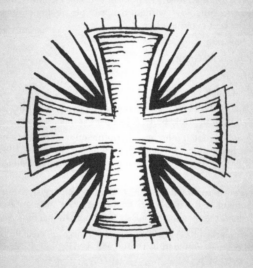

Three Books in One

CLARENCE H. BENSON AND ROBERT J. MORGAN

CROSSWAY BOOKS

WHEATON, ILLINOIS

Exploring Theology: A Guide for Systematic Theology and Apologetics

Copyright © 2003, 2004 by Evangelical Training Association

Previously published as separate books:
The One True God © 2004
Biblical Faith © 2003
Evidence and Truth © 2003

Three-in-one edition first published 2007.

Published by Crossway Books
        a publishing ministry of Good News Publishers
        1300 Crescent Street
        Wheaton, Illinois 60187

Cover design: Jon McGrath

Cover illustration: Jessie McGrath

First printing 2007

Printed in the United States of America

The One True God and *Biblical Faith*: unless noted otherwise, Scripture quotations are taken from the Holy Bible, *King James Version*.

Evidence and Truth: unless noted otherwise, Scripture quotations are from *The Holy Bible: New International Version.*® Copyright © 1973, 1978, 1984 by International Bible Society. Used by permission of Zondervan Publishing House. All rights reserved.

The "NIV" and "New International Version" trademarks are registered in the United States Patent and Trademark Office by International Bible Society. Use of either trademark requires the permission of International Bible Society.

Scripture quotations marked NASB are from *The New American Standard Bible*® Copyright © The Lockman Foundation 1960, 1962, 1963, 1968, 1971, 1972, 1973, 1975, 1977, 1995. Used by permission.

Scripture references marked ASV are from the *American Standard Version* of the Bible.

ISBN 13: 978-1-58134-962-7
ISBN 10: 1-58134-962-9

Library of Congress Cataloging-in-Publication Data
Exploring theology : a guide for systematic theology and apologetics :
three books in one / Clarence H. Benson and Robert J. Morgan.
    p. cm.
   ISBN 978-1-58134-962-7 (tpb)
   1. Theology, Doctrinal—Popular works. 2. Bible—Theology.
3. Apologetics. 4. Trinity—Biblical teaching. I. Benson, Clarence
Herbert, 1879–1954. One true God. II. Benson, Clarence Herbert,
1879–1954. Biblical faith. III. Morgan, Robert J., 1952–   . Beyond
reasonalbe doubt! IV. Title.
BT77.E97   2007
230—dc22   2007016749

VP		17	16	15	14	13	12	11	10	09	08	07
15	14	13	12	11	10	9	8	7	6	5	4	3	2	1

EXPLORING THEOLOGY

CONTENTS

Book One

The One True God

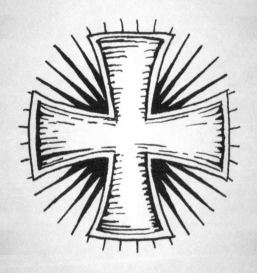

CLARENCE H. BENSON

Chapter One

THE NATURE
OF GOD

THE STUDY OF GOD is the greatest one in which man can engage. It is one subject that is truly inexhaustible. The source for all knowledge of God is God Himself, who has chosen to reveal Himself to men through the universe that He created and through the Scriptures that He inspired. Theologians speak of *natural theology* (that which can be known of God through nature) and *revealed theology* (that which can be known of God through the Scriptures).

Certain evidences of God rise from man's observation of the world about him. To those who have eyes to see, "the heavens declare the glory of God; and the firmament showeth his handiwork" (Ps. 19:1). God is the great need of the vast creation in which we live, and consequently He must exist. One might as well think of throwing a rope into the air and climbing up it or building a tower on nothing and expecting it to stand as to explain creation without a creator.

Is knowledge of nature or natural theology sufficient for a knowledge of God? Read Romans 1:18-25. Here is a picture of the heathen to whom God speaks through nature. The statement of Paul that "the world by wisdom knew not God" (1 Cor. 1:21) is strictly true of the history of religious systems. No heathen religion ever embodied the true conception of God, though some have had most monstrous ideas of Him. Man needs the revelation of God's Word and God's Son to really know God.

GOD IS A LIVING BEING

Shown by Nature

There is much evidence in nature to substantiate faith in the existence of God. Using facts found in nature, Christian theologians over the centuries have developed rational arguments to attest God's existence. The most enduring of these are:

The Cosmological Argument

For every effect there must be a corresponding cause. Since the universe (cosmos) is an effect, there must be a cause adequate to bring it into existence. That cause is God.

THE TELEOLOGICAL ARGUMENT

The Greek word for "bring to an end, finish, complete, carry out" is *teleo*. Our world reveals intelligence, harmony, and purpose. From the evidences of design and purpose in the universe as studied through the telescope and the microscope, it must be concluded that the cause or creator is intelligent.

THE MORAL ARGUMENT

Since man is a moral being, possessing a sense of right and wrong, his creator and judge must be moral.

THE ONTOLOGICAL ARGUMENT

Since the concept of the absolute being is necessary in man's thinking, such an absolute being must in point of fact exist. If this is not the case, then all of man's reasoning is merely relative. The Greek word *ontos* means "in point of fact" or "in reality" or "truly."

THE RELIGIOUS ARGUMENT

Archaeologists and anthropologists tell us that mankind throughout history has been religious. No culture has been or now is totally devoid of religion. Since the phenomenon of religion is universal, there must be some truth to it.

Perhaps none of these arguments alone carries compelling proof, but together they testify forcibly to the reasonableness of Christian belief in a living God.

Affirmed by Scripture

Scripture gives unqualified affirmation to the existence of God. The opening phrase of Genesis, "In the beginning God," sets forth the basic assumption of the Bible, and in the rest of the Scriptures it is never denied or even debated. So indelibly impressed on virtually every page of the Word is the Living God that to consent to its teachings is to brand atheism as sheer heresy. The best that the Bible can say of the atheist is that he is a fool whose reasoning stems from the heart rather than the mind (Ps. 14:1; 53:1).

GOD IS A PERSONAL BEING

The fact that God is a person is of great consequence. It is because God is a person that revelation, fellowship, and prayer are not only possible but also meaningful. God is not mere energy or blind force, nor is He the sum total of everything (pantheism). Rather God is a person who speaks, hears, sends, and blesses among other activities. Because God is a person, man can trust Him, know Him, love Him, worship Him, and serve Him. The fact that God is a person is clearly revealed in the Scriptures.

The Multitude of Biblical Inferences

Throughout the Bible names and personal pronouns are ascribed to God. These names and personal pronouns undeniably prove that He is a person. In addition to this, He is everywhere pictured as possessing the three essentials of personality—intellect, emotion, and will. The Bible clearly asserts that God knows (Ps. 139:1-6), God feels (Nahum 1:2-3; John 3:16), and God wills (1 Thess. 4:3; 5:18).

Explicit Biblical Statement (Exod. 3:13-14)

Moses had been commissioned to declare to enslaved Israel that the God of their fathers had sent him to deliver them from bondage. Moses said to God, "Behold . . . they shall say to me, What is his name? what shall I say unto them?" God's answer was, "I AM THAT I AM. . . . Thus shalt thou say unto the children of Israel, I AM hath sent me unto you."

This name is most significant. The main idea is that of self-existence and personality. The words signify the eternal God, "which art, and wast, and art to come" (Rev. 11:17). This likely is the origin of the Hebrew personal name for God, *Jehovah*. This name occurs in the Old Testament over six thousand times. Each occurrence is a testimony to the personality of God.

GOD IS A SPIRIT BEING

The Teaching of Christ (Luke 24:39; John 4:24)

Grammatically simple but theologically profound is the statement, "God is spirit" (literal translation), uttered by the Lord in response to the Samaritan woman's query. This remarkable statement deals directly with the nature of God as is clearly seen when "a," the indefinite article, which is never found in the Greek, is deleted. In His very essence God is spirit.

The basic meaning of *spirit* is clarified by the Lord's remark to His followers after the resurrection. When they saw Him, they were terrified, thinking Him to be a spirit or ghost. He banished those fears by stating that "a spirit hath not flesh and bones, as ye see me have." From this it is apparent that spirit stands in contrast to that which is material or corporeal. God, being spirit, is not composed of material parts. For this reason it is true that "no man hath seen God at any time" (John 1:18).

The Second Commandment (Exod. 20:4–5; Ps. 145:3)

The Ten Commandments are best understood in the light of the nature of God. The second commandment illustrates this principle. Because God is spirit, He cannot faithfully be represented by anything that is material. Any tangible, visible object, no matter how cleverly fashioned, serves only to distort the worshiper's comprehension of God. Not only is the concept distorted by the image, but it is also limited. That which is material is limited to time and space, whereas God, being spirit, is limited by neither.

The Image of God (2 Cor. 4:4; Col. 1:15)

If God were of a material or bodily nature, He could be reproduced. But God is not of the nature of the material world since He cannot be seen with material eyes (John 1:18). In fact, Moses was told that no man could look upon God's face and live (Exod. 33:20). If God is spirit, what is meant by the statement that man was made in the image of God (Gen. 1:27)? Elsewhere the Bible declares that this image consists of righteousness, knowledge, and holiness (Col. 3:10; Eph. 4:24). The image of God in man, therefore, consists in personal and moral likeness rather than in physical resemblance.

GOD IS ONE BEING

Christianity vs. Polytheism (Deut. 6:4–5; 1 Kings 8:60;
Isa. 42:8–9; 44:6–8; 45:5–6, 14; 46:9; Mark 12:29–30;
John 10:30; 1 Cor. 8:4; Eph. 4:6; 1 Tim. 2:5)

There was abundant reason for the first commandment to be thundered from Sinai's summit. The worship of the sun, as the most prominent and most powerful agent in the kingdom of nature, was widely disseminated through the nations of the ancient world. In Egypt the sun was worshiped under the title Ra. Baal of the Phoenicians, Molech of the Ammonites, Hadad of the Syrians, and Bel of the Babylonians were also deities of the sun. The worship of the sun and moon and other heavenly bodies is one of the sins most unsparingly denounced in Scripture. One of the first warnings to Israel was to take heed "lest thou lift up thine eyes unto heaven, and when thou seest the sun, and the moon, and the stars, even all the host of heaven, shouldest be driven to worship them, and serve them" (Deut. 4:19). The utter overthrow of the nation was predicted should this law be violated, and as for the nation, so for the individual. Any man, woman, or child who worshiped the sun or moon or any of the hosts of heaven, when convicted of working "such abomination," was to be put to death (Deut. 17:2-5).

Israel lived in the midst of polytheistic nations (Josh. 24:2, 14-15; Judg. 10:6; 2 Kings 17:33). It appears that the great purpose in their being called out as a chosen and separate people was to witness to the unity of God. No other truth receives more prominence in the Old Testament. More than fifty passages teach that God is one, that there is no other, and that He has no equal.

It is to be expected, then, if the Lord is one God, that the first and great commandment is the unity of all man's powers in concert and concentration on loving God (Deut. 6:4-5; Mark 12:29-30). An undivided God justly claims the undivided allegiance and worship of His creatures. He will not recognize any other claimant to divine honor: "My glory will I not give to another, neither my praise to graven images" (Isa. 42:8). All human religion is an abomination to God, and it is not for us to try to discover how much good there is in beliefs that fail to give God His undisputed right to exclusive worship. God will not accept a niche in the pantheon of heathendom. He must be all or nothing.

Christianity vs. Unitarianism (Gen. 1:26; 3:22; Isa. 6:8; Matt. 3:16-17; 2 Cor. 13:14)

From the earliest centuries of the church, evangelical Christians have insisted upon the doctrine of the Trinity. This doctrine has been defined by A. H. Strong: "In the nature of the One God there are three eternal distinctions . . . and these three are equal. The doctrine of the Trinity does not on one hand assert that three persons are united as one person, or three beings in one being, or three Gods in one God (tritheism); nor on the other hand that God merely manifests himself in three different ways (modal Trinity of manifestations); but rather that there are three eternal distinctions in the substance of God" (*Systematic Theology* [Philadelphia: Judson Press, 1907], p. 144). The Trinitarian doctrine has been assailed vigorously by various types of Unitarians through the centuries. Unitarianism charges that Trinitarianism is nothing more than tritheism or veiled sophisticated polytheism, thus violating the oneness of God.

While the term *trinity* is not a biblical expression, the doctrine of the Trinity is biblical. It is totally a product of revelation that man's reason could never discover. The doctrine is to be believed because the inspired Scriptures teach it. It is one of the most profound and difficult mysteries in the Word of God. Although the truth of the Trinity lies outside the capacity of our minds to fully comprehend and explain, the doctrine is clearly taught in the Bible. God is unique in this respect. There is nothing in nature that perfectly illustrates this aspect of God's being. Examples such as a circle divided into three parts; light, heat, energy; three musical notes comprising a chord; ice, water, steam; the body, soul, and spirit of man all fall short of clarifying the truth they seek to illustrate.

Although the Old Testament is not as explicit as the New Testament in this area of truth, there are strong inferences that are best explained in the light of the Trinity. The plural pronouns *us* and *our* (Gen. 1:26; 11:7; Isa. 6:8) cannot speak of creatures such as men and angels and hence must speak of God. Passages referring to the Messiah (Isa. 9:6; Micah 5:2; Ps. 45:6-7) indicate that He is one with Jehovah and yet distinct from Him. The Angel of Jehovah is described in a similar manner (Gen. 16:9, 13; 22:11, 16; 31:11-13; 48:15-16; Ex. 3:2, 4-5; Judg. 13:20-22). The Hebrew word for God, *Elohim*, is actually a plural form, although generally it takes a singular verb. These and other inferences in the Old Testament may find an explanation in the doctrine of the Trinity.

It is in the New Testament that the truth becomes more precise. Clearly the New Testament teaches the complete deity of the Father, Son, and Holy Spirit while at the same time distinguishing between them. Only the doctrine of the Trinity does justice to the plain teachings of the New Testament.

That the doctrine of the Trinity is taught in Scripture, there can be no doubt. By comparing Scripture with Scripture, it can be known even if it cannot be perfectly understood. In subsequent lessons we shall see how frequently and plainly the Bible teaches not only that Jesus Christ and the Holy Spirit possess the same essence as God the Father, but that they are equal with Him in power and glory. One illustration will suffice at this time: The Father is God (Rom. 1:7). The Son is God (Heb. 1:8). The Holy Spirit is God (Acts 5:3-4). The New Testament clearly recognizes each member of the Trinity as true Deity and presents its message upon this premise.

REVIEW QUESTIONS

1. In what two ways can a knowledge of God be secured?
2. What is our most complete source for knowledge of God?

3. What are the rational arguments for the existence of God?
4. What is the basic assumption of the Scriptures?
5. Give biblical evidence to prove that God is a person.
6. Of what practical significance is the fact that God is a person?
7. What is meant by *spirit*?
8. How does the second commandment indicate that God is a spirit?
9. What is meant by the statement that man was made in the image of God?
10. How did the call of Israel witness to the unity of God?
11. Briefly state the doctrine of the Trinity in your own words.
12. Why is the doctrine of the Trinity to be believed?

APPLYING DOCTRINE TO LIFE

1. Why is it imperative that Christians know about the nature of God?
2. How should knowledge of God affect one's life and ministry?

Chapter Two

THE INFINITUDE
OF GOD

THE PSALMIST WROTE, "Great is the LORD, and greatly to be praised; and his greatness is unsearchable" (Ps. 145:3). Even the atomic age with its vast scientific knowledge does not change this humble confession. The Bible clearly sets forth the attributes of God, but each characteristic has a dimension that is beyond human comprehension. All that God is, He is to the perfect or infinite degree. Man being finite in his being and understanding cannot measure God. He only can stand in awe of His greatness. To acknowledge this unsearchable, limitless dimension, we speak of the infinitude of God.

GOD IS ETERNAL

To confess that God is eternal is to affirm that His life is infinite. We cannot fathom the unknown future, but we might think back as far as the mind can go and try to imagine eternity. We speak of Genesis as the book of the beginnings. We read of the beginning of the nations, the beginning of man, the beginning of creation. But that was not the beginning. We may go back to the time when the angels were created—those sublime, empyreal (or celestial) sons of God, who were present to sing an oratorio on that prehistoric day when the earth was created (Job 38:7). But that was not the beginning. We may enter eternity where God the Creator dwelt alone, with all creation resting in His mighty, gigantic thought. We may go back, back, back as far as our imagination can fly and yet never arrive at the beginning, for there is no beginning or end to eternity.

While God has created such immortal beings as angels and men, He alone is without beginning and thus may be said to be the sole inhabitant of eternity. Men have a past, present, and future. God knows only the present, for both past and future are now to Him. Men are everlasting; God is eternal (Deut. 32:40; Ps. 90:2; 1 Tim. 6:16).

Alpha and omega are the first and last letters of the Greek alphabet, the language in which the New Testament was originally written. The use of these letters in Revelation 1:8 indicates that God was at the very beginning and will be at the end of all time. While eternity has neither beginning nor end, time has both. Time is swallowed up in eternity, and none can comprehend eternity but the eternal God.

GOD IS IMMUTABLE

Only God is unchanging and unchangeable. God is above all causes of change and even the possibility of it. This unchangeableness or immutability of God is closely associated with His immensity (He exceeds space to the infinite degree) and eternity (He exceeds time to the infinite degree). In contrast to the ever-changing world, of Him it can be said, "They shall be changed: But thou art the same" (Ps. 102:26-27).

God Cannot Change His Nature

As an infinite and absolute being, self-existent and absolutely independent, God is exalted above all the causes and even the possibilities of a change. He can neither increase nor decrease. He is subject to no process of development or self-evolution. His knowledge and power can never be greater or less. He can be neither wiser nor holier; He cannot be more righteous or more merciful than He ever has been or ever will be. He is absolutely above all law that governs time and change, for His word is law.

God cannot change in His relation to men and women. What encouragement would there be to lift up our eyes to one who was of one mind today and another mind tomorrow? Would we trust a vacillating ruler? It was because God is unchangeable in His mercy that there was hope for apostate Israel: "I am the LORD, I change not; therefore ye sons of Jacob are not consumed" (Mal. 3:6).

God Cannot Change His Word (Ps. 119:160; Matt. 5:18; John 10:35b)

It is the most natural thing in the world for a human's word to be broken. Why is it that our friends and relatives have a legal, written form for the slightest business transactions? Isn't it because we may fully expect man's spoken word to be broken? Is not man a changeable creature? How many times have we been deceived by those in whom we placed confidence? Is not man a limited creature? Does he not often find himself a victim of circumstances and unable to fulfill his obligations, however much he may desire to do so? Altogether, then, it is not only possible but quite probable that man's word will be broken. In sharp contrast we find that the word of God remains the same.

God Cannot Change His Will (1 Sam. 15:11; Jer. 26:13)

If God cannot change, how do we explain the Bible passages that speak of God as "repenting"?

This repentant attitude of God does not involve any real change in His character and purpose. He ever hates sin and ever pities and loves the sinner. This attitude is just as true before as after the sinner's repentance. There is no change fundamentally in God's attitude, although He may change his *dealings* in view of man's change. For example, God's attitude toward the wickedness of Israel did not change. He hated her sin, and because she persisted in associating herself with sin, of necessity she shared its penalties.

But when Israel, whom God always loved and pitied, repented and separated herself from her sin, God's dealing with her in consequence changed. As Strong says, "God's immutability is not that of the stone, that has no internal experience, but rather that of the column of mercury that rises and falls with every change in the temperature of the surrounding atmosphere" (*Systematic Theology*, p. 258). God may will a change, but He cannot change His will.

GOD IS OMNISCIENT

By *omniscience* is meant that God's knowledge is infinite. The knowledge of God is as precise, minute, and certain as it is vast and all-embracing. All that He says and does is absolutely true and right. He is too wise to make any mistakes. He can neither err nor fail. We have but to dwell upon this vast subject to cry out like Paul in wonder and astonishment, "O the depth of the riches both of the wisdom and knowledge of God" (Rom. 11:33).

God Knows All the Past (Acts 15:18; 1 John 3:20)

Man is a forgetful creature. Even with the benefit of papers and books with which to refresh his memory, he remembers little of the past. True, he may study what has been recorded on the pages of history. He may dig down and unearth the archives of ancient nations to learn something about the past. But how imperfect his knowledge, and how quickly he forgets it!

God Knows All the Present

GOD'S PERFECT KNOWLEDGE OF NATURE
(GEN. 15:5; PS. 147:4-5; ISA. 40:26)

God challenged Abraham to count the stars, that he might have some conception of the great numbers who would constitute his descendants.

But no scientist of Abraham's day would have ventured to compare the stars with the sands of the sea (Gen. 22:17). Hipparchus, the ancient astronomer, counted 1,022 stars, and later Ptolemy recorded 1,026. Jeremiah's declaration that the host of heaven could not be numbered (Jer. 33:22) would seem a scientific inaccuracy were it not for the fact that our latest instruments have revealed an almost inconceivable and incalculable number of stars.

But while man even today cannot count the stars, God not only knows the number but knows the names of every one of them. Can you conceive of any man having sufficient knowledge to call each one of the millions of inhabitants of this globe by name? And yet God knows the names of all the stars in our own galaxy, and an incalculable number in ten million other galaxies.

GOD'S PERFECT KNOWLEDGE OF MEN

(1) Man's ways (Job 24:23; Ps. 119:168; 139:3; Prov. 5:21; Heb. 4:13).

(2) Man's words (Ps. 19:14; 139:4).

(3) Man's thoughts (Ps. 139:2; Luke 11:17; 1 Cor. 3:20).

(4) Man's desires (Acts 1:24; Rom. 8:27).

God Knows All the Future (Isa. 41:21-23; 42:9; 46:10; 48:5-7)

In no way is the Bible better attested as the Word of God than in its revelation of God's foreknowledge. More than one-fourth of the Bible is prophecy. We have but to read what God said would be the end of Babylon and Nineveh and then walk through the ruins of these once magnificent cities to realize God's foreknowledge.

No prophet gives us a greater glimpse of God's foreknowledge than Isaiah. Judah was to be carried away by the powerful armies of Babylon. All the prophets had declared that, but it was left for Isaiah to challenge the gods of Babylon, if they were gods at all, to declare things to come.

Very minutely Isaiah foretells the coming of Cyrus, the conqueror of Babylon (45:1-4; 46:11). This prophecy was spoken when Assyria, and not Babylon, was in the ascendancy, and it was spoken of Persia, an inferior nation. In fact, the name of Cyrus was revealed 180 years before he was born.

Christ again and again predicted His crucifixion and resurrection (Matt. 16:21; 17:22-23; 20:17-19; 26:1-2; Mark 10:33-34). He thus proved not only that He knew the future, but that He was God. These predictions were so seemingly improbable and even impossible that the disciples were not able to comprehend them (Mark 8:31-33; 9:31-32).

Not a thing shall transpire in the next thousand years that is not already known to the infinite mind of God. Not a deed shall be transacted tomorrow or the next day or the next—there is nothing that shall transpire in eternity—but God knows it altogether.

God's Right Use of Knowledge (Isa. 40:13-14)

With all man's knowledge, he lacks the necessary wisdom to make a right use of that knowledge. Man is constantly making mistakes. "To err is human." But not so with God; His wisdom is infinite. Only God is removed beyond the possibility of making a mistake. He never experiments; He never changes His plans. The ages have not taught Him anything, and He cannot improve upon what He has already done, for His wisdom assures perfection in the first place.

GOD'S WISDOM IN CREATION (PROV. 3:19; ISA. 40:12)

In a musical instrument there is first the skill of the workman in the construction, then of the artisan in tuning its strings, and finally the technique of the musician in expressing the beauty of its tones. So in the works of creation we see the wisdom of God first in framing the world, then in tuning its parts to perfect harmony, and finally in expressing its marvelous utility in His wise government of all its creatures. The wisdom of creation appears in:

Its Variety (Ps. 104:24; 1 Cor. 15:41)

One never completes his studies of zoology or botany, for there appear to be endless species of creatures and a countless variety of plants. There are wonderful similarities, and yet even more marvelous differences in two leaves growing on the same tree. Even "one star differeth from another star in glory" (1 Cor. 15:41).

Its Beauty and Harmony (Eccl. 3:11)

The lilies of the field are more beautiful and fragrant than the most exquisite artificial flower. The movements of the planets in perfect harmony with each other are what constitute the safety and sublimity of the solar system.

Its Fitness and Usefulness (Prov. 30:24-28)

Divine wisdom is even more marvelous in its purposes than in its creation. There is a spider on the wall, but he takes hold on king's palaces and spins his web to rid the world of noxious flies. There is a tiny sea creature under the water, but it builds an island. The star in the sky guides a great vessel.

God's Wisdom in Providence (Ps. 104:13-14, 27- 28)

This can be shown in a multitude of ways. One example is the earth. We know how thin a covering of the surface of the earth is the atmosphere, that envelope of gases surrounding the earth, which sustains life. The atmosphere, so little appreciated because of its seeming abundance, is the medium of both light and sound and the means of both heat and protection.

THE MEDIUM OF LIGHT

If it were not for the air surrounding us, it would be dark except where the sun shines directly upon us. At sunrise, we would be plunged into immediate daylight, and at sunset into immediate darkness. It would not get lighter or darker gradually; there would be no dawn or twilight.

THE MEDIUM OF SOUND

If it were not for the air, we could never make or hear a sound of any kind. All sounds are made and carried by air vibrations.

THE MEANS OF HEAT

The atmosphere serves as a blanket to hold the heat of the sun. Except for this air-blanket around the earth, the daytime heat would be too great, and the cold at night would be too severe for life to exist on the earth. It is the atmosphere that makes artificial heat possible.

THE MEANS OF PROTECTION

Were there no atmosphere, thousands of meteorites, traveling in space and attracted to the earth, would fall with deadly impact upon its surface. The atmosphere serves as a cushion to arrest their velocity and break the violence of their fall.

God's Wisdom in Redemption

CHRIST, THE WISDOM OF GOD (1 COR. 1:24)

Wise men went to Jerusalem to find the King of kings, but the poor, humble shepherds went to Bethlehem and found Christ at once. God chose a lowly manger instead of a king's splendid palace as the birthplace of His Son. None was poorer, none humbler, none more lowly from an earthly standpoint than the only Redeemer of God's elect. Therefore, no one can say Christianity is only for the wise, the wealthy, or the noble. God makes it possible for all sinners to be saved and makes their salvation depend not upon their wisdom but upon their faith.

THE CHURCH, THE WISDOM OF GOD (1 COR. 1:21)

God chose twelve uneducated men to evangelize the world, to make it evident that it is the wisdom of the Gospel and not the wisdom of men that wins human hearts. God chose not warriors but weaklings to proclaim the Gospel, and the "foolishness" of their message conquered continents. They spread the Gospel, and the Lord received the glory—not the apostles.

GOD IS OMNIPOTENT

God's power is infinite and has no bounds or limitations except His own will. For Him to think is to act; to resolve is to execute. "Hath he said, and shall he not do it?" (Num. 23:19). He speaks, and it is done. Since His wisdom is perfect, He does not experiment but once for all executes a work that cannot be improved.

God's Power in Creation (Ps. 33:4-9; Isa. 40:12-17)

The first chapter of Genesis is not the only account of creation in the Bible. God's marvelous wisdom and power in the construction of the earth are reiterated again and again. The psalmist declared that by God's word the heavens were made and that the starry host was brought into existence "by the breath of his mouth."

When we are inclined to feel the world is getting larger and man is growing great, we would do well to read Isaiah 40. Note specifically how God's power is magnified in verses 12-17.

God's Power in Providence (Jer. 32:17-24)

Jeremiah was in prison when he offered this wonderful prayer. This was in the last days of Jerusalem, when the city was being besieged by Nebuchadnezzar. Because the faithful prophet persisted in proclaiming the ultimate capture of the city, he was imprisoned. But his sad predicament did not lessen his faith in the Almighty. He approached God with an acknowledgment that there is nothing too hard for Him who made the heaven and the earth (v. 17), and it is interesting to notice that when his prayer was finished, God answered him in the same language of His omnipotence (v. 27). Jeremiah magnified God's power in His specific dealings with Israel (vv. 20-24).

God's Power over Nature (Ps. 107:25-29; Matt. 8:24-27)

In Psalm 107 we have a picture of a storm at sea. The towering waves threaten to overwhelm the vessel as it rides one moment on the crest of the billow and then drops down to the depths beneath. The sailors stagger on deck like "a drunken man, and are at their wits' end." But how quickly the storm subsides and the waves are still when God is asked to intervene. God's special intervention in the laws of nature is called a miracle. These miracles in nature were not limited to the time of Christ, for many today can testify to remarkable answers to prayer: when rain has been provided, a scourge of insects has been stayed, or a forest fire has been diverted.

God's Power over Man (Exod. 5:2; 12:30-31; Dan. 4:30-37)

Some of the world's greatest monarchs defied Almighty God only to discover that all kings owe their place and power to God (Prov. 8:15-16). When the great Napoleon set out to conquer Russia at the head of the Grand Army of Europe, someone reminded him that "man proposes, but God disposes." The conqueror of Europe replied, "I am he that both proposes and disposes." His magnificent army seemed invincible, but God used tiny snowflakes to overwhelm it. The flower of European militia perished in the snowbanks of Russia. And God also used a storm to defeat the invincible Armada of Philip II of Spain.

God's Power over Satan (Job 1:10, 12; 2:6; Luke 22:31-32)

Satan, a fallen angel and the prince of the powers of darkness, is called "the god of this world" (2 Cor. 4:4), so completely does he dominate it. But Satan has no power over any of God's children except as God allows. This fact is clearly established in the cases of Job and Peter. God can set a limit to the power of Satan, just as He can stop the raging waves of the ocean. One day the Lord God omnipotent will reign over heaven and earth, and the devil will be "cast into the lake of fire and brimstone, where the beast and the false prophet are, and shall be tormented day and night for ever and ever" (Rev. 20:10).

God's Power in Redemption (Acts 9:3-6; 16:30-34)

How quickly God transformed the lives of Saul the persecutor and the jailer of Philippi who was about to commit suicide! Thousands today could give similar testimony to the saving power of God. One of the most convincing accounts of the grace of God is that of the transformation of the savage, spear-ruled Auca Indians who came under the influence of the Gospel through the martyrdom of five missionaries in Ecuador in 1956. This dramatic account is told in story and picture in Elisabeth Elliot's The Savage My Kinsman.

God's Power to Will

God's omnipotence is dependent upon His will. Even greater than God's omnipotence is His perfect character that controls it. Character is not so much made up of impulses as restraints. God's high moral character makes it impossible for Him to misuse His omnipotence. God's will, then, is dependent upon His character.

- God is infinitely wise and cannot will what is foolish.
- God is infinitely just and cannot will what is unfair.
- God is infinitely good and cannot will what is evil.
- God is infinitely pure and cannot will what is unholy.

GOD IS OMNIPRESENT

The omnipresence of God is closely associated with His omnipotence and omniscience. "Can any hide himself in secret places that I shall not see him? Do not I fill heaven and earth? saith the LORD" (Jer. 23:24). All-seeing presupposes God being always present. Pantheists declare that God is everything, but Scripture teaches that the Creator is apart from His creation. Astronomers have been unable to measure the bounds of the universe; thus it is most difficult for men to comprehend this attribute of God. We must simply accept the scriptural statement of the fact. The 139th Psalm speaks of the omniscience of God (vv. 1-6) and the omnipotence of God (vv. 13-19) but dwells particularly on His omnipresence (vv. 7-12). David realized that he was never out of the sight of God any more than he was outside of the range of His knowledge and power. In these and many other Scriptures (including Job 22:12-14; Jer. 23:23-24) it is clearly taught that God is everywhere personally present and acting.

REVIEW QUESTIONS

1. What is meant by the infinitude of God?
2. How is *everlasting* different from *eternal*?
3. Name three things God cannot change.
4. How does the fact that God is immutable benefit the believer?
5. About what three periods of time does God know everything?
6. What does God know about the stars?
7. How does God's foreknowledge prove that the Bible is the Word of God?
8. How does God's wisdom eliminate the possibility of His making a mistake?

9. How is God's wisdom shown in the events associated with the coming of Christ?
10. What suggestions of God's power in creation are shown in Isaiah 40?
11. Illustrate ways in which God's will is dependent upon His character.
12. What is the scriptural teaching concerning the omnipresence of God?

APPLYING DOCTRINE TO LIFE

1. What personal witness should be presented to a person who does not believe in the existence of God?
2. How should the omniscience of God affect one's life and ministry?

Chapter Three

THE HOLINESS, RIGHTEOUSNESS, AND JUSTICE OF GOD

IF WE WERE ABSOLUTELY convinced that it were possible to find on earth any man without a fault, we would make arrangements to meet him. If there could be found a human being incapable of making a mistake, would we not want him for a friend? But we well know that such a person does not exist. Diogenes, a Greek cynic, won an imperishable name for himself by carrying a lighted lantern around the streets of Athens by day, looking for an honest man. He never found such a person. In fact, Diogenes himself was banished from his country for coining counterfeit money.

There may be a man—yes, many men—who have no desire or intention of committing a single wrong; but, alas, there is no man of whom it can be said, "He *cannot* do wrong."

We have seen that God is incapable of making intellectual mistakes because of His omniscience. It is equally impossible for Him to make moral mistakes because of His holiness. And it is just as impossible for Him to render a wrong decision regarding the mistakes of others, because of His justice. "Shall not the Judge of all the earth do right?" asked Abraham when the destruction of Sodom had been revealed to him (Gen. 18:25). Yes, the Judge of all the earth shall do right. We shall now learn that His *holiness* places His character above possible reproach, while His *justice* makes His judgment absolutely infallible.

GOD'S HOLINESS

To be holy is to possess not one virtue or grace, but all. Even some of the best of men, who have become noted for some outstanding virtue, were pitifully lacking in others. Socrates was a model Greek but was cruel to his wife and children. Plato and Aristotle were teachers of wisdom but tolerant of the licentiousness of their fellow countrymen. Cato was proverbial for his honesty but was cruel to his slaves. The strongest men have some weakness of character that unfits them for perfect holiness. The crown of supremacy belongs to God, not only by an arbitrary act of coronation, but by His own inherent fitness to wear it.

God's Holiness Taught by Express Statement (Josh. 24:19; 1 Sam. 2:2; Job 36:23; Ps. 99:9; Isa. 5:16; Ezek. 39:7; Rev. 4:8)

IN THE OLD TESTAMENT

The holiness of God is emphasized throughout the Old Testament. God is called the Holy One of Israel about thirty times in Isaiah and is so called in Jeremiah and Ezekiel as well. In contrast to the idolatrous nations around it, the chosen nation was constantly impressed with the two great distinguishing characteristics of Israel's God.

- He was *one* God.
- He was a *holy* God.

After the law had failed to bring Israel to see the holiness of God, the prophets were sent especially to impress upon the people this all-important fact. To the prophets, God was the absolutely Holy One, the One with eyes too pure to behold evil, the One swift to punish sin.

IN THE NEW TESTAMENT

The attributes of holiness are ascribed to each of the three persons of the Trinity.

- God the Father is the Holy One (John 17:11).
- God the Son is the Holy One (Acts 3:14).
- God the Spirit is the Holy One (Acts 13:52).

The truth that God is holy is a fundamental truth of the Bible—of the Old Testament and the New Testament, of the Jewish religion and of the Christian faith.

God's Holiness Taught in the Ten Commandments (Exod. 19:10-13; 20:7-11)

The strict orders that were given to Israel in regard to approaching Sinai when God came down to utter the Ten Commandments with His own voice were meant to impress the people with His holiness. While the first and second commandments made emphatic the *unity* of God, the third and fourth emphasized the *holiness* of God. What pertains unto God—His *name* and His *day*—must be kept holy. It is well to be reminded of these important commandments as well as those that relate to murder and theft.

God's Holiness Taught in the Ceremonial Law
(Exod. 39:30; Lev. 11:44-45; 19:2)

The theme of the book of Leviticus is holiness, a word that occurs eighty-seven times in its twenty-seven chapters. Its keynote is, "Ye shall be holy: for I the LORD your God am holy" (19:2). This and the other books of the Pentateuch set forth God's holiness.

The plan of the tabernacle also presented God's holiness. God's presence was especially manifested in a particular room known as the Holy of Holies, which no one could enter but the high priest, and he only once a year (Exod. 26:33; Lev. 16:2).

God's Holiness Taught in Personal Visions

In the visions of Himself that God granted men in the Scriptures, the characteristic that most impressed them was divine holiness. ·

MOSES' VISION (EXOD. 33:18-23)

The glory of the Lord, which Moses was privileged to see, was in reality the glory of His holiness.

ISAIAH'S VISION (ISA. 6:1-5)

Isaiah was one of the holiest men in all Israel, but when he caught a glimpse of the glory of God, he realized and confessed his own sinfulness, as well as that of his people.

JOHN'S VISION (REV. 4:8-11)

Every glimpse of heaven that John was permitted to see and record is a picture of the glory of God and the recognition of His holiness by all the inhabitants of that place.

God's Holiness Taught by the Punishment of Profane Men
NADAB AND ABIHU (LEV. 10:1-3)

Nadab and Abihu were guilty of the sin of presumption. They debased their holy office of priesthood by offering strange fire before the Lord. Even though they were the sons of Aaron, it was necessary for these profane men to meet a sudden and miraculous death by fire from heaven.

KORAH, DATHAN, AND ABIRAM (NUM. 16:4-12, 31-33)

Korah, Dathan, and Abiram also debased their high office of priesthood, by rebelling against the authority of Moses and Aaron. Moses in his humility suggested that the Lord would decide between Korah and his company and Moses and Aaron. We need to note especially the warning Moses gave to these rebellious sons of Levi. "Seemeth it but a small thing unto you, that the God of Israel hath separated you from the congregation of Israel, to bring you near to himself to do the service of the tabernacle of the LORD, and to stand before the congregation to minister unto them?" (Num. 16:9). God's immediate punishment followed when the earth opened her mouth and swallowed up Korah and all the men who were associated with him in the rebellion.

UZZIAH (2 CHRON. 26:16-21)

Uzziah, the king of Judah, usurped the office of priesthood and ventured to burn incense unto the Lord. While he was engaged in this forbidden act, the priests and the congregation observed the marks of leprosy upon his face, and he remained a leper until the day of his death.

God's Holiness Taught by the Provision of a Redeemer
(Job 19:25-26; Isa. 59:1-2, 20; Rom. 5:8-11)

Sin is an abomination in the light of God's perfect holiness; hence the sinner must be separated from God. The sinner and God are at opposite poles of the moral universe. How can God punish sin and yet be reconciled to the sinner? The answer is Jesus Christ, the only Redeemer of God's elect. The cross shows how much God loves holiness. The cross exhibits God's holiness even as it does His love. God's love to sinners will never be appreciated until seen in the light of His blazing wrath against sin. Christ died not merely for our sins, but that He might provide us with that righteousness in which God delights.

GOD'S RIGHTEOUSNESS

Righteousness is the expression of God's holiness. Holiness has to do with God's character, but His holiness is expressed by righteousness in His relation to man. The righteousness of God may be said to be His *love of holiness*. This is shown by:

God's Hatred of Sin (Ps. 5:4; 11:5; Prov. 6:16; Hab. 1:13)

The presence and power of sin should be apparent to everyone. Sin is the ultimate cause of every sickness and every sorrow (Gen. 3:16-19). Sin is the undertaker that digs every grave and officiates at every funeral. Sin is the occasion of all want and wretchedness, all pain and privation. There are some men who say there is no heaven. They wish to know nothing better than this earth. If this is heaven, it is a very strange one— this world of sickness, sorrow, and sin. The man who has that idea is to be pitied. This world, which some think is heaven, has nothing in it to satisfy the soul. The more men see of it, the less they think of it. They go all over it and then want to get out of it. Thousands every year commit suicide in order to get away from it.

Not only are the evidences and effects of sin all about us, but we find that sin abounds within us (Rom. 3:23). Surely we are not so blind as to imagine ourselves perfect. We might sooner number the grains of sand on the seashore than the iniquities of one man's life. Even if we could number man's sins, no one could estimate his guilt. In God's sight the guilt of one sin—even such a one as some foolishly call a little sin— merits His eternal displeasure (Jas. 2:10).

God's whole nature is turned in utter abhorrence against sin. He is immaculately pure and cannot be tempted with evil. In fact, if there is any difference in the attributes of God, that of His holiness seems to occupy first place. It is easy to comprehend the awfulness of sin once we realize the moral perfection of God's holiness. His name is Holy, and He dwells in the high and holy place only with those who are holy.

God's Provision of a Holy Habitation (Ps. 5:4; 47:8; Isa. 63:15; Rev. 4)

Where does God dwell? We have already seen that God is omnipresent, but in His immeasurable dominion there is one place that could be called God's habitation. We learn from the Bible that there are three heavens. The first, as mentioned in the first chapter of Genesis, has reference to the immediate atmosphere serving the earth—an indispensable part of life. The second is the celestial heaven, which includes not only the solar system but the stars, constellations, and systems that constitute the boundless universe. But above all these and apart from them is the place reserved for the very special presence of God. Perhaps the most impressive description of the enthroned God in the presence of His worshipful attendants is in Revelation 4. Our limited senses as now constituted are too dull to comprehend the glory and majesty of this scene. In these headquarters of the immensity of creation, God dwells in a habitation of holiness.

Men who do not want to be holy on earth cannot hope to enter heaven. Even if they were admitted, they would not feel at home. As George Whitefield, the great preacher, once declared, "The unholy man would be so unhappy in heaven that he would ask God to let him run down to hell for shelter." Only those who "hunger and thirst after righteousness" "shall be filled" with the happiness and holiness of heaven (Matt. 5:6).

GOD'S JUSTICE

God's justice is the result of His holiness. While the righteousness of God may be said to be His love of holiness, the justice of God is His judgment of sin. This is seen in His:

Upholding Righteousness (Deut. 10:17-18; Ps. 89:14; 97:2)

God's love of righteousness requires that there be absolute justice and unerring judgment in heaven. His clear sense of right and wrong will not permit Him to show any partiality. He is no respecter of persons and cannot be bribed or influenced to do anything but what is absolutely just. He is the great champion of righteousness and justice.

Protecting the Righteous (Gen. 18:24-26; Ps. 96:11-13)

In order to uphold righteousness, God must protect the righteous, those who have God's righteousness reckoned to them by believing on Jesus Christ (Rom. 10:10; 1 Cor. 1:30; Phil. 3:9), both in heaven and on earth. The day will come when the righteous will be separated from the *presence* of sin. In the meantime God protects them from the *power* of sin.

Abraham declared that the Judge of all the earth does right. This was proved in His protection of the righteous.

LOT (GEN. 18—19; 2 PET. 2:7-8)

Abraham's earnest prayer for his nephew was answered, not in the sparing of the intensely wicked city of Sodom as anticipated, but by the miraculous escape of Lot.

DAVID (1 SAM. 17:37)

Whether David was contending with a lion or a bear or the giant Goliath, his life was secure because of God's protection.

DANIEL (DAN. 6:22)

The safest place in Babylon for Daniel was in the lions' den, for he was assured of God's protection there, just as Shadrach, Meshach, and Abednego had been protected in the fiery furnace (Dan. 3:28).

PETER (ACTS 12:11)

How peacefully Peter slept in the Jerusalem prison, although he was chained to four soldiers and had been sentenced to be executed on the next day. His life was preserved until his work was finished.

PAUL (ACTS 27:21-25)

The last chapters of Acts find Paul threatened by death again and again. Forty Jews took an oath that they would neither eat nor drink until they had slain the fearless apostle. The Roman government rescued and protected him, but this availed little when a terrible storm threatened to sink the ship and all its human cargo to the depths of the sea. Having escaped all this, his life was again in jeopardy when a deadly viper fastened itself on his hand. God wanted Paul in Rome, and the apostle was assured of His protection until he reached that city.

God not only protects righteous individuals but also righteous nations. Again and again He protected His chosen people, Israel. In like manner He has protected His church, and "the gates of hell shall not prevail against it" (Matt. 16:18).

Rewarding the Righteous (Ps. 11:4-5, 7; Matt. 5:6; 13:43; Rom. 14:10; 1 Cor. 3:12-15; 2 Cor. 5:10; 2 Tim. 4:8)

The Lord is said to try or test man's righteousness to see whether it is genuine. Happy indeed is the believer who desires righteousness and hates wickedness, for he shall be rewarded by an entrance into God's kingdom of righteousness. God has also promised a crown of righteousness to all who await with joy and expectation the coming of the righteous Judge to execute justice upon the earth. Here we are not always rewarded, but at the judgment seat of Christ we shall receive full reward for all the good we have done—not for self-glory, but for Christ's glory. The righteousness of God is a guarantee of all this.

Punishing the Wicked (Ps. 7:11-17; 11:6; Matt. 25:46)

There is such a thing as the wrath of God. God is holy, infinitely holy, and He infinitely hates sin. We get glimpses of what God's hatred of sin must be in our own burning indignation at some outrage. But God's wrath at the smallest sin is infinitely greater than our anger at the most shocking crime. God must punish sin or He no longer can be God. If He tolerates sin or fails to punish the sinner, He must henceforth abdicate His throne of holiness and justice. The kindness of a king demands the punishment of those who are guilty. Even the wicked will admit the justice of their punishment.

There is no better illustration of this than the case of Pharaoh (Exod. 9:27). After the plague of hail, he sent for Moses and Aaron and confessed, "I have sinned this time: the LORD is righteous, and I and my people are wicked." Pharaoh was not a repentant sinner. He later died in open rebellion against God. But Pharaoh here acknowledged the perfect justice of God in punishing him. And so it will be with every sinner at last. Every mouth will be stopped, and all the world will become guilty before God (Rom. 3:19).

REVIEW QUESTIONS

1. With what two great distinguishing characteristics of God was Israel constantly impressed?
2. How is God's holiness taught in the Ten Commandments?
3. In what ways did the ceremonial law give instruction in holiness?
4. What three men had visions of God's holiness?
5. Give three illustrations of the punishment of profane men as evidence of God's holiness.
6. How does the provision of a Redeemer suggest God's holiness?
7. What do we mean by God's righteousness?
8. In what two ways does God show His righteousness?
9. What are the three heavens mentioned in Scripture?
10. What do we mean by God's justice?
11. In what four ways does God manifest His justice?
12. What five Bible characters illustrate God's protection of the righteous?

APPLYING DOCTRINE TO LIFE

1. How is the holiness, righteousness, and justice of God to be evidenced by the Spirit-filled Christian?
2. In what specific ways has your life and ministry been influenced by the fact of God's holiness?

Chapter Four

THE TRUTHFULNESS, FAITHFULNESS, AND LOVE OF GOD

WE HAVE LEARNED enough about the holiness and justice of God to realize that it is impossible for sinners to dwell with a holy God or to escape the punishment of a just God. But apart from God's holiness and justice, there are other circumstances that positively assure us that the righteous shall be rewarded and the wicked punished. How do we know there is a heaven and a hell? God's *truthfulness, faithfulness, and love,* as we shall see, prove the existence of these places.

> *The heavens declare Thy glory, Lord,*
> *In every star Thy wisdom shines;*
> *But when our eyes behold Thy Word,*
> *We read Thy name in fairer lines.*
>
> *The rolling sun, the changing light,*
> *And nights and days, Thy power confess;*
> *But the blest volume Thou hadst writ*
> *Reveals Thy justice and Thy grace.*—ISAAC WATTS

THE TRUTHFULNESS OF GOD

The truthfulness of God is evident from the following passages: Numbers 23:19; Deuteronomy 32:4; 1 Samuel 15:29; 2 Samuel 7:28; Psalm 146:6; and Titus 1:2.

The Nature of God

God is not subject to those infirmities that lead men into falsehood. He "which keepeth truth for ever" (Ps. 146:6) knows about deception and hypocrisy, so common to man. God cannot be guilty of deception because:

HE IS TOO WISE TO BE UNTRUTHFUL

Only a foolish man lies. For some present advantage he may imagine the lie to be profitable, but sooner or later be will learn that honesty is the best policy. The truth may suffer loss at first, but in the end it is triumphant, and true wisdom will prescribe honesty. Do you suppose God will choose the policy of the ignorant? Do you suppose that He who knows all things is not wise enough to choose the truth?

HE IS TOO POWERFUL TO BE UNTRUTHFUL

Someone has said that men find a lie "a present help in time of trouble," but when has God ever been in trouble? A man may lie to gain some present advantage, but when has God needed anything? He says, "Every beast of the forest is mine, and the cattle upon a thousand hills. I know all the fowls of the mountains: and the wild beasts of the field are mine. If I were hungry, I would not tell thee: for the world is mine, and the fulness thereof" (Ps. 50:10-12). Men deceive in order to win honor and fame, but God needs no glory from His thankless creatures. To Him it is the greatest disgust of His righteous soul to be praised by unholy men. His glory is great enough without stooping to lie for the respect and honor of men.

The Character of God
HE IS TOO HOLY TO BE UNTRUTHFUL

Man is not a sinner because he is untruthful, but he is untruthful because he is a sinner. His tendency to deceive is due to his corrupt and depraved nature. But God is not man, that He can lie. His absolute holiness prevents even the thought or the temptation to be untrue.

HE IS TOO HONORABLE TO BE UNTRUTHFUL (HEB. 6:13-18)

What in the above passage are the "two immutable things, in which it was impossible for God to lie"? The first of these is His divine integrity, of which we have just spoken. God prizes His integrity above all things. His word must be fulfilled at any cost, because His holy character will not permit otherwise. But the second unchangeable circumstance that makes it impossible for God to be untruthful is His oath. Here He is represented as confirming His promise to Abraham by an oath.

THE FAITHFULNESS OF GOD

The truthfulness of God is manifested in His faithfulness. In the very beginning of human history the devil insinuated that God was untruthful. But what does the record say (Deut. 7:9; 1 Kings 8:56; Ps. 36:5; Lam. 3:23; 1 Cor. 1:9; 1 Thess. 5:24; Heb. 10:23)?

God Has Been Faithful in His Promises

THE PROMISE TO ADAM (GEN. 3:15; GAL. 4:4)

God warned Adam that if he ate of the forbidden fruit, he would surely die. Satan declared that statement to be false, claiming Adam would not die. But he did die spiritually the very moment he sinned, and by his death he proved God true and Satan a liar. However, God gave the repentant Adam the promise of a Redeemer who would bruise the serpent's head, and His word was verified when Christ died and rose again.

THE PROMISES TO ABRAHAM (GEN. 15:13; EXOD. 2:24)

God promised Abraham that He would make of him a great nation and that his descendants would possess the land in which he dwelt. For a period of four hundred years, however, his children would serve strangers, and they would be in bondage and affliction until God would finally deliver them from their taskmasters. God heard the groaning of Israel in Egypt and remembered His covenant with Abraham.

THE PROMISES TO MOSES (EXOD. 3:12, 21; 4:12; 33:14)

God promised to be with Moses, to teach him what to say, to give the Israelites favor with the Egyptians, and to give them an entrance into Canaan. Moses reminded the Israelites in his farewell address of the long list of promises God made and kept with His people (Deut. 26:7-9).

THE PROMISE TO JOSHUA (JOSH. 1:1-5; 23:14)

God promised to be with Joshua as He had been with Moses. So faithful was God in His dealing with this great military leader that in his final message Joshua declared that "not one thing hath failed of all the good things which the LORD your God spake concerning you; all are come to pass unto you, and not one thing hath failed thereof."

THE PROMISE TO DAVID (2 SAM. 7:8-16)

God promised that David's son, Solomon, would build the temple. Upon the dedication of that magnificent structure, the great and wise king declared that not one word of all God's good promises that He had promised by the hand of His servant Moses had failed (1 Kings 8:56).

God Has Been Faithful in His Judgments

History also records the fact that God has never failed to keep His word regarding judgment for sin. In every instance, unheeded warnings have been followed by punishment.

THE WARNING TO THOSE WHO LIVED BEFORE THE FLOOD (GEN. 6:11-13; LUKE 17:26-27; 2 PET. 2:5)

The great catastrophe that swept away the human race, with the exception of one family, proves that overwhelming numbers do not influence God's judgments. The unbelieving world perished as He said it would. The rainbow that God hung in the skies as the memorial of His promise never again to destroy the earth with a flood (Gen. 9:12-17) also proves that God cannot lie. There have been partial floods since then, but no world devastation such as Noah witnessed.

THE WARNING TO SODOM (GEN. 18:20-21; LUKE 17:28-29; 2 PET. 2:6-8)

Lot was a silent missionary in the city of Sodom. His example was a warning against the wickedness of that city, but even his own family did not believe that God would destroy Sodom (Gen. 19:12-14). Had there been ten righteous people in Sodom, God would have kept His promise to Abraham to save the city (Gen. 18:32). But there were only four righteous ones, and God in His mercy saved them out of the doomed city (Gen. 19:16).

THE WARNING TO PHARAOH (EXOD. 5:1-3; PS. 105:26-36)

Pharaoh was the mighty and haughty potentate of the greatest nation of ancient times. Why should he pay any attention to the Lord—a tribal god, as he supposed? But Pharaoh learned that the God of Israel was the God of heaven and earth, who executes judgments according to His decree. Study the ten plagues and their advance announcements to see how accurately God kept His word.

THE WARNING TO ISRAEL (DEUT. 7:6-11; JER. 25:3-11)

Again and again God's chosen people were warned by faithful prophets, "rising early and speaking" (Jer. 25:3), that they would lose their liberty and their land if they did not repent of their national sins and return unto the Lord. And though Israel was His "peculiar treasure" (Exod. 19:5) and dearly loved for the faith of their fathers, yet God punished His children.

THE WARNING TO NINEVEH AND BABYLON

Two prophets, Nahum and Habakkuk, wrote exclusively about the impending doom of these majestic and magnificent cities of ancient days. At the time they were in the height of their power, and nothing seemed further remote than their destruction. Ask the wastes of Nineveh; turn to the mounds of Babylon! We may boldly ask the traveler, "Has He said, and hath He not done it? Has God's curse been an idle word? Have His words fallen to the ground?"

THE LOVE OF GOD

The apostle John, through the Spirit of God, penned for us some of the most profound insights into the nature of God in remarkably short statements: God is spirit (John 4:24), God is light (1 John 1:5), and God is love (1 John 4:8). Of all the characteristics of the divine nature, none moves the human heart or reaches our deepest need more than love. Small wonder that John 3:16 has been the favorite text for multitudes of believers. That verse magnifies not the infinite wisdom, absolute power, or immaculate holiness of God, but the greatness of His love.

Whom Does God Love?

HIS SON (MATT. 3:17; 17:5; MARK 1:11; 9:7; LUKE 9:35; 20:13; JOHN 5:20; 15:9; 17:24)

Every time the voice from heaven witnessed to the fact that Jesus was the Christ, it spoke of Him as the *beloved* Son. At His baptism and again at the Transfiguration we hear this expression of endearment, as well as testimony of approval. Christ also referred to the love of the Father for Him, in speaking both to the unbelieving Jews and to the sympathetic disciples.

"In the beginning God created the heaven" (Gen. 1:1), but the day that He began to love the Son was long before this. Of course, if the love of God is eternal, as His very nature requires, then that love must have had an eternal object to love. So Christ in addressing the Father says, "Thou lovedst me before the foundation of the world" (John 17:24).

HIS CHILDREN (DEUT. 7:6-8; JOHN 14:21-23; 16:27; 17:23; 1 JOHN 3:1-2)

Moses declared that God had chosen Israel above all the peoples that were on the earth not because of their numbers or any commendable characteristic, but simply because He loved them. Moreover, He loved them because He first loved Abraham, Isaac, and Jacob, their fathers (Deut. 4:37) and was keeping His covenant with them.

In His farewell address, Christ had much to say about the love of the Father for the Son, but He reached the climax when He said, "He that loveth me shall be loved of my Father" (John 14:21). Three times He compared the Father's love for the disciples with God's love for the Son. If we truly believe these words, we shall realize that we are not on the outskirts of God's love but in its very midst. There stands Christ in the very center of God's love, and He draws us to Himself, that we might enjoy the same warmth of love that the Father lavishes upon Him.

What honor that in this incalculable, incomprehensible universe there should be found intelligent beings so highly honored as to be called sons of God! Wherever this term is found in the Old Testament, invariably it refers to the angels. When we think of the majesty of these celestial, eternal creatures, we are not surprised that they are called the sons of God. The marvel is that this term should now be associated with such vastly subordinate creatures as constitute the human race. No wonder the apostle cried, "Behold, what manner of love the Father hath bestowed upon us, that we should be called the sons of God" (1 John 3:1). Sons of God! Heirs of glory! Princes of supreme sovereignty! Participants of endless bliss!

HIS ENEMIES (JOHN 3:16; ROM. 5:8)

"For God so loved the world" was a startling truth to Nicodemus, who thought God was concerned only about the Jews (John 3:16). God loved not the Jew only, but also the Gentile; not a part of the world, but every man in it, irrespective of his moral character.

God takes no pleasure in the death of His enemies but is "longsuffering to us-ward, not willing that any should perish, but that all should come to repentance" (2 Pet. 3:9). Christ's mission to this earth was for the rebellious sinner: "While we were yet sinners, Christ died for us" (Rom. 5:8). Thus God commended His love toward wayward ones.

How Does God Love?

BY HIS GOODNESS (PS. 25:8; 33:5; 34:8; 65:9; 68:19; 119:68; 145:7; MATT. 5:45; ACTS 14:17)

The smiles of God's benevolence are upon all creation. God's hand feeds all His creatures. He sweetens the clover top to the cattle's taste, provides the mountain stream from which the deer may drink, pours nectar into the cup of the honeysuckle to refresh the hummingbird, and spreads a banquet of blossoms for the honeybee.

And how good God is to the human race! The necessities of life are provided in abundance. Man has all the air and all the water he needs; the heat and light of the glorious sunshine are provided—all without money and without price. We are created amid conditions that are just suited to our life and fitted to make us happy. The light is suited to the eye, the ear to the atmosphere.

BY HIS DISCIPLINE (PROV. 3:12; HEB. 12:6-11; REV. 3:19)

God cares enough for His children to guide them and correct them. Earth is not our permanent home. It is only a place in which we are being prepared for a future state. School is good for a child, although the study may at times be tedious. The discipline of suffering is good for man, although at the time it is not joyous but grievous. Men have said, "If God would only tell me that He loves me!" Well, if He has sent you sorrow or pain, He has told you that He loves you. "Happy is the man whom God correcteth" (Job 5:17). This is a deep, reassuring truth—that He orders each particular blow or weight or sorrow or fretting care or harassing discomfort or unrest in His all-wise love, fitting each trial to our own particular temperament. It is not merely an all-wise God, unseen, unfelt, at a distance, who guides all things in perfect wisdom for the good of each individual creature that He has made. Rather God manifests individual, infinite, personal love. He who loves us infinitely, loves us individually.

BY HIS MERCY (DEUT. 4:31; PS. 86:5; 103:8, 17-18; 145:8-9; 2 PET. 3:9)

Mercy is kindness for the miserable—pity, compassion, forbearance, gentleness. It is synonymous with the term "loving-kindness," so frequently found in Scripture. Loving-kindness is the attribute of God that leads Him to bestow upon His obedient children constant and choice blessings. "He that trusteth in the LORD, mercy shall compass him about" (Ps. 32:10). This act of trust on the part of the believer protects him just as in the case of a parent and a child. The moment we throw ourselves on God, we are enveloped in His mercy. Mercy is our environment and protects us like a fiery wall, so that no evil can break through. God's mercy is seen, too, not only in healing the sick in answer to prayer when it is His will to do so (Phil. 2:27), but also in comforting sorrowing loved ones (2 Cor. 1:4).

Mercy is exercised also toward the disobedient, by long-suffering and forbearance. If God should deal with them in justice, they would be cut off immediately. "Nevertheless for thy great mercies' sake thou didst not utterly consume them, nor forsake them; for thou art a gracious and merciful God" (Neh. 9:31). "It is of the LORD's mercies that we are not consumed" (Lam. 3:22). The sinner is already condemned, but God in mercy is seemingly reluctant to carry out the sentence. He spares him as long as it is right that a condemned man should live. It was through His mercy that God spared Sodom until Lot could escape. It was by His mercy that the Canaanites were permitted to live four hundred years after their land had been given to Abraham for a possession. God is slow to execute sentence, even when He has declared it.

BY HIS GRACE (PS. 84:11; ACTS 11:20-23; 13:43; ROM. 3:24-25; 1 TIM. 1:14)

Grace is unmerited favor. It is unexpected love exercised toward the unworthy. Mercy is the term more frequently used in the Old Testament, since God's loving-kindness was primarily exercised toward His chosen people Israel. Grace, on the other hand, is emphasized in the New Testament, since the term receives its largest use in expressing God's unmerited favor to the Gentiles. God showed mercy to Israel because of His covenant with Abraham, but He showed grace to those who had no claims on Him. When the disobedient Jews claimed their rights as children of Abraham, John the Baptist declared that God could raise up children out of stones (Matt. 3:9). Even the Jews, under the terms of the old covenant, were not justified by works or covenant rights but by the grace of God expressed in the atonement of His beloved Son (Rom. 3:21-25). God showed His regard for Israel by giving the nation His law, and His mercy to those who disobeyed as well as those who obeyed it, but *grace* and truth came by Jesus Christ (John 1:17).

THE GRACE OF GOD (2 COR. 8:9; EPH. 1:7)

The grace of our Lord Jesus Christ was expressed by the fact that "though he was rich, yet for your sakes he became poor, that ye through his poverty might become rich" (2 Cor. 8:9). The riches of God's grace were expressed by the forgiveness of our sins, by redemption through the blood of Christ. Grace was God's disrobing Himself of all His splendor and coming down to the earth as an unwelcome guest to show His love for a rebellious people (Phil. 2:5-8). Grace is God dressed in the crimson robes of a dying Redeemer, courting the love of the unholy and unlovely. Grace is God's lay-ing aside His glory, that He might express His abhorrence of man's sin by enduring its penalties instead of inflicting them. Grace is God's following the unbeliever through life, exhibiting His wounded hands and feet to prove and plead His love. Grace is the Good Shepherd going out into the wilderness after the wayward sheep before there is any alarm felt because of its danger or any desire on its part to return.

THE RICHES OF GOD'S GRACE (EPH. 2:4-7)

The riches of God's grace include not only the condescension and redemption of the Lord Jesus Christ, but the resurrection, exaltation, and glorification of the humble believer. Grace is so amazing, so marvelous that it will be the theme of admiration and wonder in the ages to come. It is only when we understand something of the greatness of God—his greatness in power and pomp and possessions—that we can realize something of the riches of His grace in giving such insignificant, unworthy, and even rebellious creatures the unmerited privilege of sharing His glory (Titus 3:3-7). The song of heaven, the hymn of eternity, will be the song of the redeemed, rejoicing in the grace of God (Rev. 5:9-10).

REVIEW QUESTIONS

1. Prove the truthfulness of God by His nature.
2. How does the character of God guarantee His truthfulness?
3. Give five illustrations of God's faithfulness in His promises.
4. Give five illustrations that prove God has been faithful in His judgments.
5. How did God fulfill His promise to Adam?
6. How was God's faithfulness seen in the Flood?
7. Why is the love of God said to be the greatest of all His attributes?
8. Whom does God love?
9. What Bible passages teach about God's love for His children?
10. How do we know that God loves His enemies?
11. How does God love?
12. What was the grace of God in Jesus Christ?

APPLYING DOCTRINE TO LIFE

1. How are the truthfulness, faithfulness, and love of God to be evidenced by the Spirit-filled Christian?
2. Compare the relative importance of God's faithfulness and yours in your relationships and ministry to others.

Chapter Five

THE WORKS
OF GOD

PSALM 19 PROCLAIMS that God is the author of two books—the book of nature and the book of His own self-revelation, the Word of God. The book of nature is a large and fascinating volume containing many chapters such as astronomy, geology, and botany. To master the content of any one of these would require years. Our concern, however, is to study God's work of creation in the light of biblical knowledge. Eight characteristics of creation will be noted. These not only witness to the handiwork of the Creator but also represent some attribute of His divine nature.

GOD'S WORK OF CREATION

God's work of creation is the making of all things out of nothing by the word of His power in the span of six days, and proclaiming all of it very good.

The Method of Creation—the Power of God (Ps. 33:6-9; 115:3; Jer. 10:12-13)

"And God said" introduces nine verses of the creation chapter (Gen. 1). It was the infinite power of God that gave His word immediate obedience. "He spake, and it was done" (Ps. 33:9). No waiting millions of years for some tedious process of evolution. God's power produced immediate and complete results.

The fallacy of the evolutionary theory lies in the fact that men arrive at conclusions by inferences drawn from facts. The truth is that the similarity between men and other species merely proves a common creator, not a common ancestor; a common author, not a common derivation. Works of art by the same artist are usually recognized because of similarities. But the real marvel of creation is the diversity and not the resemblance of its constituent parts. Man's inventions need to be patented to prevent reproduction, so prone is human nature to copy; but the Master Mind is inexhaustible in its types and patterns.

The Plan of Creation—the Wisdom of God (Job 26:7; 36:26-29; 38:36-41; Ps. 40:5; 95:5; 104:24; Prov. 3:19)

In Job we read of the marvel of gravitation and "the balancings of the clouds" (37:16). Life is possible upon this globe only because of its atmosphere and its proper distance from the sun. How is the latter maintained? By gravitation, an invisible cable five thousand miles in diameter and ninety-three million miles in length. To prepare a connection of such vast proportions is beyond the resources of man; even if it were completed, he would not have the power to attach it to the sun.

The divine wisdom in planning the system for watering the earth is equally marvelous. Three-fourths of the earth's surface is water. But how can it be liberated from its saline impurities and carried to the parched portions of the earth? Who that had never before seen a cloud or a shower could have solved this problem? The efficient plan conceived by the Great Engineer would never have entered the human mind. And how can these tons upon tons of water, purified and elevated, be sustained without destructive discharge upon the earth? Had not God in His wisdom put a check on rainfall, every rain cloud, with its devastating dangers, would be an object of terror to all who behold it.

The Perfection of Original Creation—the Holiness of God (Gen. 1:31; Deut. 32:4; Isa. 45:18; Jer. 4:23-26)

Why should not a perfect God create a perfect universe? He must be perfect in Himself, and therefore He could not create anything imperfect. In fact, we are told that "God saw every thing that he had made, and, behold, it was very good" (Gen. 1:31). There is not a suggestion in the Bible that anything that came from the hands of God was imperfect. Instead we find the word "good" and "very good" used again and again to denote the perfection of His work.

God allowed Job to understand (Job 38:4-7) that when He created the earth, it was so marvelously perfect that "the morning stars sang together, and all the sons of God shouted for joy." Do you suppose that these highly intelligent angels shouted over a chaotic mass such as our evolutionists would have us think originally constituted the earth? No; it was a beautiful world, a perfect creation that called forth the Creator's praise on the morning of creation.

The Vastness of Creation—the Immensity of God (Job 22:12; Ps. 8:3-4;
92:5; 145:3; Rev. 15:3)

Job's would-be comforter, Eliphaz, recognized thousands of years ago
that the stars were inconceivably remote. The sun and its system of
planets comprise a very minute part of the millions of orbs that constitute our universe. Our Milk Way is only one of many galaxies that cover
space, each one with a retinue of countless billions of stars. In fact, we do
not know the confines of this vast universe or how many stars there
are. Though men have made great advances into space, they acknowledge that creation is immeasurable and well-nigh incomprehensible.
No wonder an eminent American astronomer exclaimed, "Our greatest
debt to astronomy is that it has shown us what a vast thing creation is,
and what a small part of the Creator's work is this little earth upon
which we live." God Himself best describes the vastness of His creation,
for it was He who "meted out heaven with the span, and comprehended
the dust of the earth in a measure, and weighed the mountains in scales,
and the hills in a balance" (Isa. 40:12).

Regularity in Creation—the Unchangeableness of God (Gen. 8:22;
Job 38:37; Ps. 74:16-17; Eccl. 1:5-7)

In the memory of man, has the return of the seasons ever failed or the day
ceased to follow the night? In some places on the earth the recurring
rains come with such regularity during the rainy seasons that it is said
that one can set his watch by the time of occurrence of the daily thun-
derstorm. People who insist that a permanent change in climate has
taken place during their lifetime are in error. We have learned from a
study of statistics that wet and dry, cold and hot periods come in cycles.
Planets and their moons move with such regularity that we can determine eclipses to a minute a thousand years from now. Sunspot periods
recur in cycles, and stars proceed on their charted courses with a change-
less velocity. Some of the stars fluctuate in brightness, going through a
period of sudden rise of brilliancy, and then slowly falling to dimness,
in time ranging from a few hours to fifty days. Such system and regularity speak of the unchangeableness of God.

Variety in Creation—the Exhaustlessness of God (Job 38:22;
Isa. 40:26, 28; 1 Cor. 15:41)

None of the planets is like another, and "one star differeth from another
star in glory" (1 Cor. 15:41). It is estimated that in our galaxy alone there
are enough stars for every one of the billions of people of the earth to
be given hundreds of stars to rule. And yet these gigantic suns differ so

much from one another in distance, diameter, direction, velocity, and substance that God "calleth them all by names by the greatness of his might" (Isa. 40:26). Could we ever count the leaves on the trees? Could we even estimate the number in a single forest? And yet no two leaves are exactly alike, although they may have enough in common to classify them. Botanists have identified more than a third of a million different species of plants. We are bewildered at the thought of the countless variety of sizes, forms, and colors that such a vast host exhibit and are overwhelmed at the discovery that even the individuals of the same species differ. There are about five thousand species of grass, and no two blades of the same species are alike. We cannot count the snowflakes. However, we can catch some and examine these marvels of nature. While we would observe that they always show six sides, their variations seem unlimited, and no two designs appear alike.

Usefulness in Creation—the Goodness of God (Deut. 8:7-9;
Job 37:17; Matt. 5:45; Acts 14:17)

Every green blade that springs from the ground serves a definite purpose. Have we ever realized how lavishly God has provided in creation for the necessities of life? Men could not live an hour without air or water and could scarcely exist without the heat and light of the sun. But there is an abundant supply of all of these vital commodities provided without money and without price. Even when economic recessions and depressions have come, they were not occasioned by man's lack of any of life's essentials. Man's difficulties come about through a scarcity of money, the love of which, the Bible tells us, is "the root of all evil" (1 Tim. 6:10). God has provided the human race with vast resources in productive soil, recurring showers, and stimulating sunshine. Our debt to nature is far greater than most men imagine. It has been estimated that after the average man has deducted the contribution of nature and the contribution of society toward the production of his commodity, he will find that he has not put more than two and one-half percent into it himself.

Purpose in Creation—the Glory of God (Ps. 19:1; 145:10-11; Prov. 16:4;
Isa. 44:24; Rom. 11:36; Col. 1:16; Rev. 4:11)

"All things were created by him, and for him" (Col. 1:16). Whatever we have is from God and should be used and employed for Him. We should use all things with due thankfulness to the generous Giver, employing them in our service soberly and wisely, considering that they stand related to God as their Creator and are His workmanship.

Truly man's chief end, like that of all other creatures, is to glorify

God and enjoy Him forever. We cannot enjoy God unless we recognize His sovereignty and proprietorship in all the wonderful things that He has made for His honor and glory, as well as for our pleasure.

GOD'S WORK OF PROVIDENCE

Little things that have determined lives and shaped the destiny of nations are not accidents. They constitute the evidence that God is directing the affairs of this world. Though His greatness is unsearchable and the immensity of His creation incomprehensible, He is still interested in all His creatures and all their actions. God's provision for His creatures and His protection for and guidance of them are called the *works of providence*. These are even greater evidences of His existence, greater instructors of His character, and greater marvels of His nature than the works of creation. Men who cannot see God in creation can hardly fail to recognize Him in His works of providence.

Providential Provision (Deut. 8:3-4, 15-16; Job 38:41; Ps. 65:9-13; 104:10-16, 21, 27-28; Matt. 6:26; Acts 14:17)

Psalm 104 is a eulogy of God's marvelous provision for His creatures. Water is the great necessity of the animal world. A horse can live twenty-five days on water, but only five days when food is provided without water. However, the Creator has interspersed springs, creeks, and waterways among the hills where there is good pasturage to be found. "They give drink to every beast of the field: the wild asses quench their thirst. By them shall the fowls . . . have their habitation." In time these watercourses would run dry; so "he watereth the hills from his chambers," and the refreshing rainfall "causeth the grass to grow for the cattle, and herb for the service of man: that he may bring forth food out of the earth." Not only the domestic animals, but "the young lions roar after their prey, and seek their meat from God." Even the innumerable creatures of the ocean wait upon God, that He may give them their food in due season.

Much of the animal world makes no provision for the future. The ravens neither sow nor reap, neither have storehouse nor barn, "yet your heavenly Father feedeth them" (Matt. 6:26). Experience has taught them that God will provide faithfully and abundantly. If God cares for the birds, how much more will He care for us? The value of the sparrow of which our Lord spoke (Matt. 10:29) is just about as little as anything that could come under appraisement. Two of them were sold for a farthing, which is less than a penny in our currency. Moreover, these common birds that have neither song nor plumage are the least desirable of the winged creatures. In many places they are regarded as a nuisance, fit only for food for the other creatures. Yet God cares for them!

> *Said the robin to the sparrow,*
> *"I should really like to know,*
> *Why these anxious human beings*
> *Rush about and worry so?"*
> *Said the sparrow to the robin,*
> *"Friend, I think that it must be*
> *That they have no heavenly Father*
> *Such as cares for you and me."*

God's gracious provision for mankind is seen in the remarkable capacity most plants have to reproduce. The common grain-bearing plants often yield from sixty to one hundredfold. One castor oil plant will produce fifteen hundred, and one sunflower four thousand seeds in a single season. From one grain of corn, if it and all its produce were from year to year planted and duly cultivated in favorable soil and climate, sufficient seed might be raised in five years to plant hills of corn with three grains in every yard of dry land upon the face of the globe. In the creative fiat, "Let the earth bring forth grass, the herb yielding seed . . . after his kind" (Gen. 1:11), God made abundant provision not only to perpetuate vegetation but also to meet the wants of all His creatures. Poverty is not the institution of heaven. The causes lie with men.

Not only does God make general provision for all mankind, but He especially cares for the needs of His children. When the chosen people were in the barren wilderness of the Sinai peninsula, special arrangements were necessary to feed a multitude of two million men, women, and children. The manna that was supplied day by day for forty years met every requirement. It was pleasant to the taste, it was nourishing, and there was enough for all. This miracle, not only of food but also of clothes (Deut. 8:3-4), is an irrefutable proof of all that the Bible assumes concerning the personality, love, and power of God, as well as His faithfulness and deep concern for all His children. The murmurings and dissatisfaction of the Israelites concerning the manna teach lessons of great value to us. "Man did eat angels' food" (Ps. 78:25), and his dissatisfaction with it revealed a rebellious nature that would be unhappy in heaven.

Providential Protection

Psalm 91 is a eulogy of God's marvelous protection of His children—those who dwell "in the secret place of the Most High." "Because he hath set his love upon [you] . . . he shall give his angels charge over thee, to keep thee in all thy ways" (vv. 14, 11). Christ spoke of the guardian angels of children (Matt. 18:10), and older ones are assured that these heavenly beings are surrounding and protecting them also (Heb. 1:14). Protection is afforded against harm and disease and evil.

AGAINST HARM (2 KINGS 6:14-17; 2 CHRON. 16:9; PS. 34:7; 41:2; 91:5; 125:2; ZECH. 2:5; LUKE 21:18)

You will remember how God protected Elisha when the entire Syrian army came to capture the prophet. For months this man of God had been revealing the Syrian war plans to the king of Israel. Now the Syrian host of horses and chariots and infantry surrounded the city in which the prophet resided. What a terrible sight greeted the eye of the prophet's servant the next morning—a vast army seeking the life of one man! In his terror he cried, "Alas, my master! how shall we do?" "Fear not," said Elisha, "for they that be with us are more than they that be with them" (2 Kings 6:15-16).

Impossible? Perhaps to those who know nothing about the providence of God! Elisha's servant was such a one, and so the prophet prayed that his eyes might be opened to see the heavenly host that covered the mountains to protect him from the Syrian army. Such is the divine protection God affords His children.

AGAINST DISEASE (EXOD. 15:26; DEUT. 7:15; PS. 91:6, 10)

"What is your life?" Well does the writer of old answer the question: "It is even a vapour, that appeareth for a little time, and then vanisheth away" (Jas. 4:14). Your own breath is a picture of the flimsy thing that men call life.

Justinian, an emperor of Rome, died by going into a room that had been newly painted. Adrian, a pope, was strangled to death by a fly. There are a thousand gates to death. Men have been choked by a grape seed and carried off by a whiff of foul air. Germs of fatal diseases are all about us. It is only God's providence that keeps us from contracting all the diseases with which we come in contact. God is taking better care of us than we can take of ourselves. His care exceeds that of the dearest friends and the best physicians. Look at a mother. How careful she is! If her child has a little cough, she notices it; the slightest weakness is sure to be observed. But she has never thought of numbering the hairs of her child's head. The absence of two or three of them would give her no concern. However, God is so concerned for us that He numbers the hairs on our heads (Matt. 10:30).

AGAINST EVIL (PS. 91:10; 121:3-8; 1 COR. 10:13)

Psalm 121 is "the Traveler's Psalm." In some homes this Scripture is read when a member of the family is about to go on a journey. It is not so much a prayer as a meditation upon God's providence. "He that keepeth thee will not slumber." His protecting care not only keeps from harm, but from evil too. "The LORD shall preserve thee from all evil: he shall preserve thy soul."

Have we ever considered how frequently God's providence has protected us in times of temptation? Providence has not permitted the temptation to come at times when we would have been overwhelmed by it. At other times when the temptation has come, God has providentially given us supernatural strength to resist it. With the temptation there has been provided a way of escape, so we were able to bear it (1 Cor. 10:13). Many a man's character has been saved by God's providence. The best man who ever lived little knows how much he owed for preservation to this providence, another aspect of God's grace. The Lord has not led us into temptation but has delivered us from evil.

Providential Guidance (Gen. 45:7; Est. 4:14; Ps. 37:5, 23-25; Dan. 2:21)

Psalm 37 is called the "Fret Not Psalm." Not only are its forty verses introduced by the two words, "Fret not," but its entire content speaks of God's providential direction in the lives of those who trust in Him. The good man is exhorted to commit his way unto the Lord, to trust in Him, and He shall bring it to pass. God has a plan for each child of His and will guide him and direct him once he is surrendered.

Joseph was fully surrendered to God's program for his life, although he knew very little of what God intended to do with him. God had in mind that Joseph should be governor of Egypt. How was this to be done? The first thing was that Joseph's brethren must hate him. Next they must put him into a pit. Why wasn't he killed? Why was Reuben delayed in rescuing him? Because God planned to have the Ishmaelites come along at the right moment and purchase him. Why were the Ishmaelites going to Egypt? Why did they sell Joseph to Potiphar? Why was Joseph falsely accused and thrown into prison? How was it that both the butler and the baker offended the king? Why did they both dream? Why did they happen to ask Joseph to interpret their dreams? Why did the butler, when released, forget all about Joseph? Why did Pharaoh dream? These are all connecting links of providence. If Joseph had not been put into the pit, he would never have been the servant of Potiphar; if he had never been thrown into prison, he never would have interpreted the butler's dream; and if Pharaoh had not dreamed, Joseph would never have been sent for. As someone has said, "God put Joseph into prison so Pharaoh could find him when he wanted him." How well Joseph recognized this providential leading is indicated by his statement to his brethren: "Be not grieved . . . that ye sold me hither: for God did send me before you to preserve life" (Gen. 45:5).

REVIEW QUESTIONS

1. What was the method of creation?
2. What was the plan of creation?
3. How do we know that the original creation was perfect?
4. How does astronomy corroborate the Bible in revealing the vastness of creation?
5. Contrast regularity with variety in creation.
6. What Scripture passages declare God's purpose in creation?
7. What do we mean by the works of providence?
8. Give some illustrations of God's providential provisions.
9. What do God's providential provisions reveal about His nature?
10. In what three ways does God exercise His providential protection?
11. How is Psalm 37 true today for the believer in experiencing God's providential direction?
12. In what ways was the providence of God evidenced in Joseph's life?

APPLYING DOCTRINE TO LIFE

1. How would you witness to an unbeliever concerning the question of evolution vs. God's creative work by His Word?
2. How might an understanding of God's providence affect a believer's life?

Chapter Six

THE PREEXISTENCE AND INCARNATION OF CHRIST

THE QUESTION FOR TODAY is not, did Christ live? There is too much established evidence to question the fact that He lived. The keystone of Christianity is Jesus Christ. No other man occupies the same position with regard to any religion that Christ occupies in regard to Christianity. He is at once its founder and its subject. Jesus Christ is the great figure of the centuries, and every system of theology and philosophy must take account of Him. Men may oppose Him and reject His claim, but they cannot ignore Him.

THE PREEXISTENCE OF CHRIST

The perennial question, then, for every man, woman, and child, all to whom "a name which is above every name" (Phil. 2:9) has gone, is, "What think ye of Christ? whose son is he?" (Matt. 22:42). A man's parentage ordinarily makes very little difference to us. He rises or falls according to his own ability and efficiency. Our estimate of Shakespeare or Lincoln is no greater because we know their ancestry. But it is different with Jesus Christ. His practical relationship to the world is bound up in His origin. His life suggests and His words lay claim to a superhuman lineage. He did not acknowledge Joseph, the carpenter of Nazareth, as His father. His sinless life and the far-reaching accomplishments of His death are grounded in the fact of His eternal preexistence.

Evidence of the Preexistent Christ

PERSONAL TESTIMONY

There are numerous New Testament witnesses to a preexisting Christ.

CHRIST HIMSELF (JOHN 6:32-38, 41-50)

Probably the greatest gathering our Lord ever addressed was the occasion when His prolonged message and ministry prompted the feeding of the hungry thousands. He used this widely recognized miracle to press home the truth that He was the Bread of Life who had come down from heaven. When the Jews objected to this extraordinary claim, contending that they knew His father and mother, He ignored their arguments and once more reiterated that He was the Living Bread from heaven, and therefore greater than the heavenly manna that had supplied their temporal needs.

PETER (1 PET. 1:19-20)

Outstanding among the disciples was Peter. Not only did he write two epistles and contribute to the preparation of a Gospel, but his name is found more frequently in the New Testament than that of any other human character. He believed in the preexistence of Christ, for he declares that He "was foreordained before the foundation of the world, but was manifest in these last times."

JOHN THE BAPTIST (JOHN 1:27-30)

John the Baptist was the most popular preacher of his day. He was the most discussed man of the hour, for multitudes from "Jerusalem, and all Judea, and all the region round about Jordan" (Matt. 3:5) went out to hear him. Yet he was constantly referring to a far greater person who was to come after him. He declared, "After me cometh a man which is preferred before me: for he was before me" (John 1:30). In other words, he used the fact of Christ's preexistence as the argument for Christ's superiority to himself.

JOHN THE APOSTLE (JOHN 1:1-2, 18; 1 JOHN 1:1-2)

Instead of opening his narrative with the ministry of Christ or tracing His genealogy from Adam or Abraham, John pushes back His existence to the beginning of all beginnings. The beginning of the first book in the Bible is, "In the beginning God," and the beginning of the fourth Gospel is, "In the beginning was the Word." God, then, and the Word must have coexisted in the very beginning. And what John declares in his Gospel he also records in his first epistle. To his mind it was a marvelous privilege to have actually seen and heard and touched the one and only Eternal Being.

PAUL (1 COR. 8:6; 2 TIM. 1:9)

It was a vision of the risen Christ that converted the greatest of Jewish scholars and transformed him from Saul the cruel persecutor to Paul the heroic missionary. Yet Paul also seems to have had a full realization of the preexistence of Christ, for he declares that "he is before all things, and by him all things consist" (Col. 1:17).

Prophetic Witnesses

There are not only New Testament witnesses, but also Old Testament witnesses to a preexisting Christ.

DAVID (PS. 40:6-8; HEB. 10:5-10)

David was permitted to draw aside the curtain of time and clearly see the crucifixion of Christ one thousand years ahead of time (Ps. 22). But he was also permitted to look back into the council of eternity. He saw that majestic scene of God the Father, God the Son, and God the Holy Spirit discussing the salvation of a sin-cursed world. No burnt offerings or sacrifices would suffice for its salvation. None but a sinless being could be accepted to atone for guilt-stained creatures. Who then could go? The Holy One of God. Who then would go? Listen! It is the voice of God the Son who speaks: "Lo, I come . . . to do thy will, O my God" (Ps. 40:7-8).

MICAH (MIC. 5:2)

The prophets were not only given details of our Lord's earthly advent, but it also appears that they too recognized His preexistence. In announcing that Bethlehem would be the birthplace of the Messiah of Israel, the prophet Micah strikingly adds that He was to be One "whose goings forth have been from of old, from everlasting."

The Eternity of the Preexistent Christ

Not only is there trustworthy evidence of the preexistence of Christ, but there also is testimony to the fact that He shared the eternity of God.

THE ONE EVER-PRESENT (JOHN 8:56-58)

When Moses asked for a message to prove that he was God's ambassador, he was told to declare to the children of Israel that "I AM hath sent me unto you" (Exod. 3:13-14). This is another way of declaring that with God there is neither past nor future, but an eternal present. When the Jews argued with Christ that He was not yet fifty years old and therefore could not possibly have seen Abraham, His memorable reply was,

"Before Abraham was, I am" (John 8:58). When the writer to the Hebrews asserted that our Lord was a priest after the order of Melchisedec rather than of Aaron, it was only to claim for Him an existence that had "neither beginning of days, nor end of life" (Heb. 7:3).

THE ALPHA AND OMEGA (HEB. 13:8; REV. 1:8; 22:13)

The preexistence as well as the immutability of our Lord was declared in that brief and striking statement, "Jesus Christ the same yesterday, and to-day, and for ever" (Heb. 13:8). At the beginning and again at the end of the Revelation of Jesus Christ that was given to His servant at Patmos, John was told to write, "I am Alpha and Omega . . . the first and the last." This is a clear testimony to His eternal preexistence.

Adoration of the Preexistent Christ

Before our Lord became flesh and dwelt among men, He existed in a state of glory and was an object of worship.

WORSHIP (HEB. 1:4-6, 13-14)

While on earth, our Lord was accorded worship (Matt. 2:11; 14:33; 28:9; Luke 24:52), and it is noteworthy that He never protested against it. Long before this, however, He was the object of worship by the angels. He was higher than they; "he hath . . . obtained a more excellent name than they" (Heb. 1:4), for He was the Father's Son and occupied the place of honor by His side.

GLORY (JOHN 1:14; 17:5, 24)

The glory of God implies the full expression of God's life—all its beauty, purity, holiness, majesty, power, and other attributes in manifestation. We might say that Christ's cloak of humanity that He wore while on earth was a mantle covering the glory to which He was accustomed at all other times. The transfiguration of which all the Gospel writers speak (John 1:14) was the brief removal of His earthly garment as witnessed by the three privileged disciples on the Mount of Transfiguration (Matt. 17:1-5).

At the close of His earthly ministry, our Lord concluded His farewell address with an intercessory prayer in which He requested that the disciples might behold the glory that He shared with the Father "before the world was" (John 17:5). Twice He made this petition, reiterating His preexistence by adding, "Thou lovedst me before the foundation of the world" (v. 24).

Activities of the Preexistent Christ

The preexistence of Christ is further revealed by the work attributed to Him. His was not an inactive existence, but one in which He shared the activities of the Father and the Holy Spirit.

THE CREATOR (JOHN 1:3; COL. 1:16-18; HEB. 1:2, 10; 2:10)

In a former chapter we attempted to fathom the greatness of God's creation, a work that is immeasurable and well-nigh incomprehensible. We were amazed and awed not only by its immensity but by its perfection, its variety, and its utility. And yet we need to be reminded that our Lord and Savior Jesus Christ shared in all this mighty and marvelous work and that "all things were made by him; and without him was not any thing made that was made" (John 1:3). His activities not only included the visible universe of galaxies, but the invisible principalities and heavenly thrones (Col. 1:16), which may be far more marvelous and majestic than that which mortal eye can discern. Moreover, all these wonderful works were not only made *by* Him, but also *for* Him (Col. 1:16; Heb. 2:10).

THE CONTROLLER (COL. 1:17; HEB. 1:3)

We have studied about the providential provision, protection, and guidance afforded God's creatures. We learned for our comfort and assurance that God controls not only the movements of the heavenly bodies, but the destinies of the nations. But this great task of governing and sustaining the universe and all creatures, human and angelic, is a work of God the Son fully as much as of God the Father. Jesus demonstrated this by His miracles when He was on earth, for the winds and waves obeyed Him, and the demons were subject to His command. Long before this, He controlled the planets in their orbits, and He ordained and sustained their fields of gravitation.

THE INCARNATION OF CHRIST

The word *incarnation* comes from the Latin and literally means "embodiment," or the assumption of humanity. That He whom the heaven of heavens cannot contain should voluntarily imprison Himself upon a mere particle of His immeasurable creation, that He whose brilliant majesty is brighter than the sun should cover His glory with the cloak of human flesh is inconceivable and well-nigh unbelievable, were it not for the facts that plainly testify to its truth.

Human Parentage

GENEALOGIES (MATT. 1:1-16; LUKE 3:23-38)

The human ancestry of Christ is traced by two of the Gospel writers. Matthew opens his narrative with a genealogy to prove that Jesus Christ as the son of David was heir to the throne of Israel and as the son of Abraham was the child of promise in whom all families of the earth were to be blessed. Luke does not stop at David or Abraham but goes back to the first man, who was the father of Jews and Gentiles alike.

BORN OF A WOMAN (MATT. 1:18-20; LUKE 1:26-35;
JOHN 1:14; GAL. 4:4)

Not only do we have express statements to this fact in Acts and the epistles, but the Gospel writers provide the details. Both Matthew and Luke testify that this birth was different from all ordinary births. Joseph, we are told, was engaged but not yet married to Mary, and naturally he was deeply grieved when he was led to believe that the young girl he loved had been unfaithful to him. Perhaps as he lay awake at night, trying to plan some way of putting her away privately to save her from death—which was the penalty of the Jewish law—an angel appeared to him and explained the creative act whereby God broke through the chain of human generations and brought into the world a supernatural being. We read that Joseph accepted the explanation and that his marriage to Mary was not consummated until after Jesus was born. Luke describes the appearance of the angel Gabriel to Mary and his announcement of the miraculous birth of Jesus. When Mary questioned such an impossible circumstance, the angel reminded her that "with God nothing shall be impossible" (Luke 1:37).

By being "made of a woman" (Gal. 4:4), Christ for all time honored motherhood, and the word *mother* was to become one of the sweetest notes on the human tongue. Why did Titian, the Italian artist, when sketching the Madonna, give her an Italian face? Why did Rubens give his Madonna a German face? Why did Reynolds in his Madonna favor the English? Undoubtedly because each believed that his own mother was the best type of Mary, the mother of Christ.

Human Development (Luke 2:40-42, 52)

From the human standpoint, Jesus grew in the same manner as other children. He subjected Himself to the laws that govern physical and intellectual development. Although His sinless nature influenced His development, it is clear that He received training along the lines of ordinary human progress—instruction, study, thought. In this great condescension, He greatly honored childhood. He who was omnipotent once had a child's beaming eye, a child's light limbs, and a child's soft hair. The greatest gift God ever gave to this world was once a little child. He was of such value that heaven took notice, and angels, breaking through the clouds, came down to look at him.

Human Characteristics

THE APPEARANCE OF A MAN (MATT. 14:24-27; LUKE 24:36-43; JOHN 4:9; 20:15, 19-20; PHIL. 2:8)

Paul said Christ "was made in the likeness of men" (Phil. 2:7), and we find that to His friends and relatives He appeared as a man. The woman of Samaria designated Him as a Jew by His features and language (John 4:9). Even when He appeared as an apparition in the darkness of the night, walking on the stormy sea, He relieved the fears of the terrified disciples by speaking to them and then joining them in the boat (Matt. 14:24-27, 32).

We possess no photograph of Him, but the four Gospels do not lead us to believe that He was different in appearance from ordinary men. Only at the time of His transfiguration do they point out that "the fashion of his countenance was altered" (Luke 9:29). After the resurrection Jesus seems still to have retained the form of a man. Mary at the tomb mistook Him for the gardener (John 20:15). The two disciples on the way to Emmaus thought He was a traveler, "a stranger in Jerusalem" (Luke 24:18). Even when He miraculously appeared in the upper room behind barred doors, the disciples were given evidence of His humanity by His eating in their presence and of His being the crucified Jesus by the exhibition of His wounds (Luke 24:36-43; John 20:19-20).

THE GARMENT OF FLESH (JOHN 1:14; HEB. 2:14, 16; 10:5)

The New Testament bears clear testimony to the genuine humanity of Christ. The apostle John declared that "The Word was made flesh, and dwelt among us." He further warned against denial of the Incarnation (1 John 4:2-3). The writer to the Hebrews likewise stressed the fact of the Incarnation when he stated that the Son of God "took not on him the nature of angels; but he took on him the seed of Abraham" (2:16). The object of God's redemptive plan was fallen man, not fallen angels. Therefore, God's Son became man in order that he might die in man's place, bearing the just penalty for man's sin (2 Cor. 5:21). Because He became man, He could die as man's substitute; because He is God the Son, His work on the cross has eternal value. Further, through the incarnation of the Son of God and His death on the cross, Satan's power over man was broken (Heb. 2:14-15).

Human Limitations

It is important that we think correctly concerning the person of the Incarnate Son of God. He is at once God and man. He was no less God because of His assumption of humanity; and the genuineness of His humanity was not affected by His deity. Any limitations that Scripture speaks of were self-imposed and were the result of His will to operate on those occasions in the sphere of His humanity. Also, it should be noted that such human limitations ceased after the resurrection. His glorified humanity is not subject to hunger, thirst, weariness, pain, or death.

PHYSICAL

Scripture indicates that our Lord subjected Himself to the limitations and needs of the human body, even though He could have exercised His power to overcome those limitations and provide for those needs.

He hungered (Matt. 4:2; 21:18). Although He provided food for the multitudes, He experienced the same need for food.

He thirsted (John 4:7). He needed to quench His thirst with the water of this world, even though He possessed and offered to men the water of life.

He was weary and slept (Matt. 8:24; John 4:6).

He experienced pain and death (1 Cor. 15:3; 1 Pet. 4:1).

MENTAL (MARK 13:32; LUKE 2:52)

Because our Lord was both God and man, He possessed seemingly contradictory attributes. He was both infinite and finite. On occasion He manifested omnipotence; on other occasions he evidenced weakness. In like manner, the Scriptures present Him both as omniscient (Matt. 9:3-4; John 1:47-49; 10:15) and as subject to increasing knowledge, and on certain occasions as lacking knowledge (Mark 11:13; 13:32; Luke 2:52). Obviously, Christ purposefully limited Himself on these occasions for reasons known only to Himself.

Human Recognition

The Lord Jesus Christ was universally recognized as a man. Note that he was spoken of as:

JESUS OF NAZARETH (LUKE 18:37; 24:19; JOHN 18:5)

As He had spent all His life, except the last three years, in the town of Nazareth, He was identified with that place. In fact, so few were aware that He was born in Bethlehem that His enemies used the accepted belief of His coming from Galilee as an argument against His being the Messiah. Prophecy had declared that Christ should come "out of the town of Bethlehem, where David was," but so prevailing was the belief that He was a native of Nazareth that even the faith of the scholarly Nicodemus was confronted by this apparent fact (John 7:40-52).

THE SON OF JOSEPH (LUKE 3:23; JOHN 6:42)

The filial obedience and close attachment of our Lord to Joseph and Mary led everyone to suppose that He was "the carpenter's son" (Matt. 13:55). Even the younger half brothers and sisters who were brought up with Jesus in the family at Nazareth refused to accept Him as the Messiah during His earthly ministry. While in the beginning they were doubtless perplexed, later they came to regard him as a fanatic and dreamer (Mark 3:21; John 7:3-5).

THE SON OF MAN (MATT. 26:63-64; JOHN 1:49-51)

No less than eighty times in the Gospels did Jesus call Himself the Son of Man. He seems to have preferred this designation to all others, for even when acquiescing to the recognition that He was the Son of God, He sometimes immediately afterward substituted the title Son of Man. While we recognize the fact that there is something official in the title Son of Man—something connected with His relationship to the kingdom of God—nevertheless, our Lord's persistent use of this term makes it evident that He most earnestly desired to identify Himself with the sons of men.

REVIEW QUESTIONS

1. What is Christ's testimony as to His preexistence?
2. Name four New Testament writers who spoke of Christ's preexistence.
3. In what respect was David a prophetic witness of the council of eternity?
4. What Scripture passages teach the eternal existence of Christ?
5. How do we know that Christ was worshiped by the angels and that he shared the glory of God?
6. In what respect was Christ the Creator and the Controller of the universe?

7. What is meant by the incarnation of Christ?
8. What was the purpose of the genealogies in Matthew and Luke?
9. What were some of the human characteristics of our Lord?
10. Give four illustrations of the physical limitations of our Lord.
11. How does Christ's perfect humanity and deity affect our redemption?
12. How does Jesus' use of the title *Son of Man* show His interest in men?

APPLYING DOCTRINE TO LIFE

1. How does Christ's incarnation help you relate to Him?
2. In what ways would you recognize Christ if He were to appear as a man in your church?

Chapter Seven

THE DEITY OF CHRIST

IT IS REPORTED THAT when Marshal Ney entered the presence of Napoleon after directing a masterful retreat from Moscow, the emperor caught him in his arms exclaiming, "The bravest of the brave." But Napoleon was wrong. The bravest of the brave was that humble Galilean who stood calmly before the Jewish council and signed His death warrant by acknowledging that He was the Son of God. The Jewish Sanhedrin condemned Christ to death because they believed Him to be a blasphemer and an impostor. He was crucified because He claimed to be the *Son of God*, thereby asserting His deity. "We have a law," the Jews said to Pilate, "and by our law he ought to die, because he made himself the Son of God" (John 19:7).

Jesus might have saved His life if He had not *insisted* that He was the Son of God. But He refused to deny the truth, which meant the suffering and shame of a criminal's crucifixion. His was the greatest of all confessions. A year earlier Peter had made a good confession, but now he was in the courtyard denying his Lord because his life was endangered. Had Peter been asked for counsel, he no doubt would have advised Jesus to conceal His real identity that fatal night. But Jesus refused to compromise. He confessed that He was the Son of God and did not flinch when put to the crucial test. He was truly the hero of heroes.

Jesus was put to death as an impostor and blasphemer because He claimed to be the Son of God. What evidence is there to support this claim, which was most presumptuous if it were not true? The Gospel writers make it plain.

JESUS A SUPERNATURAL PERSON

His Virgin Birth (Matt. 1:22-23; Luke 1:34-35)

We must not lose sight of the fact that there was something supernatural surrounding the birth of Christ. He was the predicted seed of the woman, not of the man (Gen. 3:15; Luke 1:34). No laws of heredity are sufficient to account for this birth. This was so exceptional and so significant that seven hundred years earlier, the prophet Isaiah had declared that the sign of the Messiah would be His virgin birth (Isa. 7:14). The fact that the virgin birth is attested by the Scriptures, tradition, and creeds and that it is in perfect harmony with all the other facts of Christ's wonderful life should be sufficient evidence of its truth.

His Marvelous Knowledge (John 2:24-25; 4:16-19; 7:45-46; 16:30)

The poverty of Jesus' parents prevented their providing Him with more than a common education. Yet He knew more than the wisest and most scholarly men of His day. When the chief priests sent officers to arrest Him, they were so amazed at His wisdom that they hesitated to take Him into custody. When they were asked by the Pharisees why they returned without Him, they declared, "Never man spake like this man" (John 7:46). The woman of Samaria was so impressed by His knowledge of her home life that she told her friends, "Come, see a man, which told me all things that ever I did: is not this the Christ?" (John 4:29). His disciples, who had come to know Him better than anyone else, declared on the last night He was with them, "Now are we sure that thou knowest all things" (John 16:30).

His Marvelous Power

Jesus pointed to His miracles as evidence that He was a supernatural person. He said, "The works that I do in my Father's name, they bear witness of me. . . . If I do not the works of my Father, believe me not. But if I do, though ye believe not me, believe the works" (John 10:25, 37-38). No less than thirty-six miracles are recorded. How many more there may have been, we do not know, but these are sufficient to establish His marvelous power.

POWER OVER DISEASE (LUKE 4:39)

He healed the sick, including the dread, incurable malady of leprosy. He caused the deaf to hear, the dumb to speak, and the blind to see.

POWER OVER NATURE (MATT. 8:26-27; 14:25, 32-33; LUKE 24:51)

The winds and the waves obeyed His voice, and He defied the power of gravitation by walking on the water and, at the end, ascended into the clouds.

POWER OVER DEMONS (MARK 5:8-13; LUKE 4:31-36)

Even the spirit world was in subjection to His word. Out of one unfortunate man a legion of demons were cast, and these upon entering two thousand swine rushed them to their destruction in the sea.

POWER OVER DEATH (MARK 5:35, 41-42; LUKE 7:12-15; JOHN 11:32, 43-44)

Three instances of Jesus' raising the dead are recorded: the daughter of Jairus, who had been dead but a few hours; the son of the widow of Nain, as the funeral procession was bearing his coffin to the grave; the beloved Lazarus, who had been buried four days and was restored to life.

HIS OWN DEATH AND RESURRECTION (JOHN 10:18)

When asked for a sign to prove that He was the Son of God, Jesus cited the experience of Jonah as an illustration of His impending death and resurrection (Matt. 12:38-40). That He could predict His resurrection and then carry it to fulfillment was truly the greatest manifestation of power over death and the grave that has ever been witnessed by humanity.

His Astonishing Authority (Matt. 7:29)

Again and again it is recorded that the people marveled because Christ spoke "as one having authority, and not as the scribes." Where did He get this authority, and how did it differ from the scribes?

There are four sources of authority:

- *Authority of testimony*—facts experienced.
- *Authority of opinion*—scholarship.
- *Authority of position*—recognition.
- *Authority of inspiration*—intuition.

Sometimes when facts and experiences are not obtainable as direct evidence, the opinion of a specialist is recognized as circumstantial evidence. The truth or falsity of this evidence will depend upon the character of the one who gives the testimony. The authority of circumstantial evidence also may be given weight by the position that the witness holds, thus giving him special recognition. He may be a public official or a member of the faculty of a well-known school. The authority of the scribes for the most part was dependent upon their scholarship that made them specialists in the law. They were also recognized because they were members of the Sanhedrin or held other high offices.

The authority of Christ did not depend upon opinion or position. He had received no recognition for completing a prescribed course of study. He had never been elected to office. His authority, therefore, was dependent upon the testimony of the inerrant Word of God and the Holy Spirit who inspired the Word. This gave more weight to His utterances than the authority of a scholar or the prestige of a member of the Sanhedrin. This authority was challenged when He assumed the right to forgive sins. The Pharisees justly contended that only God can forgive sins. This Jesus must have been either God or an impostor. His supernatural authority was revealed at:

HIS CONFERENCE WITH THE JEWISH TEACHERS (LUKE 2:46-49)

Even at the age of twelve, Jesus recognized that He must be about His Father's business. In these first recorded words of Jesus, there is an indication of a consciousness of the unique relationship with His heavenly Father. Note that contrary to Jewish custom, Mary, not Joseph, asked the question, "Why hast thou thus dealt with us? behold, thy father and I have sought thee sorrowing." It is remarkable to note that in His reply, Christ makes no allusion to Joseph and in fact always omits the word "father" when referring to His parents (see Matt. 12:48; Mark 3:33-34). In this incident Christ revealed the fact that it was not Joseph but God who was His Father, and He used this authority in debating with the Jewish teachers.

THE TRANSFIGURATION (LUKE 9:30-35)

On the mountain, the favorite disciples rejoiced that they had the privilege of seeing Moses and Elijah, those honored characters of the Old Testament. What an opportunity for them now to ask questions and learn from the lips of these saints the mysteries of their disappearance! But the voice from heaven silenced their curiosity by that all-important declaration, "This is my beloved Son: hear him." Eminent men though they were, the voices of Moses and Elijah were only those of human authority. Christ alone could speak with supernatural authority.

THE COMMISSION OF THE TWELVE (MARK 3:13-19)

When our Lord sent out the Twelve, He demonstrated His deity and His consequent authority by giving the disciples power over all manner of illness and demons. Certainly only God has the ability and authority to dispense such power to men. By this means Jesus was demonstrating the validity of His claim that He was "the Christ, the Son of the living God" (Matt. 16:16; cf. John 20:31).

JESUS WORSHIPED AS GOD

If Jesus were a man only, why did He permit other men to worship Him? The homage given to Him would be nothing short of sacrilegious idolatry if Christ were not God.

Worshiped after His Birth (Matt. 2:8-11)

Princely scholars from afar, with their homage and costly gifts, were not ashamed to kneel before Him in His humble home. Even King Herod recognized that this was the proper attitude in which to receive Him.

Worshiped by the Leper (Matt. 8:2)

This is the first instance recorded in our Lord's adult ministry of His being worshiped. Why did He not rebuke this act of worship and confess, as Peter later did (Acts 10:25-26), that He was but a man?

Worshiped by the Man Born Blind (John 9:32, 35-38)

It is well to notice this connection: Before the grateful beneficiary of Christ's healing power fell at His feet, our Lord revealed Himself to the man as the Son of God.

Worshiped by the Syrophoenician Woman (Mark 7:25-30)

In her conversation with Jesus concerning her demon-possessed daughter, this woman not only recognized Him as the Messiah by declaring Him the "son of David" (Matt. 15:22), but three times she addressed Him as Lord as she prostrated herself before Him. No wonder our Lord marveled at her faith and honored it by healing her daughter.

Worshiped by the Apostles

There are so many instances recorded of the apostles' worshiping Jesus that we can only name some of them at this time. Most of these took place after Peter's notable confession that Jesus was the Son of God (Matt. 16:16). His apostles and some women worshiped Jesus when:

THE STORM WAS STILLED (MATT. 14:33)

The disciples had witnessed three great miracles within the space of a few minutes. First they saw the Lord walking upon the water; next they witnessed the saving of the floundering Peter; third, they observed that the boisterous wind had suddenly ceased. In awe and admiration they worshiped Him.

ZEBEDEE'S SONS SOUGHT KINGDOM HONORS (MATT. 20:20)

The mother of Zebedee's sons was ambitious. She wanted to see James and John sitting beside the Lord Jesus Christ on the throne of His kingdom. Perhaps it was the audacity of this request and the intense desire to have it granted that caused all three to worship Him. In this request they admitted the truth of His coming kingdom and by this act of worship recognized His kingship.

THE WOMEN RECOGNIZED THEIR RISEN LORD (MATT. 28:5-9)

Last at the cross and first at the tomb, these faithful women in their worship not only acknowledged His resurrection but testified to His divinity.

THE RISEN CHRIST APPEARED ON A MOUNTAIN (MATT. 28:16-17)

The risen Lord directed the women to tell the disciples that He would go before them into Galilee and meet them there on a mountain. When the disciples gathered at the appointed place and beheld their risen Lord, they worshiped Him.

HE FINALLY ASCENDED TO HEAVEN (LUKE 24:51-52)

The last act of our Lord, as He parted from His disciples, was that of loving benediction; and the last attitude of the disciples, as they saw Him ascending above the clouds, was one of admiration and worship.

JESUS RECOGNIZED AS GOD

Four different groups or personages declared that Jesus was God. It has been argued by those who reject Christ as God that in all times people have sought to deify men who have commanded their admiration and affection. But Christ's exaltation was not one of man's creations. His was a wider field of recognition than the admiration of a few followers. This acceptance of deity recognized our Lord's prehistoric existence and was not based on elevation attained by human veneration.

The Testimony of Men
JOHN THE BAPTIST (JOHN 1:29-30)

Not only did the great evangelist bear witness to the prehistoric existence of Christ and the eternal plan to make the God-man the Savior of the world, but our Lord in His debate with the Jews expressly called attention to this testimony to prove His deity (John 5:33-35).

NATHANAEL (JOHN 1:49)

Before Nathanael became a follower of Jesus, he confessed that the much discussed Teacher was not only the Messiah but also the Son of God.

PETER (MATT. 16:16)

Peter was the spokesman for the Twelve, and in this great public confession he declared the belief of the other disciples.

THOMAS (JOHN 20:28)

How quick Thomas was to worship Jesus when he recognized that the crucified man was the living God!

THE ROMAN CENTURION (MARK 15:39)

Even the official executioner of Jesus substantiated the testimony of friends that the man suffering the death of a criminal was truly the Son of God.

The Testimony of Angels (Luke 2:10-11)

The message of the angels heard by the shepherds on the night of Jesus' birth proclaimed His deity. The angel who appeared to Mary and later to Joseph also recognized Him as God.

The Testimony of the Devil and Demons (Matt. 4:3; Luke 4:3, 41)

Satan himself on three occasions admitted Jesus to be the Son of God as he vainly tempted Him to use powers and assume prerogatives that already rightfully belong to Him.

Poor demon-possessed people cried out that Jesus was the Son of God, for the demons in them knew that He was Christ (Luke 4:34, 41). But while their testimony was admitted as true, it was not encouraged by our Lord, for He wanted men to make this discovery for themselves.

The Testimony of God

Three times the voice of God was heard from heaven during our Lord's ministry, and on each occasion it was to confirm the fact that Jesus was the Son of God. God's voice was heard at:
- *Jesus' baptism* (Matt. 3:13-17; Luke 3:22).
- *His transfiguration* (Matt. 17:5; Luke 9:35).
- *The last Passover* (John 12:27-28).

Both John and Peter call attention to the great significance of the Transfiguration, not only because of the spoken acknowledgment of

Christ's deity, but because of the heavenly honor and glory that were accorded Him on that occasion (John 1:14; 2 Pet. 1:16-18). Of the high value of this testimony John writes further, "If we receive the witness of men, the witness of God is greater: for this is the witness of God which he hath testified of his Son" (1 John 5:9).

JESUS CLAIMED TO BE GOD

If Jesus was not God He was nothing less than an impostor, for He distinctly declared again and again that He was God. Let us examine His testimony before three distinct groups.

Before His Apostles (John 14:7-11)

Jesus was constantly speaking of His heavenly Father in His conversations with the apostles as well as in His controversies with the Jews. In His farewell address He urged His apostles to accept His statements concerning His relation to the Father, or at least to accept Him on the basis of His miracles. "Believe me that I am in the Father, and the Father in me: or else believe me for the very works' sake" (John 14:11).

Before the Jews (John 10:22-25, 30-33)

At the Feast of Dedication the Jews asked Jesus the pointed question, "How long dost thou make us to doubt? If thou be the Christ, tell us plainly." Jesus again called attention to His statements to this effect, as well as to the miracles that were offered to substantiate His claims. "I told you, and ye believed not: the works that I do in my Father's name, they bear witness of me." A few minutes later He said, "I and my Father are one." What did the Jews understand Him to mean by such a remark? There was no question in their minds, for they picked up stones to hurl at Him for blasphemy, or as they themselves admitted, "Because that thou, being a man, makest thyself God."

Before the Council (Luke 22:66-71)

We have already seen that this hero of heroes refused the opportunity to clear Himself and go free by speaking a falsehood. When He persisted that He was the Son of God, the Jews declared that He had indicted Himself by His own confession and was therefore worthy of death. This testimony before the high priest was the culmination of all His repeated claims to be nothing less than God.

REVIEW QUESTIONS

1. What testimony of our Lord before the Jewish Sanhedrin led to His condemnation?
2. Name three facts that proclaim Christ a supernatural person.
3. In what five ways was His marvelous power manifested?
4. How did the authority of our Lord differ from that of the scribes and Pharisees?
5. How was the authority of Christ revealed at the Transfiguration?
6. Give five incidents in which Jesus was worshiped as God.
7. On what three occasions was our Lord worshiped after His resurrection?
8. What five individuals testified that Jesus was God?
9. What superhuman beings also acknowledged Christ as God?
10. What were the three occasions on which God spoke from heaven, and for what purpose?
11. Name three incidents when Christ claimed to be God.
12. Why must we conclude that Jesus is God?

APPLYING DOCTRINE TO LIFE

1. What can you do to prepare yourself and other believers to meet the attacks of false cults who deny the deity of Christ?
2. What benefits accrue to the believer as the result of the deity of Christ?

Chapter Eight

THE SACRIFICIAL DEATH OF CHRIST

JESUS CHRIST CRUCIFIED is a foundational and fundamental doctrine of the Christian church. The cross is the insignia of our faith. Other great men have been valued for their lives. Christ's greatest blessing to men came through His death.

The cross pervades all Scripture. The Mosaic instructions foreshadow its meaning. The historical books prove its necessity. The Psalms picture its reality. The prophets describe its coming. The Gospels announce its presence. The Acts proclaim its power. The Epistles explain its purpose. Revelation sees the consummation of its blessings.

It is often said, "Cut the Bible anywhere, and it bleeds; it is red with redemption truth." One out of every forty-four verses in the New Testament deals with the sacrificial death of Christ. It is mentioned in all 175 times.

While the incarnation divides time, the cross divides eternity. Christ was foreordained as the Lamb slain before the foundation of the world (1 Pet. 1:19-20); and as the Lamb once slain, He will be the theme of endless praise (Rev. 5:13).

It was unreasonable to expect that crucifixion would be employed for the execution of the Messiah. Stoning was the common method of capital punishment among the Jews (Lev. 20:2; Deut. 13:6-10; 17:2-5), and there are illustrations of its use in the Old Testament (Lev. 24:11-14; Num. 15:32-36; 1 Kings 12:18; 21:13; 2 Chron. 24:20-21). Stoning was especially stipulated in the Mosaic law as punishment for idolatry and blasphemy. The Jews requested that our Lord give them permission to stone a sinful woman (John 8:4-5), and on another occasion they took up stones to hurl at Him when He declared that He was equal with God (John 10:30-33).

Crucifixion was unknown to the Jews when the earliest prophecies of our Lord's death were recorded. The Romans, who introduced this bar-

barous method of capital punishment, were then hardly in existence. But by a circumstance of events that made the Romans the rulers of the world, the Jews in Christ's time, with other conquered nations, were paying tribute to Caesar. As a province of Rome, the right of such a dependent nation to execute its criminals was no longer permitted. Hence the Jews were required to secure the aid of the Roman governor before their prisoners could be put to death. By these strange and unexpected circumstances our Lord was led out to be crucified by the Romans rather than being stoned by the Jews.

Christ said, "Greater love hath no man than this, that a man lay down his life for his friends" (John 15:13). "But God commendeth his love toward us, in that, while we were yet *sinners,* Christ died for us" (Rom. 5:8, emphasis added). Some have given their lives for their friends, but think of Christ's amazing love for His *enemies.* He came down from the heights of heaven to the lowly cross and bowed His sacred head in shameful, agonizing death. His was the great sacrifice for mankind. God gave His dearly beloved Son for this great sacrifice, so that "whosoever believeth in him should not perish, but have everlasting life" (John 3:16).

THE PROMINENCE OF THE SACRIFICE

The Purpose of the Incarnation

Why was Christ born? The name that Joseph was commanded to give Him indicated He was to be the Savior of His people (Matt. 1:21). He Himself declared that He had come to give His life as a ransom for many (Matt. 20:28). From the beginning of His ministry Christ realized that the cross would terminate His life.

A Mystery to the Old Testament Prophets

One of the great proofs of the verbal inspiration of the Bible is that the writers did not always understand the message God gave them to record. It appears that the death of Christ, which was predicted centuries before He appeared, was a great mystery to the prophets (1 Pet. 1:10-12). Even the angels were not fully advised as to the plan and purpose of the world's greatest tragedy, but it was of such significance that they desired further information about it (v. 12).

A Mystery to the Disciples

There is no better proof that the Bible is the Word of God than the sacrifice of our Lord on Calvary, which was clearly described by the psalmists and prophets centuries before it took place. Our Lord particularly calls attention to this fact (Luke 24:44). The marvel of the mystery is that the disciples failed to understand the passages in the Old Testament that predicted the history of Jesus Christ and yet described with wonderful literalness His sufferings and glory. These passages are remarkable in view of the fact that the Jews did not expect their long looked-for Messiah to be put to death but rather thought He would reign as king. Even the disciples could not comprehend the many references our Lord made to His death.

The truth of the matter is that the Old Testament had much to say about a coming King and prophesied about a crucified Savior. The angel who announced to Mary the birth of Jesus said nothing about His premature death but instead predicted, "He shall be great, and shall be called the Son of the Highest: and the Lord shall give unto him the throne of his father David: And he shall reign over the house of Jacob for ever; and of his kingdom there shall be no end" (Luke 1:32-33). No wonder Mary pondered these things in her heart, and no wonder that a sword pierced her own perplexed soul (see Luke 2:35) as she stood at the cross and beheld the suffering of her uncrowned Son.

Its Place in the Gospels

A study of the Gospels impresses one with the silence concerning many years of Christ's life and the emphasis upon the last week of his life. If, as some contend, the life rather than the death of Christ is the important subject, is it not strange that each of the Gospel writers gave the briefest accounts of the events in Jesus' life but described in detail the events connected with His death? That the atonement was the all-important purpose of Christ's coming is proved by the fact that John, having related incidents and conversations that others omitted, joined with Matthew, Mark, and Luke in making much of our Lord's last week in Jerusalem. Of the twenty-one chapters in John, ten describe the events leading up to the crucifixion and resurrection.

Paul made the cross the theme of his first and many other sermons (see 1 Cor. 15:1-4). Like Peter at Pentecost, Paul particularly pointed out that Christ's death was "according to the scriptures."

PROPHECY CONCERNING THE SACRIFICE

More than a third of the Old Testament is prophecy, with Christ its central theme. Note the relationship of the Old Testament to the last book of the New Testament: In the one the Savior and King is prophesied; in the other, the Savior and King is glorified. The work of the Savior was predicted in three ways.

By Symbol

When Paul said that "the law was our schoolmaster to bring us unto Christ" (Gal. 3:24), he included the ceremonial law. The shedding of blood by the offering of animal sacrifices for the redemption of sin was a symbol of the great Sacrifice (Lev. 1:2, 11, 15; 8:15) and a constant emphasis on the all-important truth that "without shedding of blood is no remission" of sin (Heb. 9:11-14, 19-22). The office of the high priest was instituted so there would be a representative of the people to offer up sacrifices. As the great High Priest, our Lord offered Himself as the all-sufficient sacrifice for sin.

By Type

There are said to be 333 striking Old Testament pictures of Christ's sacrificial death. In the beginning of human history, only sacrifices requiring the shedding of blood met with God's approval. Cain's offering did not typify the sacrifice of life and was not acceptable (Heb. 9:22; 11:4). Let us consider two outstanding types:

THE PASSOVER LAMB

The lamb required for the celebration of the Passover (Exod. 12:5-7, 13) was an appropriate type of the great Sacrifice, typifying the sinless Lamb of God whose blood would save from eternal death. In the substitution of the Lord's Supper for the Passover, Christ became the Paschal Lamb.

THE BRAZEN SERPENT

The fiery serpents that invaded the camp of Israel were representative of sin and its fatal consequences. The brazen serpent erected by Moses (Num. 21:9) represented the Sin-bearer who was "made . . . sin for us" (2 Cor. 5:21) in order to remove the penalty of sin. Christ indicated that it was a picture of the crucifixion—the uplifted cross (John 3:14-15).

By Word

Just what experiences our Lord passed through we learn not so much from the Gospel narrators, who wrote what they saw and heard, but from the prophets who recorded the story by divine inspiration centuries before it took place. Prophecy provides another Gospel that is corroborative and supplementary to Matthew, Mark, Luke, and John. In the

New Testament we see only glimpses of the terrible conflicts of our Lord on the cross; in the Old Testament we see all His anguish. In the Gospels we have what Christ said and did, and what was said and done to Him; in prophecy we see His inner life—what He thought, and how He felt, and how He lived in the presence of His God and Father.

THE SAVIOR PIERCED (PS. 22:16; ZECH. 12:10; LUKE 24:40; JOHN 19:34)

What a picture is given us of the mob closing in at the foot of the cross. They were on all sides, like the packs of dogs in Palestine that were accustomed to surrounding their prey. There He was in the center with hands and feet pierced. Yet those scarred hands were to be evidence to the disciples that the risen Lord was the very man who had passed through this terrible ordeal. And there shall come a time when the Jews, who have long rejected Jesus Christ as their Messiah, shall recognize Him as the same one they had pierced. When they recognize the awful mistake of the centuries, "they shall mourn for him, as one mourneth for his only son. . . . In that day shall there be a great mourning in Jerusalem" (Zech. 12:10-11).

THE SAVIOR THIRSTING (PS. 22:14-15; 69:21; MATT. 27:34, 48; JOHN 19:28-29)

Note the words of John: "Jesus knowing that all things were now accomplished, that the scripture might be fulfilled, saith, I thirst" (John 19:28). He did not give vent to His own suffering until He knew that all He had come to do for man's salvation had been accomplished. And here is recorded both in prophecy and history the one kindness shown to our suffering Lord as He hung on the cross: When He cried of His thirst, someone offered Him an opiate that would have lessened the physical pain. But we note that He refused the vinegar, which was mingled with gall. He bore the full penalty of our sins in every respect.

THE SAVIOR STRIPPED (PS. 22:17-18; 34:20; LUKE 23:34; JOHN 19:23-24, 32-37)

Seated in front of the cross, the Roman soldiers, the lowest strata of Roman citizenry, the men whose lives were characterized by violence and sin, gambled for His clothing. Though these men cared not for God or His Word or the dying Son of God upon the cross, they fulfilled that Word that day, for the prophet had declared, "They part my garments among them, and cast lots upon my vesture" (Ps. 22:18).

And yet the same unseen power that caused the soldiers to gamble over the Savior's garments later withheld the hammer blows that would have broken His limbs. Not only had the prophet declared that not a bone of His would be broken, but centuries earlier when Israel fled from Egypt, not a bone of the paschal lamb was broken. When the Lamb who was slain from the foundation of the world became Israel's Passover, it was fitting that He should be offered up in the same manner. Here again we see the marvel of God's providence, for if our Lord had been stoned to death or had even suffered bone-breaking bodily injury from one of the boulders with which the Jews had threatened Him, He would no longer have been the perfect Lamb for the Passover sacrifice. Thus in the substitution of crucifixion for stoning, Christ in His death became a perfect antitype of the paschal lamb.

THE SAVIOR HUMILIATED (ISA. 53:12; MARK 15:27-28; LUKE 22:37; 23:34A)

In Isaiah 53 there are at least ten predictions regarding the humiliation of the King of Glory. The crowning insult was numbering Him with the transgressors. What it meant to the absolutely holy Son of God to be crucified between thieves we cannot fathom. It was the outrage of the ages. It was an indignity that this world had never seen before and never will again. But in the midst of His humiliation He became a Savior of the transgressors with whom He was numbered.

THE PROVISION OF THE SACRIFICE

The Lamb Provided for Abraham

A bearded patriarch rose early one morning and awakened his son, so they could begin the three-day journey to the mount of which God had spoken (Gen. 22:1-13). God had commanded him to slay his only son as a sacrifice on a mountain altar. Finally they arrived at the appointed place. Imagine the anguish of the father's heart when the son broke the silence with his innocent question: "My father . . . behold the fire and the wood: but where is the lamb for a burnt offering?" How Abraham must have stifled his emotions as he said brokenly, "My son, God will provide himself a lamb."

The Lamb Provided for the World

Abraham spoke prophetically (see John 8:56). The ram substituted for Isaac was a type of the Lamb of God who was to be provided twenty centuries later (John 1:29). Abraham's son was spared in the moment of death.

But when God led His only begotten Son to the cross, He could not release Him from death. Can anyone measure the greatness of the love that made the everlasting Father not only place His Son on the altar but thrust the sacrificial knife into the heart of His only begotten, beloved Son?

THE PURPOSE OF THE SACRIFICE

Why was Abraham's son spared and God's Son sacrificed? Why was it necessary for our Lord Jesus Christ to suffer a painful and shameful death?

The Fulfillment of Scripture (Luke 24:25-26; 1 Cor. 15:3)

Christ's sacrifice was necessary in order to fulfill Scripture. This our Lord declared to the travelers on the road to Emmaus. This Paul wrote to the Corinthians. God's Word cannot be broken; therefore, "the Lamb slain from the foundation of the world" (Rev. 13:8) was in due time revealed so that the unchangeable decree might be executed.

The Holiness of God (Ps. 47:8; 24:3-4; Isa. 6:3)

In a former chapter we considered the perfection of God's holiness. To God, sin of every kind is awful, sullied, degrading. His whole nature turns in utter abhorrence against it. The Scriptures plainly teach that death has been the penalty of sinful creatures who have dared to venture into His holy presence. A righteous God could not possibly ignore sin. To do so would have been contrary to His own holiness and would have resulted in moral chaos in the world.

The Sinfulness of Man (Rom. 3:10-20; Gal. 3:13-14)

All men have sinned. This is the plain teaching of Scripture. There is original sin, in which all men partake of the transgression of their first parents, who not only fell from the holy estate in which they were created, but by disobeying God brought all their descendants into a state of sin and misery. The sinfulness of man was made evident in the giving of the law. The law God gave did not remove sin but only made it all the more glaring.

In view of the holiness of God and the sinfulness of man, the question naturally arises: How is the mercy of God to be manifested so that His holiness will not be compromised by His assuming a merciful attitude toward sinful men in the granting of forgiveness? If God and the sinner are to be brought together, something must be done to remove sin, for while God loves the sinner, He has and will always continue to have hatred for sin.

PROPITIATION THROUGH SACRIFICE
(ROM. 3:25; 1 JOHN 2:2; 4:10)

Propitiation means "appeasing." The mercy seat covering the ark of the covenant was a type of Christ. The Hebrew word *kaphar* or *kapporeth* was translated in New Testament Greek as *hilasterion*. Both words convey "covering" and are discussed in the context of reconciliation with God, or propitiation (Exod. 25:17, 22; Heb. 9:5; Rom. 3:25). The death of Christ for man's sin satisfied the demands of God's holiness and righteousness relative to the sin question and the offending sinner. Therefore, all who come to God through faith on the basis of that gracious cross-work receive the forgiveness of sins and the gift of eternal life and are given a perfect standing in God's sight (justification). Christ's death is the righteous ground on which a righteous God can justify sinners without compromising His holiness and righteousness. It must always be remembered that "the carnal mind is enmity against God," and "to be carnally minded is death" (Rom. 8:6-7). God can have no dealings with man until his sin is removed, and only Christ's blood is sufficient for this.

Sufficient for All (Heb. 2:9)

Christ tasted death for every man, and sinners of all sorts, degrees, and conditions may have a share in the benefits of his redemptive work. The Greeks invited only the cultured, the Romans called the strong, and the Jews believed only the religious were entitled to salvation. Christ bids all to come. "Whosoever will, let him take the water of life freely" (Rev. 22:17). No one can deny the *whosoever* of the Gospel. The invitation to partake of the blessings of Christ's death is universal.

Efficacious to the Believer

A sovereign God who offers a gracious pardon to an undeserving sinner has a right to lay down conditions for the reception of these benefits. There must be an acceptance of God's gift. Salvation made possible by Christ's sacrificial death is unlimited, but only those who believe and accept it can be saved. Only man's unbelief limits the atonement (John 3:16-18; 5:40).

THE POWER OF THE SACRIFICE

It is almost impossible to measure the far-reaching results of the atonement. Every blessing, material or spiritual, that has come to man in the history of the world has been brought about by the death of Christ. Without it God could not have given blessings, for because of his sin man had forfeited every claim to God's benevolence. It will take eternity to appreciate all that the great sacrifice means. Observe its power over sin:

It Saves from the Penalty of Sin (Rom. 3:24; 5:1; 8:1; Titus 2:14)

Christ died in our place on Calvary, suffering the just penalty due our sin, in order that we might be delivered from the guilt, defilement, and penalty of sin through faith in Him.

It Secures from the Power of Sin (Rom. 6:6-18; 8:12)

While Satan cannot change the destiny of the believer, he still is able to tempt him with sin. But "there is power in the blood" of Jesus Christ to give every Christian victory over temptation (Heb. 2:18). Sin no longer need have dominion over the believer (Rom. 6:12-18).

It Separates from the Presence of Sin (Rev. 21:27)

The believer in Christ can look forward to the certainty of an entrance into that holy and happy habitation where no evil can gain entrance. This unmerited, indescribable place has been provided only by the death of Jesus Christ.

REVIEW QUESTIONS

1. In what respects is the crucifixion of Christ the foundation and fundamental doctrine of Christianity?
2. What was the Jewish method of execution, and why was it not employed in the death of our Lord?
3. Of what significance is it that the crucifixion was a mystery to the Old Testament prophets as well as to the disciples?
4. How large a place does the sacrificial death of Christ have in the Gospels?
5. Give two Old Testament types of the crucifixion.
6. Name four Old Testament predictions of Christ's agonizing death on the cross.
7. How was the lamb that was provided for Abraham a prophetic type of the crucifixion?
8. What three things suggest the purpose of the sacrifice?
9. What Scripture passages declare the sinfulness of man?
10. What is meant by *propitiation*?
11. If propitiation is sufficient for all, why will not all men be saved?

12. What three far-reaching benefits are secured for the believer through the sacrifice of Christ?

APPLYING DOCTRINE TO LIFE

1. What does the death of Christ mean to you?
2. How should the fact of Christ's death affect your relationships with others?

Chapter Nine

THE RESURRECTION OF CHRIST

THE RESURRECTION OF the Lord Jesus Christ is an historic fact, and as such it has been substantiated by many infallible proofs. All English-speaking people believe that eighty years before the birth of Christ, Julius Caesar, with two Roman legions, landed in Britain on the coast of Kent. No one thinks of doubting that. If eternal salvation depended on believing that fact, every student of history would accept it. Yet the actual, historic proof of this is far less complete, cogent, and convincing than is the evidence that Christ died and rose again. All Americans believe there is such a thing as the Declaration of Independence. Why? Because George Washington, Thomas Jefferson, and their contemporaries stated so. Since 1776 Americans have celebrated the Fourth of July as a memorial of national independence. But while the resurrection of Jesus Christ occurred centuries before the signing of the declaration of American independence, Easter is more widely observed today than the Fourth of July. More significant in our study is the fact that there was not one word of prophecy recorded concerning either the conquest of Britain by Julius Caesar or the gaining of American independence. The foretelling of the resurrection of Jesus Christ, together with the many other infallible proofs, such as the testimony of eyewitnesses and the remarkable attending circumstances, makes it the best attested fact in history.

THE EVIDENCE OF FULFILLED PROPHECY

Old Testament Predictions

Nothing in prophecy occupies more attention than the death and resurrection of Christ. At least twenty-five Old Testament prophecies were fulfilled in one day.

SPECIFIC PREDICTIONS (PS. 16:10; ISA. 53:9)

Isaiah had a vision of our Lord's burial. Though He died with the wicked and according to the usual proceedings would have been buried with them in the place where He was crucified, the prophet declared strangely enough that the Lord Jesus Christ would be honored with an exquisite funeral. Although the betrayal money, which the conscience-stricken Judas returned to the chief priests, was used to purchase the potter's field for the burial of the friendless (Matt. 27:3-8), the body of our Lord was not permitted such disgraceful disposal. The wealthy Joseph of Arimathaea begged the body of Jesus from Pilate and gave it the attention befitting a man of great renown and distinction. No expense was spared in the provision and preparation of the royal sepulcher. In having the body placed "in his own new tomb," this wealthy and influential disciple of our Lord bestowed upon it as much care as he would have given to his own son (Matt. 27:57-60).

Long before Isaiah saw in a vision the Savior dying with the wicked and yet buried with the wealthy, David spoke expressly about His resurrection: "For thou wilt not leave my soul in hell; neither wilt thou suffer thine Holy One to see corruption" (Ps. 16:10). Our Lord would go into Sheol (hell or the grave), but for a brief time only. His body would sink into the outer prison of the grave, but not to corruption. Death and hell would not be able to hold Him. In other words, Jesus Christ would be entombed long enough for conclusive evidence of His death, but not long enough for His body "to see corruption." The repeated mention of "the third day" in connection with the resurrection is most significant (Mark 9:31; Luke 9:22). It will be remembered that Lazarus, whom Jesus raised, had been in the grave four days and that decomposition of the body had already begun (John 11:39). Our Lord, however, was released from the tomb on the third day, before there were any signs of disintegration. Could one ask for anything more definite and more clearly defined than this?

TYPES OF PERSONAL EXPERIENCE (MATT. 12:40; HEB. 11:17-19)

The experience of Isaac was not only a type of the atonement, but also of the resurrection of Jesus Christ. From the moment that Abraham began to obey God's command to offer up his only son as a sacrifice, Isaac was a dead man. The father was fully resolved to follow out the divine instructions, believing "that God was able to raise him up, even from the dead; from whence also he received him in a figure" (Heb. 11:19). It was "on the third day" (Gen. 22:4) that God interrupted Abraham in the midst of the sacrifice, providing the substitutionary lamb and restoring the doomed son to the father's embrace.

The experience of Jonah was an even greater type of our Lord's resurrection. When the scribes and Pharisees clamored for a sign or special miracle to prove that Jesus was the Messiah, He declared that "as Jonah was three days and three nights in the whale's belly; so shall the Son of man be three days and three nights in the heart of the earth" (Matt. 12:40). Christ, the most intelligent of teachers, observed the law of apperception, or the Law of the Lesson, by teaching the unknown in terms of the known. (This law is one of the seven laws of teaching, as presented by John Milton Gregory. See his classic *The Seven Laws of Teaching*, revised edition, Baker, 1954, 1975, 1995.) It is inconceivable that He would have used a recognized myth to convince unbelieving Jews of His own burial and resurrection. Nothing is more conclusive from the reading of the Gospels than that both the disciples and the Jews accepted the experience of Jonah as fact but were reluctant to believe in the coming resurrection of Christ.

New Testament Predictions

All of the New Testament predictions regarding our Lord's resurrection were spoken by Him. The first was uttered at the very beginning of His ministry and the last on the final journey to Jerusalem only a few weeks before the crucifixion.

CHRIST'S FIRST PROPHECY (JOHN 2:18-22)

On the occasion of the Jewish Passover, our Lord indignantly drove out the desecrators of the temple who were using its sacred portals to sell their merchandise to the assembled multitudes. When the Jews challenged Him for a sign to show that He had authority for such action, Christ declared His power to rise from the dead: "Destroy this temple, and in three days I will raise it up." No one understood what He meant by these words, but after His resurrection the disciples recalled the incident and then realized that "he spake of the temple of his body." It is not to be wondered that they did not understand this hidden prophecy when they failed to grasp the plain predictions He made later.

CHRIST'S SECOND PROPHECY (MATT. 16:21; MARK 8:31; LUKE 9:22)

More than a year passed before the second prediction of the resurrection. This occurred at the height of our Lord's popularity, shortly after He had fed the five thousand and the people had attempted to make Him king. We can imagine how shocked the disciples must have been to hear that their popular leader would "suffer many things of the elders and chief priests and scribes, and be killed" (Matt. 16:21). It is little wonder that the impetuous Peter protested. The disciples were apparently so distressed and confused by the dismal thought of His death that the assurance of the Lord's resurrection made no impression on them. Yet this prediction was definite, even to the time when the resurrection would take place.

CHRIST'S THIRD PROPHECY (MATT. 17:9; LUKE 9:28-31)

After the first discouraging announcement of His death, our Lord inspired three of His disciples by a glimpse of His glory on the Mount of Transfiguration. At that time Moses and Elijah appeared and conversed with the glorified Savior. It is interesting to note that the topic of their discussion was "his decease which he should accomplish at Jerusalem" (Luke 9:31)—the theme that had been so unwelcome to the disciples. This wonderful conference on the mountaintop in which the Old Testament prophets joined was not only intended as another prediction of the crucifixion but also to give Peter, James, and John some conception of the importance of its place in God's program. When they came down from the mountain, our Lord again reminded the three disciples that He would rise from the dead, for He charged them not to speak to anyone of what they had seen until after His resurrection (Matt. 17:9).

CHRIST'S FOURTH PROPHECY (MATT. 17:22-23; MARK 9:31; LUKE 9:43-45)

Despite the association of the crucifixion and resurrection with their wonderful mountain experience, the disciples who had witnessed the Transfiguration were still unwilling to accept the announcement. Once more our Lord was obliged to speak explicitly of these coming events. Once more the disciples failed to comprehend it all. We read, "They were exceeding sorry" (Matt. 17:23). But while they had begun to realize what Christ meant when He spoke about being put to death, they still did not understand the meaning of His rising again.

CHRIST'S FIFTH PROPHECY (MATT. 20:18-19; MARK 10:34; LUKE 18:33)

Now the time drew nigh for the all-important events of the Lord's ministry to take place. He was preparing to attend His last Passover at Jerusalem. Unlike other celebrations of the feast He had observed with His disciples, this fateful one would usher in His death and resurrection. Once more He went over these vital matters with His disciples, but if they grasped His unwelcome instruction at all, it was not very clear in their minds. Scarcely had He spoken of the cross and the empty tomb when the ambitious mother of the sons of Zebedee requested that James and John be accorded the chief places in the coming kingdom (Matt. 20:20-21). Their minds were filled with thoughts of His throne and the day of His power. They were anxious to share in Christ's reward, but did not realize that they must first be partakers of His sufferings.

THE TESTIMONY OF THE ASTONISHED FRIENDS

The closest friends of Jesus did not expect that He would rise again. They considered their cause ended at the crucifixion.

The Women (Mark 16:1-11; Luke 24:1-11; John 20:11-18)

Study the various accounts of Mary Magdalene. She went to mourn, not to greet her Lord. "Who shall roll us away the stone?" the women asked (Mark 16:3). They were astonished to find it rolled away and the tomb empty. It was only after our Lord appeared personally to Mary Magdalene and the angels reminded the other women of His oft-repeated predictions of His resurrection that they were willing to believe that someone had not come and stolen the body.

The Disciples (Luke 24:13-31; John 20:1-10, 24-28)

When the women were finally convinced, they hastened to tell the disciples, but "their words seemed to them as idle tales, and they believed them not" (Luke 24:11). It was only when Peter and John came to the empty tomb and saw the discarded grave-clothes still retaining the shape of the body that they were convinced a robbery was impossible. On the way to Emmaus, Jesus' companions could not believe that Christ was with them until He broke bread and vanished out of their sight. Even when Christ finally appeared to all of the disciples in the upper room, the doubting Thomas would not believe it was anything but a hallucination. It was only after he was asked to put his fingers in the nail prints and to thrust his hand into Christ's side that he declared, "My Lord and my God" (John 20:28).

This detailed evidence of the utter *unbelief* of the disciples finally destroys the attempted theory that the risen Lord was the creation of excited, nervous, and ardent expectations. The disciples were willing to brand the women's tales as hallucinations and were far from expecting that they would eventually be convinced of what they could not previously conceive. Peter, who permitted a maid to frighten him on the eve of Calvary, possessed the courage of a lion at Pentecost. Unquestionably something most extraordinary had happened between those two days. The enthusiasm of the disciples that could not be diminished by persecution and martyrdom was not built upon a known falsehood. The resurrection was the cornerstone of their preaching.

An Eminent Scholar (1 Cor. 15:1-9)

There was an eminent scholar at that time who refused to accept the earnest, enthusiastic testimony of the disciples. He branded the resurrection as an out-and-out lie. He even went further and persecuted all who proclaimed it. But one day the attitude of this great intellect was completely changed. The living Christ called down to him from heaven and demanded a reason for his persecuting hatred. This convinced the philosopher of Tarsus that Christ had risen. He saw Christ's glory, he heard Christ's voice, and he then and there devoted his life to the task of bearing testimony to what he had seen and heard.

But this new disciple of our Lord did not content himself merely with rehearsing the things that he had seen and heard. His scholarly mind investigated all the evidences of the resurrection of Christ so that they might be set down in writing as unanswerable arguments for the years to come. He interviewed Peter and John. He questioned James, the brother of the Lord. He saw the women who were with Jesus. He visited the church of Jerusalem that had been gathered by the risen Christ. He confirmed the report that five hundred had seen Jesus at one time. So convincing were the proofs that he was able to gather that he went into heathen cities and presented them before some of the most intellectual people, and they accepted them. The thousands of converts of the world's greatest missionary could have investigated every statement that Paul made and could, like him, have interviewed the living witnesses of the resurrection of Jesus Christ.

THE EVIDENCE OF CHRIST'S ENEMIES

The Precaution to Insure Christ's Death (John 19:31-37)

By this torturous means of execution (crucifixion), the victim died slowly and sometimes lingered thirty-eight to forty hours before expiring. Josephus, the Jewish historian, tells of the recovery of one of three friends for whom he had a release, after having been on the cross for some time. This circumstance encouraged some people to argue that Christ merely swooned and revived in the cooler recesses of the tomb.

The Jews were unwilling for the three criminals to remain hanging on the cross on the Sabbath day. According to their own law they were obliged to bury criminals the same day they were executed. For this reason, on the eve of the Sabbath they besought Pilate to let the soldiers complete the execution. The two thieves were immediately dispatched, but believing Jesus to be already dead, the Roman soldiers certified to this fact and thrust a spear into His side. His death, then, was positively proved by His enemies and positively pronounced by unbiased witnesses whose business it was to execute order.

The Precaution to Guard the Sepulcher (Matt. 27:62-66)

The strongest evidence of the risen Lord was the absent body. Where did it go? The disciples did not take it. They could not take it. They had no thought of such action. The Jews did not take it. On the other hand, every precaution was taken to prevent the stealing of Christ's body, for they remembered His saying that He would rise again on the third day. In order that His friends might not circulate such a report, the chief priests and Pharisees requested of Pilate that the sepulcher be sealed and a guard set over it. This was intended positively to prevent any possibilities of tampering with the body by the disciples. But the disciples, as we have seen, had no such intention. When Joseph of Arimathaea had his servants roll the great stone before the mouth of the tomb, it was like sealing up a lost cause.

The Precaution to Bribe the Authorities (Matt. 28:11-15)

Imagine the predicament of Christ's enemies when the guards told them of the terrible earthquake and the appearance of supernatural creatures who had rolled away the great stone as though it were a swinging door, and for fear of whom they were obliged to flee for their lives.

Now there was only one thing that the enemies of Christ could do. They bribed the Roman authorities, who were always willing to do anything provided they were paid sufficiently. And so the chief priests and elders, having taken counsel, advised, "Say ye, His disciples came by night, and stole him away while we slept. And if this come to the governor's ears, we will persuade him, and secure you. So they took the money, and did as they were taught." This deception by the religious leaders was designed to explain away the resurrection by making the disciples responsible for the removal of Christ's dead body. In these religious leaders we have a fulfillment of the words of Christ that they would not be persuaded "though one rose from the dead" (Luke 16:31).

THE EVIDENCE OF THE IMPARTIAL WITNESSES (ACTS 5:34-40)

The Witness of Gamaliel

So great an impression did the preaching of the resurrection make upon the people of Jerusalem that the great lawyer Gamaliel said to the authorities who tried to crush it, "Let them alone: for if this counsel or this work be of men, it will come to nought: But if it be of God, ye cannot overthrow it; lest haply ye be found even to fight against God" (Acts 5:38).

But the apostles were not left alone; they were hunted and persecuted and slain. Nevertheless, their work did not come to nought. Based upon faith in the resurrection, millions of men, women, and children have been loved, sought out, and blessed.

The Witness of the Church

The Christian church is a great witnessing fact to the resurrection. Where did it get its missionary life? It was received from the risen Christ who said, "Go into all the world and preach the gospel to every creature" (see Matt. 28:19). What gospel does it bring to the world? The Gospel of the resurrection: "If thou shalt confess with thy mouth the Lord Jesus . . . thou shalt be saved" (Rom. 10:9). Upon this creed the great Christian church has been established.

The Witness of the Lord's Day

How does worship on the first day of the week prove the resurrection? For centuries the Jews had recognized the seventh day as the day of rest and worship. But the resurrection was such an important factor in the life of the church that Christians began worshiping on the first day of the week to commemorate the resurrection of Christ.

The Witness of Easter

The very observance of Easter in Europe, America, and Australia, and even in Asia and Africa, where millions of people are neither friends nor foes of Christ, is overwhelming evidence of the resurrection. Why does the domestic world, the commercial world, and the social world make so much of this great event if there be no risen Lord and no hope of a resurrection body? This year all over the civilized world people will mark time with a number. What does this mean? Why would the years be calculated from the birth and death of Jesus Christ rather than from any other great figure of history—such as Julius Caesar, Alexander the Great, or even George Washington? Jesus Christ was no ordinary man, and he changed the course of time and gave the world its calendar.

Every time a date is written, it is a witness to the resurrection of Jesus Christ! Explanation can be given on no other ground than that corroborated by reliable witnesses that Jesus was the Son of God and that He arose from the dead as He predicted.

REVIEW QUESTIONS

1. How do we know that the resurrection of Christ is better established as an historic fact than the Declaration of Independence?
2. What specific predictions of the resurrection are found in the Old Testament?
3. In what respects were Isaac and Jonah types of the resurrection?
4. How many prophecies did our Lord make concerning His resurrection? When was the first one uttered, and on what occasion was the last?
5. What evidence is there that the friends of our Lord did not believe in the resurrection?
6. What finally convinced Peter and John of this fact?
7. What circumstance led Paul to believe in the resurrection?
8. How did the enemies of Christ show some faith in his predictions?
9. What was the witness of Gamaliel to the resurrection?
10. How did the Christian church get its missionary life from the resurrection?
11. How does the observance of the Lord's Day prove the resurrection?
12. How is the observance of Easter a witness to the resurrection?

APPLYING DOCTRINE TO LIFE

1. What effect does the resurrection of Christ have upon the Christian's present and future experience?
2. What should be a Christian's attitude toward Sunday activities in the light of the resurrection?

Chapter Ten

THE RETURN AND
REIGN OF CHRIST

IN EMPHASIZING THE sacrificial death of the Lord Jesus Christ, many
have overlooked the importance of His second coming in the future to
reign as King over all the earth. Some have concluded that when Christ
was born as the King of the Jews and rejected by His own people, the
divine plan for a kingdom was abandoned and the church substituted.
Others make no distinction between the church and the kingdom. These
views are not the teaching of Scripture. Christ is both Savior and King.
The Great Sacrifice accomplished, the High Priest is now in heaven. We
anticipate His future entrance as King into His kingdom.

The prophets of the Old Testament were perplexed, Peter tells us,
because the Holy Spirit revealed unto them both "the sufferings of
Christ, and the glory that should follow" (1 Pet. 1:10-11). They could
not understand how the Messiah could be both Sacrifice and King. They
little dreamed that there would be a long interval of time between the
crucifixion and the coronation, when the church—a mystery not
revealed to the prophets—would have its day and accomplish its purpose. It was not until the day of transfiguration that the first light illu-
minated the problem. After our Lord had disclosed to His disciples His
coming death, three of them were privileged to catch a glimpse of "the
glory that should follow" on the Mount of Transfiguration. This our Lord
declared to be a vision of "the Son of man coming in his kingdom" (Matt.
16:28), and Peter later associated it with the "coming of our Lord Jesus
Christ," an event still future (2 Pet. 1:16-18).

THE RETURN OF CHRIST
*His Coming Assured (Matt. 24:29-30; Mark 14:62; Luke 17:24-25;
21:25-27; 1 Thess. 4:13-18; Heb. 9:28)*

No less than three hundred references in the New Testament assure us
of the second coming of the Lord Jesus Christ. In addition to His own

specific statements, all of the writers in the New Testament refer to it, while the book of Revelation is the "unveiling" (the literal translation of the Greek word translated "revelation") of His glorious person. While the terrible Tribulation period and other impending events are predicted as sure and certain signs of His coming, the exact day and hour is not revealed. The frequent use of the word "watch" in the New Testament teaches us that the second coming of the Lord must always be regarded as imminent. Like the motion to adjourn in parliamentary law, it takes precedence over any other event.

His Coming in Person (Zech. 14:4; Acts 1:11; Rev. 1:7)

Forty days after His resurrection, Jesus was talking with an assembled group of His disciples and followers when suddenly, before their eyes, He was taken up into heaven, and a cloud received Him out of their sight. As the disciples stood there staring up in amazement, two angels said to them, "Ye men of Galilee, why stand ye gazing up into heaven? This same Jesus, which is taken up from you into heaven, shall so come *in like manner* as ye have seen him go into heaven" (Acts 1:11, emphasis added).

In the moment of their keenest desolation and loss, this promise was given to the disciples. It also comes to us and to believers of every generation as an assurance that Christ will literally come again. His coming will not be just a spiritual visitation, but a personal return. From the earth He ascended, and to the earth He will return: "And his feet shall stand in that day upon the Mount of Olives, which is before Jerusalem on the east" (Zech. 14:4). With a real body He left them, and with a real body He will come back; it shall be a resurrected and glorified body, but we shall recognize Him just as truly as Thomas did when he was shown the nail prints in the Lord's hands.

They saw Him go away into heaven, and every eye shall clearly see Him when He descends from heaven to the earth. "Behold, he cometh with clouds; and every eye shall see him, and they also which pierced him: and all kindreds of the earth shall wail because of him" (Rev. 1:7).

His Coming with His Saints (Jude 14-15; Rev. 19:14)

When the Son of Man comes in the clouds of heaven with power and great glory, He will not come alone. "Behold, the Lord cometh with ten thousands of his saints" (Jude 14). John saw them and wrote, "And the armies which were in heaven followed him upon white horses, clothed in fine linen, white and clean" (Rev. 19:14). The armies, then, must be the saints—not the church alone, but the saints of Old Testament times, as well as those slain by the Beast in the Great Tribulation. All follow in the train of their now triumphant Lord, when He comes to put down Satan and his followers forever and to reign in righteousness.

The Great Captain will be mounted on a white horse, and the saints likewise will ride forth on horses of all white, for they are all royal and righteous, through Him, and will come forth to share in His work of conquering, judging, and ruling. They will wear no armor, for they are immortal, but will be clothed in fine linen, white, and clean, for their garments have been washed in the blood of the Lamb.

Have you ever seen those strange conceptions of the future life of the saved that picture them reclining idly on a golden street or playing a harp by a crystal stream? We are not saved to eternal idleness, nor to the feverish rush of activity such as we know here on earth. But there will be a place for each of us in God's plan for the eternal ages. We cannot look that far ahead now, but from what is revealed, we see that the saints will have important work to do in the day of the establishing of Christ's kingdom. John here pictures them sharing in the battle and triumph that bring in the kingdom. Paul tells us that the saved shall share in judging the world (1 Cor. 6:2). We also read that the saints shall reign with Him (Rev. 20:6) and that "his servants shall serve him" (Rev. 22:3).

His Coming in Power and Glory (Matt. 24:29-31; 26:64; Mark 8:38; Luke 21:25-27)

A number of the passages to which we have already referred have spoken of the power and the glory of the second coming of our Lord. Now we turn to still others. Matthew, Mark, and Luke all record Christ's prophecy of His coming back to earth at the end of the days of tribulation, and in this prediction He speaks of His coming with great power and glory.

Again, in that infamous trial to which the holy Son of God was subjected, when the high priest sought to force Christ to answer whether or not He was the Christ, the Son of God, Jesus said to His accusers, "Hereafter shall ye see the Son of man sitting on the right hand of power, and coming in the clouds of heaven" (Matt. 26:64). Peter speaks of the Transfiguration as a glimpse of "the power and coming of our Lord Jesus Christ" (2 Pet. 1:16). All this power and glory will be in sharp contrast to His first appearance here on earth as the Son of Man.

Think what will be the feeling of those who have made light of Christ! Imagine the agony of soul of those who mocked Him in Pilate's hall and helped hang Him on the tree! John mentions in particular that they who pierced Him shall see Him in the hour of His triumph (Rev. 1:7).

Not only man will tremble in the presence of such great power and glory, but the whole universe will shake. The Mount of Olives will cleave in two, the hills and the mountains will move, the stars will fall from their places, and the sun and moon will hide their faces.

His Coming in Judgment (Ps. 2; Zeph. 1:14–18; Matt. 16:27;
2 Thess. 1:7-10; Jude 15)

Why will the nations wail at the sign of His appearing? Why will God laugh while "the heathen rage . . . the kings of the earth set themselves, and the rulers take counsel together, against the LORD, and against his anointed"? Because when He comes in power and great glory to judge the world, He will break the rebellious "with a rod of iron" and "dash" the ungodly "in pieces like a potter's vessel," as the psalmist expresses it in that prophetic psalm (2) of the Messiah's return to establish His kingdom.

Read Zephaniah's graphic account (1:14-18) of when the Lord comes "to execute judgment upon all, and to convince all that are ungodly among them of all their ungodly deeds which they have ungodly committed, and of all their hard speeches which ungodly sinners have spoken against him" (Jude 15).

Paul, writing to the Thessalonians, says that "the Lord Jesus shall be revealed . . . in flaming fire taking vengeance on them that know not God, and that obey not the gospel of our Lord Jesus Christ: who shall be punished with everlasting destruction from the presence of the Lord, and from the glory of his power" (2 Thess. 1:7-9).

The doctrine of the second coming of Christ is not popular. It is a sad prospect for any but those who are truly born again. Men like to talk about the gentle Galilean and the pattern of His noble life here on earth, but not of the Great Judge returning in power to pour out divine wrath and vengeance on this sinful world. Christ will come to restore all the blessings that were lost in the Fall and to usher in the Millennium, but judgment must precede blessing, and there can be no universal righteousness until Satan and his ungodly followers are vanquished completely.

THE REIGN OF CHRIST

The Throne of Christ

THE THRONE OF DAVID (2 SAM. 7:10-17; PS. 89:3-4; ISA. 9:6-7;
JER. 23:5; AMOS 9:11; LUKE 1:32-33; JOHN 18:37; 19:19-22)

Nothing is plainer in all Scripture than the message of the angel to Mary that her child "shall be called the Son of the Highest: and the Lord God shall give unto him the throne of his father David" (Luke 1:32). One thousand years earlier, God had covenanted with David that He would establish his kingdom *forever* through a ruler that would come from his own family. This covenant was confirmed by the prophets. Amos goes so far as to speak of the restoration of the house of David, which in his day was already tottering. When Nebuchadnezzar carried away into captivity the royal family of Judah, he little realized that in that remnant, in due time, there was to be born a king far greater than himself.

No man of the house of David had more right to the throne than Jesus Christ. In Matthew 1:1-16 we have the royal line from David to Joseph. The man who had a right to the throne when Christ was born was Joseph, the carpenter. However, it was not to Joseph but to Mary that the coming of the King was announced. Joseph was not the father of the divine King, and therefore no claim to the throne could be made through him. But Luke 3:23-31 gives us the genealogy of Joseph's father-in-law, or Mary's father. He too was a direct descendant of David through Nathan, a brother of Solomon. It is through this connection that Jesus Christ could lay valid claim to the throne of David. And we find that was just what He was expected to do.

When Jesus was finally born, wise men came from the East saying, "Where is he that is born King of the Jews?" Herod was so alarmed, fearing the royal child might dethrone him, that he slaughtered all the innocent babes of Bethlehem (Matt. 2:1-8, 16).

A little later we find John the Baptist announcing that "the kingdom of heaven is at hand" (Matt. 3:2). The King Himself used the same expression at the beginning of His public ministry and later directed His disciples to proclaim that message. Eight times the King was acclaimed "the son of David," and during His last week His royal rights were notably recognized. He admitted to Pilate that He had been born to sit on a throne—the throne of His father David—and the Roman governor wrote that title in three languages and thus proclaimed to the world that Christ was the King. All the protests of the Jews that this significant statement be modified were in vain. Christ was King even in death.

THE THRONE AT JERUSALEM (ISA. 24:23; JER. 3:17; JOEL 3:16; AMOS 1:2; MIC. 4:7)

From some of the songs that are sung or sermons that are preached today, one would receive the impression that *Zion* is simply a synonym for heaven. However, in most Bible references Zion is identical with Jerusalem. From the time the stronghold of Zion was captured by David (2 Sam. 5:7) and hallowed by placing the ark of the covenant in it, there has been an interchange of the names of this mountain and the city of which it is a part (Ps. 135:21; Isa. 30:19; Zech. 1:14).

The throne of David that the angel promised for the Son of Mary was to be in Jerusalem. So the prophets had stated, and so the people believed. After our Lord had performed the marvelous miracle of feeding the five thousand, the multitude was so firmly convinced that He was the promised Messiah that they endeavored to take Him by force to make Him King (John 6:14-15).

THE KINGDOM OF CHRIST

A Universal Kingdom (Ps. 72:8-11; Dan. 2:44; 7:14; Zech. 14:9; Rev. 11:15)

This kingdom will not be limited to the confines of Solomon's domain, nor will the King reign merely over Israel. "He shall have dominion also from sea to sea. . . . The kings of Tarshish and of the isles shall bring presents: the kings of Sheba and Seba shall offer gifts . . . all kings shall fall down before him: all nations shall serve him" (Ps. 72:8-11).

Babylon, Persia, Greece, and Rome established world kingdoms, but although more than twenty centuries have elapsed, no nation has been able to control the world. Mohammed attempted it, and so did Napoleon, but all the efforts of world conquerors have failed. The unbroken word of prophecy long ago predicted that the God of heaven will set up a kingdom that will never be destroyed or inherited by others but will consume all other kingdoms. It is only when the kingdoms of this world become the kingdoms of our Lord Jesus Christ that this prophecy will be fulfilled.

A Millennial Kingdom (Isa. 65:20, 22-23; Rev. 20:4-6)

Six times in Revelation 20 we are told that the Lord will reign a thousand years. Because this coming age will last a thousand years, it has been called by the Latin word *millennium*. While this specific number is not found elsewhere in Scripture, there are a multitude of promises for Israel, for the nations of the earth, and even for all creation that will require a millennium of years to be fulfilled.

A Peaceful Kingdom

The Prince of Peace will be on the throne, and consequently there will be:

DESTRUCTION OF ALL ARMAMENTS (ISA. 2:4; MIC. 4:3)

There cannot be a warless world as long as nations continue to build armaments for the destruction of the human race. The Prince of Peace "shall rebuke strong nations afar off," and of their own accord they "shall beat their swords into plowshares, and their spears into pruning hooks" (Mic. 4:3). The books and newspapers of that day will not be filled with accounts of warring nations, and it will be literally true that they shall learn war no more.

UNIVERSAL KNOWLEDGE OF GOD (JER. 31:34; HAB. 2:14)

During the Kingdom Age Christ will be recognized in all His perfection and knowledge; consequently there will be a general knowledge of God. "After those days, saith the LORD, I will put my law in their inward parts, and write it in their hearts; and will be their God, and they shall be my people . . . for they shall all know me, from the least of them unto the greatest of them" (Jer. 31:33-34). The apostle Paul in the New Testament also speaks of this coming day when "at the name of Jesus every knee should bow, of things in heaven, and things in earth, and things under the earth; and that every tongue should confess that Jesus Christ is Lord, to the glory of God the Father" (Phil. 2:10-11).

INDIVIDUAL SECURITY (1 KINGS 4:25; MIC. 4:4)

The families of Judah and Israel enjoyed the most prosperous tranquillity during all the days of Solomon, whose reign is a type of that of Christ's age of glory. Under the wise administration of an impartial judge, there will be an equitable division of the land, and every man will be a proprietor. Not only will he have a possession of his own, but his life and property will be secure. The vine and the fig tree are mentioned rather than a house to signify that there will be no need for a shelter. Men will be safe even in the fields and open air.

A Righteous Kingdom (Ps. 72:2-4, 12-14; Isa. 11:1-5; 61:11; Jer. 23:5)

In these days it is impossible for human governments and rulers to govern righteously. Our courts are unable to get at the facts, even when all concerned are honestly trying to do so. Often lying witnesses and fraudulent lawyers and even untrustworthy judges conspire to thwart the course of justice. Might often makes right, and wealth covers wickedness. But the King of the millennial kingdom will have all wisdom to know and all power to accomplish. He and His associate judges will not need to hear evidence or depend on witnesses, nor will it be necessary to employ armies or police forces to execute justice (Isa. 11:3-4). Judgment will be meted out without delay on everyone who violates the laws. "He shall deliver the needy when he crieth; the poor also and him that hath no helper" (Ps. 72:12).

Can we who seek first the kingdom of God and His righteousness and pray, "Thy kingdom come" possibly picture the joy of a thousand years of peace? The government of an absolute monarch too wise to make any mistakes and too good to be unkind, yet powerful enough to secure the absolute submission of all, will be perfect.

REVIEW QUESTIONS

1. How many references to the second coming of the Lord Jesus Christ are in the New Testament?
2. What statement was made on the occasion of our Lord's ascension that would indicate His return in person?
3. What two passages in Scripture state that He will return with His saints?
4. What did the Gospel writers say about His return in power and glory?
5. How do we know that the second coming will be for judgment upon unbelievers?
6. What is meant by the throne of David, and where is it to be established?
7. How are the throne rights of Christ revealed in the genealogies of Matthew and Luke?
8. How do we know that Christ's kingdom will be universal?
9. What passages in Scripture state the length of Christ's reign upon earth?
10. What three circumstances will make it possible for this to be a reign of peace?
11. From what Scriptures do we know that there will be universal knowledge of God?
12. What assurance is given that Christ's reign will be a righteous reign?

APPLYING DOCTRINE TO LIFE

1. How can a Christian "watch" for Christ's return while busy in everyday life and ministry?
2. What are you doing for the Lord now that will not be necessary after His second coming?

Chapter Eleven

THE PERSONALITY
AND POWER OF
THE HOLY SPIRIT

THERE ARE SOME THINGS that we cannot see but that we most certainly believe. In fact, four of our five senses may be closed to the reality of certain facts that our fifth sense proclaims.

No one has seen a pain, heard it, or smelled it, but one can *feel* a pain. The wind cannot be seen, but we know that it bends the trees and tosses the waves. Electricity cannot be seen, but we know that it exists, as is evident by its power all about us.

THE PERSONALITY OF THE HOLY SPIRIT

No one has ever seen the Holy Spirit. But the evidences of His presence and power are conclusive to all who are willing to give unbiased thought to the phenomena that His presence brings to pass.

We have learned that the three persons of the Godhead are equal in power and glory. We have already studied many of their common attributes; so now we need to study only those attributes of the Holy Spirit that relate especially to the believer in Christ. Because some would not only deny the deity but also the *personality of the Holy Spirit*, it is essential to begin our study at this point.

The lessons on God's works of creation and providence helped us understand the personality of God. The incarnation, miracles, and resurrection are conclusive evidence of the personality of Jesus Christ. But the acts and workings of the Holy Spirit are so secret and mystical—so much is said about His influence, gifts, and power—that some have hastily concluded that He is a manifestation or influence of the divine nature rather than a person. His being called "breath," "wind," and "power" and His association with symbols such as "oil," "fire," and "water" have erroneously led some to think of Him as an impersonal influence emanating from God.

Is it essential to know whether or not the Holy Spirit is a person? If the Holy Spirit is a person, He is worthy of our worship, faith, and love, and the Christian has no right to withhold honor due Him. If the Holy Spirit is a person, infinitely wise, holy, and loving, then it should be our concern that He possess us and use us to His honor and glory. It makes all the difference in the world whether we vainly struggle to possess the Holy Spirit or whether the Holy Spirit possesses us.

Trinity of Persons

How many times we have sung the "Doxology" without thinking of the words! Surely we should not sing this tribute of adoration to the Trinity without realizing that we have ascribed to the Holy Spirit the same devout praise that is accorded to the Father and to the Son. Furthermore, the singing of the "Gloria" is the proclamation both of the deity and the personality of the Holy Spirit. "Glory be to the Father, and to the Son, and to the Holy Ghost." If we grant personality to the Father and to the Son, of necessity the third person of the Godhead must be included. The Bible provides proof in:

CREATION (GEN. 1:26)

When God created man He said, "Let us make man," not "Let me." The three members of the Godhead said, "Let us unitedly become the Creator of man." In the plan of redemption it was the same three persons speaking with one consent: "Let us save man." It is a source of sweet comfort to think that it was not one person but the glorious Trinity who declared this.

BAPTISM (MATT. 28:19)

Baptism is administered in the name of the Father and of the Son and of the Holy Ghost. No one thinks of the Holy Spirit as a power or a force in this connection. He is a person.

BENEDICTION (2 COR. 13:14)

How familiar is the benediction taken from the Scriptures with which many services are concluded! Here again the Holy Spirit is ascribed an equal place with that of the Father and the Son. "The grace of the Lord Jesus Christ, and the love of God, and the communion of the Holy Ghost, be with you all."

Divine Attributes

Not only is personality ascribed to the Holy Spirit through His association with the other members of the Godhead, but the attributes of the divine nature are also recorded of Him.

HE IS ETERNAL (HEB. 9:14)

It is important to note that though the believer possesses eternal life, he had a beginning in time. Actually all men, though creatures of time, will exist forever either in bliss or in judgment. However, God has neither beginning nor end but eternally exists.

HE IS OMNIPRESENT (PS. 139:7-10)

The Holy Spirit is everywhere present. "Whither shall I go from thy spirit? or whither shall I flee from thy presence?"

HE IS OMNIPOTENT

The virgin birth of our Lord (Luke 1:35) was made possible by the omnipotence of the Holy Spirit, who has no limitations in power.

We marvel at the unpromising group of men our Lord chose to carry on His work after His departure. They were men without learning, money, or influence. Moreover, despite His revelation of Himself to them, they were so lacking in faith and courage that they deserted Him at the hour of His arrest and trial. Yet these men later created such a stir, not only in Jerusalem but throughout Asia and Europe, that people said, "These that have turned the world upside down are come hither also" (Acts 17:6). It was not these men who transformed the world but the omnipotent power of the Holy Spirit working through them (Acts 4:31-33).

HE IS OMNISCIENT

Paul, a great scholar, intellectually well-equipped to deal with the keen-minded Greeks, humbly acknowledged to them that his preaching "was not with enticing words of man's wisdom, but in demonstration of the Spirit and of power" (1 Cor. 2:1-11).

Personal Characteristics

PERSONAL ADDRESS

The Greek word for *spirit* is neuter and should be accompanied by a neuter pronoun. However, contrary to ordinary usage, the masculine pronoun is used twelve times in John 16:7-8, 13-14. This is not just personification, but a definite assertion of the personality of the Holy Spirit. This does not mean that the third person of the Trinity has hands and feet like a man. We must distinguish between personality and corporeality. A *person* can think, feel, and exercise willpower. All these functions are attributed to the Holy Spirit in Scripture.

PERSONAL ATTRIBUTES

INTELLECT

The Holy Spirit has a mind (Rom. 8:27)—the unique possession of a person. He searches the deepest truths of God and possesses enough knowledge of His counsels to understand His purposes (1 Cor. 2:10-11). Could a mere influence do this?

EMOTION (ROM. 15:30)

Have you ever thought of "the love of the Spirit" (Rom. 15:30)? The love of the Father was infinitely great. His love was broad enough to encompass everyone in the entire world and great enough to give His only begotten, beloved Son for their salvation. The love of the Son was also inconceivably great. His love caused Him to leave the glory of heaven and come and die for sinful men. Yet the great love of the Father would have been in vain, and the self-sacrificing love of the Son to no purpose, if it had not been for the great, patient, infinite love of the blessed Spirit working in our hearts. The love of Father, Son, and Holy Spirit is expressed in the divine program for the salvation of the sinner.

WILL

The Holy Spirit has a will of His own (1 Cor. 12:11; Acts 16:6-7). It is quite different with the angels that do God's commandments, hearkening unto the voice of "his word" (Ps. 103:20).

Paul desired to preach in the province of Asia, but the Holy Spirit willed otherwise. Later he was privileged to minister for two years in Ephesus, a key city there (Acts 19:10).

HUMAN ATTITUDES

ABLE TO BE GRIEVED

We could not grieve the Holy Spirit if He were merely a force or an influence. Alas, we can hurt His feelings. Every unkind word, every selfish deed, every impure thought grieves the Spirit (Eph. 4:30).

ABLE TO BE RESISTED

Stephen delivered one of the most masterful sermons in the Bible and so antagonized the Jews that they stoned him to death. In his dying message he declared that generation after generation Israel had persisted in resisting the Holy Spirit (Acts 7:51).

THE POWER OF THE HOLY SPIRIT

In the Gospels the disciples are cowards; in the book of Acts they are heroes. A mere maid frightened Peter, but a few days later that same man was as bold as a lion. Courageously he stood before a multitude of three thousand and charged them with the crucifixion of the Lord Jesus Christ. What made the difference? The power of the Holy Spirit. In His parting message to the disciples just before His ascension, Christ said, "Ye shall receive power, after that the Holy Ghost is come upon you" (Acts 1:8). So conspicuous was this power in the life of Peter that Simon the magician offered him money saying, "Give me also this power." To this Peter replied, "Thy money perish with thee, because thou hast thought that the gift of God may be purchased with money" (Acts 8:18-20).

In Creation (Gen. 1:2-3; 2:7; Job 26:13; Ps. 104:30)

The Holy Spirit shared in the creation of the heavens and the earth. In other chapters we have noticed that the work of creation was attributed to God the Father and Christ the Son. This is not contradictory but is one more proof of the Trinity. "Let *us* make man" (Gen. 1:26, emphasis added).

All the stars of heaven are said to have been placed up above by the Spirit, and one particular constellation, called the "crooked serpent" (Job 26:13), is especially pointed out as His handiwork. We do not know how remote the time of creation was, nor through what various stages of existence our planets have passed, but we do read that at the beginning of creation, "the earth was without form, and void; and darkness was upon the face of the deep" (Gen. 1:2). It was then that "the Spirit of God moved upon the face of the waters" (Gen. 1:2), bringing order out of chaos and causing darkness to disappear. All this happened before the creation of man. It was the Spirit of God who breathed into man the very life of his existence, and it is the same Spirit who perpetuates life and "renewest the face of the earth" by the creation of all life (Ps. 104:30).

In Regeneration (John 3:3-5; Eph. 3:16; Titus 3:5)

Nicodemus was a rich man and was held in high esteem among the people. He had education and honor, for he was one of the seventy who sat in the highest council of the Jews. But he lacked one thing—life from God. Christ told him that he must be born again. In his natural birth he was born to die. Why? Because by one man (Adam) "sin entered into the world, and death by sin; and so death passed upon all men, for that all have sinned" (Rom. 5:12).

Regeneration, then, is re-creation. If creation is the work of the Holy Spirit, it is not surprising that the work of re-creation is also ascribed to Him. Men cannot create themselves or re-create themselves. Men cannot create a tiny gnat or a grain of sand; nor can we find a thing that has created itself. Nothing but the power of the Holy Spirit is equal to this task.

We must distinguish between Christ's work *for* us and the Holy Spirit's work *in* us. Without the sacrifice upon Golgotha, it would have been impossible for man to be saved. Without the work of the Holy Spirit it would be equally impossible. The Holy Spirit creates in our hearts the faith through which we recognize and receive salvation.

Regeneration is never separated from faith. The moment a man really believes on Christ, however feebly, he is regenerated by the Holy Spirit. The weakness of his faith may make him unconscious of the change, just as a newborn infant knows little or nothing about himself or herself. But where there is faith there is always a new birth, and where there is not faith there is no regeneration.

In Inspiration

Since the Holy Spirit is the author of the Scriptures, it is not surprising to find a peculiar power emanating from the Bible that is not found in any other book (Jer. 5:14; 23:29; 2 Cor. 3:6; 1 Thess. 1:5; Heb. 4:12).

A poor man in South Africa once came to Mr. Moffat, the missionary, with a distressed look. Mr. Moffat asked him what was the matter, and he replied, "My dog has swallowed three leaves of the New Testament."

"Why cry over that?"

"Because it will spoil the dog. He was a good hunter, but it will make him tame now, the same as it makes all the people tame around here. It will spoil him as a hunter."

The man had seen the wonderful effect of the reading and preaching of the Bible—that it made people quiet and contented—and he was afraid it would have the same effect upon his dog.

Thousands of men and women have been converted simply from reading the Word of God. It was that which first awakened Martin Luther to the emptiness of the Roman Catholic doctrine of works and gave him courage to nail his Ninety-five Theses upon the door of the Wittenberg Cathedral in defiance of the powerful Church of Rome.

In Witnessing

When the Holy Spirit descended upon our Lord at His baptism, it was to attest or witness to the fact that He was the Son of God. Afterward, when the Lord stilled the storm, healed the sick, raised the dead, and cast out demons, it was done by the power of the Holy Spirit (Isa. 61:1; Zech. 4:6; Luke 4:16-21). These were works of attestation, works that authenticated or bore witness to His power.

When Christ declared in His farewell address that His disciples would perform even greater works than He had done (John 14:12), it was because the same Holy Spirit who empowered Him would rest upon them. Just before He left them, He announced that they would receive power after the Holy Ghost had come upon them, and they would be witnesses for Him (Acts 1:8). Ten days later the Holy Spirit came like a mighty rushing wind, and His great power was soon evident, not only in Jerusalem, but in Judea and Samaria and the regions beyond. "With great power gave the apostles witness of the resurrection of the Lord Jesus" (Acts 4:33). But the disciples fully realized the secret of their power and were not ashamed to disclose it. "We are his witnesses of these things; and so is also the Holy Ghost, whom God hath given to them that obey him" (Acts 5:32). The Holy Spirit, as our Lord predicted, convicted that great multitude at Pentecost "of sin, and of righteousness, and of judgment" (John 16:8).

The Holy Spirit attested to the message and ministry of the disciples by many miraculous deeds (Heb. 2:4). Not only were the disciples given the ability to speak in the languages of eighteen different nationalities represented at Pentecost, but miracles of life and healing followed. Peter healed Aeneas and raised Dorcas from the dead. So numerous were the healings of the sick that invalids lined the streets where Peter walked, so the efficacy of his shadow falling on them might afford recovery (Acts 5:12-16). Prison doors were thrown open, and prisoners were released, to the astonishment of the authorities who had taken every precaution to prevent an escape. Again and again Paul and his companions were miraculously saved from stoning, from prison, from shipwreck. These are the acts not of the apostles, but of the Holy Spirit (see Rom. 15:18-19), who was the might and marvel of the early church.

In the Resurrection

The resurrection of Christ is ascribed to the work of the Holy Spirit. We may be perplexed to find that sometimes the resurrection of Christ is ascribed to Himself; because of His own power He could not be held by the bond of death. He willingly laid down His life, and He had the power to take it up again (John 10:17). But in another portion of Scripture our Lord's resurrection is ascribed to God the Father. Jesus is the one "whom

God hath raised from the dead" (Acts 3:15); "Him hath God exalted" (Acts 5:31). Scripture also teaches that Christ was raised by the Holy Spirit (Rom. 1:4; 8:11; 1 Pet. 3:18). This difference in the divine record, rather than contradicting the truth, merely confirms it. The difficulty is easily explained by the doctrine of the Holy Trinity, which declares that the three persons in the Godhead are the same in substance and equal in power and glory.

REVIEW QUESTIONS

1. How do we know that the Holy Spirit is a person?
2. What three Scripture passages include the Holy Spirit in the Trinity?
3. Name four divine attributes of the Holy Spirit.
4. Suggest three personal attributes of the Holy Spirit.
5. What do we mean by the human attitudes of the Holy Spirit?
6. In what five ways is the power of the Holy Spirit manifested?
7. How is the power of the Holy Spirit manifested in regeneration?
8. In what respect is the Holy Spirit the author of Scripture?
9. How did the miracles of our Lord relate to the power of the Holy Spirit?
10. How do we know that the Holy Spirit participated in the work of creation?
11. What did Christ mean when He declared to His disciples that they would perform even greater works than He had done?
12. Give scriptural evidence that the resurrection of Christ is ascribed to the work of the Holy Spirit.

APPLYING DOCTRINE TO LIFE

1. How is the personality and power of the Holy Spirit manifested in the life of a Christian?
2. How should the Spirit's authorship of the Scriptures affect a Christian's study and presentation of them?

Chapter Twelve

THE HOLY SPIRIT AND THE BELIEVER

CHRIST WAS ABOUT TO return to heaven. It was the last hour with His disciples. He was about to leave His earthly office as Teacher and Prophet. But before doing so, He wished to acquaint them with the One who would come after Him. He prepared their hearts and aroused their interest in the One who was to follow by saying, "It is expedient for you that I go away: for if I go not away, the Comforter will not come unto you; but if I depart, I will send him unto you" (John 16:7). "I will pray [to] the Father, and he shall give you another Comforter, that he may abide with you for ever" (John 14:16).

The word "Comforter," while most fitting for the needs of the grief-stricken disciples, does not fully describe the service that the Holy Spirit would render. The name *Paraclete* in the Greek has no English translation that exactly reproduces its meaning. The same word elsewhere indicates the office of Christ in heaven: "We have an *advocate* with the Father" (1 John 2:1, emphasis added). But the Holy Spirit was to be even more than a trustworthy attorney for the disciples. He was to be their Teacher, Partner, Companion—in fact, everything that Christ had been to them.

THE BELIEVER TAUGHT BY THE HOLY SPIRIT

Jesus Christ had been the official teacher of the Twelve. They did not sit at the feet of the scribes and Pharisees to learn their doctrines but listened with rapt attention to Him who spoke as "never man spake" (John 7:46). "And now," said He, "when I am gone, where will you find the great infallible teacher? Shall I set you up a pope at Rome to whom you shall go? Shall I ordain the councils of the church to solve your problems?" Christ said no such thing. In essence He said, "I am the infallible Teacher, and when I am gone I will send you another Teacher who shall be the authoritative oracle of God. He will guide you into

all truth" (see John 14:26). The promise was made in the first instance
to the apostles, but later it was applied to all believers. Each believer
may be independent of human teachers—"ye need not that any man
teach you" (1 John 2:27). It is the privilege of each of us to be "taught
of God" (John 6:45). The man who is most fully taught by God is the
one who will be most ready to listen to what God has taught others.
Why is the Holy Spirit the preeminent, infallible Teacher?

He Is the Author of the Scriptures (John 16:13; 2 Tim. 3:16; 2 Pet. 1:20-21; Rev. 2:7)

Peter tells us that the men who wrote the Scriptures were "moved" (literally "borne along") by the Holy Spirit. Paul declares that all Scripture is
"given by inspiration of God," or more literally is "God-breathed." As
God breathed into man the breath of life and made him a living soul, so the
Holy Spirit breathed into human beings a living knowledge of the things
of God. It was "what the Spirit saith unto the churches" that John was commanded to hear and record in the book of Revelation; and it was the Spirit
who was to guide the apostles into all truth and show them things to come.

He Is the Interpreter of Scripture (John 16:13-14; 1 Cor. 2:10)

As the author of all Scripture, surely the divine Spirit would be capable
of understanding it and explaining it. The best commentary on the Bible
is the Bible itself. By comparing Scripture with Scripture we may have
an infallible interpretation of all divine utterances.

He Was the Companion of Christ

Not only was Christ born of the Spirit (Luke 1:35) and raised from the
dead in the power of the Spirit (Rom. 1:4; 8:11), but He was:

ANOINTED BY THE SPIRIT (ACTS 10:38)

Before He entered upon His active ministry, our Savior was anointed by
the Holy Spirit for service.

LED BY THE SPIRIT (MATT. 4:1)

After His baptism, the Holy Spirit, who had descended upon Christ in the
form of a dove, led Him into the wilderness to be tempted by Satan.

He Instructs the Believer

ABOUT CHRIST (JOHN 15:26; 16:13-15)

The Holy Spirit reveals and glorifies Christ as cannot be done by any
other. The disciples knew Christ, but they knew Him as a man. The

Holy Spirit reveals Him in a much greater and grander manner. You may have known a man by his appearance, by his face. Now you come to know him by his character. He reveals himself by his abilities, by his integrity, by his truthfulness, as your friend.

ABOUT SPIRITUAL THINGS (1 COR. 2:9-14)

We have already observed that the Holy Spirit is the author and the interpreter of the Word of God. The inward illumination of the Holy Spirit enables us to understand the Word. It is a great mistake to try to comprehend spiritual revelation with natural understanding. A man with no aesthetic sense might as well expect to appreciate the Sistine Madonna because he is not color-blind as an unspiritual man to understand the Bible simply because he understands the language in which the Bible was written. All the wisdom of Greece could not enable the Corinthians to understand spiritual things, and all the intellects of our greatest universities will be mystified by spiritual truth without the instruction of the Holy Spirit.

He Reproves the World (John 16:7-11)

The world cannot receive or know the Holy Spirit, as He dwells only with the believer. The Holy Spirit, however, works through the believer to reprove the world:

OF SIN (JOHN 16:9)

Not necessarily of all sins, such as intemperance, greed, theft, falsehood, but of *one special sin*—the sin of rejecting Jesus Christ as the Savior of the world. Sin received new meaning when Christ came into the world (John 15:22). Christlessness in a Christian land is atheism. The Holy Spirit makes a man see that not to believe in Christ is the crowning sin, since it makes God a liar. He who believes not on Christ has rejected God's mercy and despised the grandest display of God's love.

OF RIGHTEOUSNESS (JOHN 16:10)

Christ was the only man who was truly righteous. The scribes and Pharisees emphasized keeping the law and thought they were almost perfect; but our Lord said, "Except your righteousness shall exceed the righteousness of the scribes and Pharisees, ye shall in no case enter into the kingdom of heaven" (Matt. 5:20). Now the only righteous one was about to leave the world, but the Holy Spirit was to come and convince the world of the righteousness of the Lord Jesus Christ and the unrighteousness of all others.

OF JUDGMENT (JOHN 16:11)

The death of Christ caused judgment to be passed upon Satan, and the devil realized that his kingdom was virtually overthrown. Our Lord recognized Satan as the prince of this world, and He saw him lurking behind Judas, Peter, and the Pharisees. It was Satan's "works" that Christ came to destroy (1 John 3:8), and his death-fearing subjects that He came to deliver (Heb. 2:14-15). Calvary was the decisive battlefield. Satan was judged and condemned. He now awaits sentence, which shall be executed when the kingdoms of this world become the kingdoms of our Lord Jesus Christ. The Holy Spirit will convince the world that "the prince of this world" is doomed and all his subjects with him (John 16:11).

THE BELIEVER GUIDED BY THE HOLY SPIRIT

As Jesus Christ is now the believer's advocate before God, so the Holy Spirit is God's advocate before men. Have you ever seen an earnest minister pleading with hands uplifted and eyes filled with tears? Were his skill and power acquired in college or seminary? Ah, no. It was the Holy Spirit within him advocating God's cause aright.

Guidance in Worship

The only true and acceptable worship is that which the Holy Spirit prompts and directs (Phil. 3:3, NIV, NASB, RSV margin, ESV). A man may be earnest in his worship and still not have submitted himself to the guidance of the Holy Spirit. In utter self-distrust and self-abnegation we must cast ourselves upon the Holy Spirit to lead us aright in our:

PRAYERS

The disciples did not know how to pray as they ought and said to Jesus, "Lord, teach us to pray" (Luke 11:1). We do not know how to pray as we ought, but we have another Paraclete right at hand to help (Rom. 8:26-27; Eph. 6:18; Jude 20). When we cast ourselves completely upon our Advocate, He directs our prayers, leads our desires, and guides our utterances. Those prayers that God the Holy Spirit inspires are the prayers that God the Father answers.

PRAISE

A prominent characteristic of the Spirit-filled life is thanksgiving (Eph. 5:18-20). This, like prayer, to be acceptable to God, must be directed by the Holy Spirit. One reason why the singing of psalms, done sincerely, is worship that is acceptable to God is that the Holy Spirit is the author of these immortal hymns of praise.

Guidance in the Affairs of Life

The Holy Spirit selects our field of activity and directs us to it (Acts 8:26-29; 13:2, 4; 16:6-10). He opens the door to the place where He would have us labor and closes the door to the task that we might ourselves select. He also directs us to the individual to whom God desires that we should speak. There is so much to do for Christ and so many to whom we might speak in His behalf. Physical limitations, however, curtail our efforts. How are we to know what to do and what not to do? The Holy Spirit will guide us. There are certain places we are to go and certain people to whom we are to speak. If we walk in obedience to the Word, the Holy Spirit will arrange our contacts with the very persons we can best reach with the Gospel, and not only so, but He will make those contacts at just the right time.

Guidance in Time of Trial

The disciples were not to worry about what to say when they were on trial for Christ. The Holy Spirit would be their advocate when they were brought before governors and kings. How was Stephen able to plead so ably before the blindly prejudiced council that was determined to execute him? The answer is that they were not able to resist the wisdom and the Spirit by which he spoke. The Jews hired a noted Roman lawyer named Tertullus to prosecute their case against Paul, but to no avail (Acts 24:1, 22). And how was it that this prisoner in chains could plead so powerfully before the Roman governor that Felix trembled before him and rose up hurriedly to dismiss the case (Acts 24:25)? It was not the man who pleaded, but God the Holy Spirit who was pleading through him.

THE BELIEVER CONTROLLED BY THE HOLY SPIRIT

We are told that no one can call Jesus Lord except by the Holy Ghost (1 Cor. 12:3). It is this work of leading the believer to realize the Lordship of Jesus in his life that the Spirit desires to accomplish in the life of every child of God. For it is a sad fact that while many have accepted Christ as Savior, He is not complete master of their lives. Many are delivered from the guilt of sin and from its ultimate penalty, but not all know the blessedness of His Lordship. We receive Him as Savior by faith on the ground of His finished work on Calvary; but He did that *for* us only that He might do something *in* us.

A Spirit-possessed Life—Holiness

Things were going wrong in the Corinthian church. A spirit of contention was dividing its members. The people were converted to Peter, Paul, and Apollos, and not to Christ (1 Cor. 1:12). Grave sin and immorality were prevalent. The members for the most part were interested in worldly things. What was the cause? The Holy Spirit was not allowed to exercise His power.

Paul did not tell these Corinthian Christians that they were without the Holy Spirit who had led them in the public confession of their faith to declare that Jesus was the Son of God (1 Cor. 12:3). They could not have been Christians without the Holy Spirit (Rom. 8:9). It was their failure to recognize the presence of the Holy Spirit dwelling within them (1 Cor. 3:16; 6:19) and their failure to permit Him to control their lives for which the apostle took them to task. In the foul atmosphere of that heathen city the Christians were exposed to fearful temptations and needed a superhuman power if they were to keep themselves pure.

What honor, what dignity have been conferred upon these corruptible bodies, that they should be chosen as the dwelling place of the Holy Spirit! The body of the Christian is claimed and indwelt by the God who has redeemed it, and therefore it should be treated with the same respect with which the Jews regarded the Holy of Holies. The Christian who thinks of his flesh in this way cannot fail to acquire a higher regard for it. How reverently he should guard his eyes to keep them from unlawful scenes! How zealously he should watch his tongue to keep it from evil words! How diligently he should preserve his thoughts and affections from evil, since God has claimed his members as His own and bidden him to give them wholly to Him!

A Spirit-sealed Life—Assurance

The presence of the Holy Spirit not only gives the believer power to live a holy life, well-pleasing to God, when the believer recognizes what that life is; but the Spirit takes us, as it were, by the hand and leads us into that life (Rom. 8:14, 16; Eph. 1:13; 4:30). This is the most convincing of all evidence given the Christian to prove his heavenly heritage.

Consider a martyr going to the stake—thousands of Christian martyrs have perished in this way. The crowds are mocking, but on he goes with courageous tread. Now they bind him with a chain about his waist. They heap bundles of sticks all about him. The flame is lighted, but he is speaking: "Bless the Lord, O my soul." The flames are kindling around his legs, but he lifts his hands and cries, "I know that my Redeemer lives, and though the fire devours this body, yet in my flesh shall I see God!" His body is being consumed, but he sings amid the torture, and finally cries triumphantly, "Into Thy hand I commit my spirit." What gives this man such assurance? (See 2 Tim. 2:19-21.) It is the glorious witness of the Holy Spirit that he is a son of God (Gal. 4:6).

A Spirit-filled Life—Service

The phrase "full of the Holy Ghost" is a familiar one in the New Testament. Our Lord Himself performed His earthly ministry in the Holy Spirit's fullness and power. Again and again the record states that the disciples were filled with the Holy Spirit. At Pentecost the 120 disciples "were all filled with the Holy Ghost" (Acts 2:4). This was to prepare them for the service they were to render in the founding of the church. Peter stood up and faced the great congregation that had been so outspoken in their hostility to Christ and His disciples, and the lives of three thousand were transformed in a day. A little later, when opposition had set in and the disciples were brought before the council, Peter, "filled with the Holy Ghost," made a masterly defense that resulted in their being liberated. In the prayer meeting that followed, "the place was shaken where they were assembled together; and they were all filled with the Holy Ghost" (Acts 4:8, 31).

Paul, in his letter to the Ephesians (5:18), lays that obligation on every believer in Christ when he says, "And be not drunk with wine, wherein is excess; but be filled with the Spirit." Therefore it is the privilege and obligation of every believer in Christ not only to have the Holy Spirit dwelling within him but to be filled with the Spirit.

The promise has been given—"He that believeth on me, as the scripture hath said, out of his belly shall flow rivers of living water. (But this spake he of the Spirit, which they that believe on him should receive)" (John 7:38-39). Only service done in the power of the Holy Spirit will count for eternity. We see the Spirit of God pictured as the great life-giving river that seeks an outlet for the divine outflow of life and love in everyday practical ministry to others. It begins to flow as soon as it finds a channel. It keeps flowing as long as the channel remains open.

A Victorious Life—Fruitfulness (Rom. 5:5; 8:2, 9-13; 14:17; Gal. 5:17, 22-23)

When a believer is regenerated and the Holy Spirit condescends to take up His abode in his body, he discovers that he has two natures—his bodily nature and his spiritual nature. He finds that his body is still subject to the temptations of the flesh. The struggle that goes on between the good and evil within is well depicted in the seventh chapter of Romans: "For I know that in me (that is, in my flesh), dwelleth no good thing: for to will is present with me; but how to perform that which is good I find not" (v. 18). In the terrible conflict of the seventh chapter the Holy Spirit is not taken into consideration; but He is mentioned nineteen times in connection with the life of victory described in the eighth chapter. The rule of the Holy Spirit in the life of the believer is the Christian's secret of victory over sin.

The place and prominence that the believer gives to the Holy Spirit will determine his character. We are not born with a fixed nature. Character is the result of our habits, and these are repeated actions. The character of the natural man who lives to gratify his body is a sad and sickening spectacle. The awful catalog of the works of the flesh is set forth in sharp contrast to the fruit of the Spirit (Gal. 5:19-23). The character of the spiritual man who allows the Holy Spirit to guide his life is altogether different. He produces the blessed fruit of the Christian life. There are three beautiful clusters to this fruit.

LOVE, JOY, PEACE (GAL. 5:22)

This is our Christian experience in relation to God. It is only through a walk in subjection to the Holy Spirit that the love of God is shed abroad in our hearts (Rom. 5:5) and we share the joy of the Holy Spirit (Acts 13:52) and "the peace of God, which passeth all understanding" (Phil. 4:7).

LONGSUFFERING, GENTLENESS, GOODNESS (GAL. 5:22)

This is our Christian experience in relation to our fellowmen. The Holy Spirit enables us to bear and forbear. First we give ourselves to the Lord and then to those around us. We practice kindness and courtesy to all.

FAITHFULNESS, MEEKNESS, SELF-CONTROL (GAL. 5:22-23)

This is our Christian experience in relation to ourselves. As we walk in the Spirit, we will be faithful and humble in all our duties and will exercise control over all our thoughts and actions. "Sin shall not have dominion over you" (Rom. 6:14).

REVIEW QUESTIONS

1. In what respects was the Holy Spirit to take the place of Christ in the lives of the disciples?

2. About what does the Holy Spirit instruct the believer?
3. Of what three things does the Holy Spirit reprove the world?
4. How does the Holy Spirit guide the believer in worship?
5. In what respect is the Holy Spirit a guide in the affairs of life?
6. Give several illustrations of how the Holy Spirit guided the apostles during times of trial.
7. In what four ways does the Holy Spirit control the life of the believer?
8. Show evidence that members of the church at Corinth had not as yet experienced the Spirit-possessed life.
9. What do we mean by the Spirit-sealed life?
10. What is the evidence of a Spirit-filled life?
11. What are the characteristics of a victorious life?
12. Which of the nine characteristics speak of the Christian's experience in relation to God? Which in relation to his fellowman? Which in relation to himself?

APPLYING DOCTRINE TO LIFE

1. To what measure can believers' lives be Spirit-filled today? What activities or attitudes promote a Spirit-filled life?
2. List at least five changes that should take place in your life as the result of a deepened understanding of the one true God, who exists as Father, Son, and Holy Spirit.

Biblical
Faith

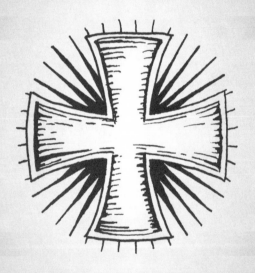

CLARENCE H. BENSON

CONTENTS

Chapter One

INSPIRATION OF
THE BIBLE

THE INSPIRATION OF the Bible is of great importance, for all Christian doctrines are developed from the Bible and rest upon it for authority. The conviction that the eternal God has revealed Himself to man has always been central in the Christian faith. Since man could never have discovered God by himself, Christians have always held that God makes Himself known to man supernaturally. The books that form the canon of the Old and New Testaments as originally written are fully inspired and entirely free from error. These books constitute the written Word of God, the only infallible rule of faith and practice.

To accept the inspiration of the Bible does not mean that every passage can be explained or understood. There are depths in God's Book that the mind of man cannot fathom, but far from being indications of weakness or failure, they serve to prove the Bible's divine origin. If the intelligence of man could master the Bible from beginning to end, it might be justifiable to question its divine origin. God has revealed a sufficient knowledge of His love and grace for believers to have both faith and hope in Him and to be assured that "if any man will do his will, he shall know of the doctrine" (John 7:17). If Christians study the Bible, not with prejudice and criticism, but with faith in and love for its Author, they will understand its message.

There is a distinction between revelation and inspiration. Revelation is the record of God's communication through men. Inspiration is God's power enabling man to record correctly the truth revealed. The word *inspiration,* used only twice in the English Bible (Job 32:8; 2 Tim. 3:16), means the "inbreathing" of God into man, so that man spoke or wrote God's revelation of truth with authority and accuracy (2 Pet. 1:21).

Not everything in the Bible has been directly revealed to men. The Bible contains history in the language of men, even of wicked men, but there is no part that is not inspired. The Spirit so directed and influenced the writers that they were kept from any error of fact or doctrine.

However, inspiration does not mean God has given His approval to every recorded statement. The Bible records the lies of Satan (for example, "Ye shall not surely die") and the misdeeds of many wicked people, some of whom God used to communicate His message. For example, the book of Job contains the truths of Jehovah, the words of Satan, the speech of Elihu, and the arguments of Job and the three friends. Satan, Job, and his three friends did not speak by inspiration of God. They spoke their own opinions. Inspiration means that no one of them is misrepresented, but that each one spoke the words attributed to him in Scripture. The fact that misdeeds like Saul's slaughter of the priests, David's numbering of the people, and Herod's massacre of the innocents are recorded in the Bible does not imply that God approved of them, but the divine record vouches for the accuracy of these facts.

THE EXTENT OF INSPIRATION

While the fact of inspiration is recognized by most churches, all do not agree on the extent of inspiration. There are various theories of inspiration.

Natural Inspiration

This theory identifies inspiration with a high order of human ability. It denies anything supernatural in the preparation of the Scriptures. It claims that the biblical writers were no more inspired than Milton, Shakespeare, or Mohammed.

However, when David said, "The Spirit of the LORD spake by me, and his word was in my tongue" (2 Sam. 23:2), he meant something more than human skill. When Isaiah announced, "thus saith the Lord" (e.g., Isa. 43:1), he claimed something higher than a great poet's eloquence. When Paul said to the Corinthians, "Which things also we speak, not in the words which man's wisdom teacheth, but which the Holy Ghost teacheth" (1 Cor. 2:13), he used language for which no parallel can be found in mere human ability.

When one compares the literature of the great secular authors with that of the Bible, the difference between the two is not one simply of degree, but of kind. The Bible is not only a higher plane of literature, but an environment that is altogether different. If the qualifications of Bible writers were the same as those of great secular writers, there would be nothing to assure the readers that Moses, David, and Paul did not make human errors or teach human views of life. The theory of natural inspiration discredits rather than supports the Word of God.

Mechanical Inspiration

This view ignores human instrumentality in the preparation of the Scriptures and claims that the writers were like robots, as insensible to what they were doing as are piano keys to a musician's touch. But consider the stern Moses, the poetic David, the lovable John, and the scholarly Paul. Careful study of the Scriptures reveals that God used these writers' individualities to reach all kinds of people.

Partial Inspiration

The theory of partial inspiration is held by some who have a superficial knowledge of the Bible and who accept scientists' theories as facts. In the face of apparent discrepancies between scientific theories and Scripture, they conclude that the Bible contains the Word of God, but that much of it is not the Word of God and therefore not necessarily accurate. They can thus accept the theory of evolution and reject as not inspired those portions of Scripture that refute it. If Jonah's experiences seem incompatible with scientific findings, or statements about the total depravity of human nature and the eternal punishment of the wicked are unacceptable, this theory of partial inspiration provides a convenient escape. But who is to decide what is and what is not inspired? The theory of partial inspiration leaves people in great uncertainty.

Plenary Inspiration

This is the belief of the Christian church. Plenary, or complete, inspiration is the opposite of partial inspiration. It claims all Scripture to be equally inspired, basing its claim upon 2 Timothy 3:16, "All scripture is given by inspiration of God."

Much has been said and written in answer to the question, does inspiration include the very words of the Bible? Were the words dictated by the Spirit, or were the writers left to choose their own words? If the entire content of the Bible is completely accurate, it can be seen at once that the words as well as the thoughts must be inspired. Some statements of Scripture are the identical words written or spoken by God Himself. The Ten Commandments were written with "the finger of God" (Exod. 31:18; cf. 32:16). The handwriting on the wall of Belshazzar's palace was written with "fingers of a man's hand" (Dan. 5:5). In the New Testament, the voice that was heard at the baptism and the transfiguration of the Lord spoke words that could not be mistaken.

Apart from the exact words, there could be no precision, particularly such precision as is demanded in the Scriptures. The declaration of the writers who were chosen of God to record the Scriptures confirms the fact that they were responsible for words rather than mere concepts.

The result of plenary inspiration is inerrancy.

THE NATURE OF INSPIRATION

Careful study will reveal several different ways God transmitted His Word to people.

Divine Utterances

In both the Old and New Testaments the exact words of God were reproduced in writing (Exod. 32:16; 1 Chron. 28:19; Dan. 5:5). The children of Israel were highly favored in being permitted to hear God's voice, about which Moses said, "Did ever people hear the voice of God speaking out of the midst of the fire, as thou hast heard, and live?" (Deut. 4:33). These divine utterances were later recorded on tables of stone by "the finger of God" (Exod. 31:18; Deut. 9:10) and carried in the ark of the covenant. In the New Testament God honored His Son by speaking from heaven at His baptism (Matt. 3:17), at His transfiguration (Matt. 17:5), and before His crucifixion (John 12:28). These divine utterances were carefully and correctly recorded by human writers.

Divine Dictation

God put into the mouths of certain men the very words they should speak and write (Exod. 4:10-15; 34:27; Isa. 8:1, 11-12; Jer. 1:7; 7:27; 13:12; 30:1-2; Ezek. 3:10-11; 24:2; Hab. 2:2). Peter says that when the prophets wrote about Christ, they actually had to study the predictions that they themselves wrote, and even then did not fully understand them (1 Pet. 1:10-12).

Even more significantly, Daniel speaks of God's dictation to him: "I heard, but I understood not." In reply to an inquiry for further explanation, God directed, "Go thy way, Daniel; for the words are closed up and sealed till the time of the end" (Dan. 12:9). Daniel was given power to record with infallible accuracy what he heard, although he did not understand it. Yet Daniel was the wise man who interpreted Nebuchadnezzar's dream and deciphered the handwriting upon the wall. His recording of God's dictation without understanding it is no inspiration of mere ideas, nor elevation of mind, nor increase of intellectual power. It is a direct and special revelation of truth from God.

Human Expression

A Scripture writer's individuality and literary style in relating divine truth was not destroyed by divine inspiration. For instance, the four

Gospel narrators differed in recording what Pilate wrote upon the cross; yet, by a careful comparison of their accounts (Matt. 27:37; Mark 15:26; Luke 23:38; John 19:19-20), the exact wording, and what part of it God wished recorded, can be determined. The complete inscription evidently was, "This is Jesus of Nazareth, the King of the Jews," but the all-important fact recorded by all four writers was that Jesus was "the King of the Jews." This was the statement that displeased the Jews, for they asked Pilate not to write it. The fact was, the Jews quoted accurately the words that applied to the argument and omitted the rest. That is just what the Gospel writers did under the guidance of the Holy Spirit. The Holy Spirit employed the attention, investigation, memory, personality, logic—in fact, all the faculties of all the writers—and worked through them.

THE CLAIMS FOR INSPIRATION

The writers themselves claimed to write the Scriptures under the direct influence of the Holy Spirit.

Old Testament Writers

One cannot read the Old Testament without being impressed with the repetition of such phrases as "Thus saith the Lord," which occurs 1,900 times. While this occurs mostly in the prophets, even in the historical books God is shown to be in close touch with His people.

It is claimed that such expressions as "the Lord said," "the Lord spoke," "the word of the Lord came" are found 3,808 times in the Old Testament. These writers claiming to have had revelations of the will of God almost always began their messages with the words, "Thus saith the Lord." Their claims are confirmed by the minuteness and detail of names, times, and places that characterize their messages, and the literal fulfillment of their predictions.

When Moses explained creation, he did not make a single reference to the theories of the origin of the universe believed in ancient Egypt or Babylon, with which no doubt he was familiar. This can only be understood by the fact that he was controlled by the Holy Spirit. In the brief chapter on creation (Gen. 1), he claims to transcribe the words of God no less than fourteen times. Elsewhere it is written again and again, "The Lord spake unto Moses," "The Lord commanded Moses."

In the historical books the Lord speaks to Joshua, Gideon, Samuel, David, Elijah, Elisha, Ezra, Nehemiah, and many others. The New Testament writers not only confirmed statements in the Old Testament, but expressly stated that they were God's utterances (e.g., Matt. 1:22-23; 2:15; Mark 12:36; Luke 1:70; Acts 1:16).

New Testament Writers

The New Testament contains more than 280 quotations from thirty of the thirty-nine Old Testament books, spread over eighteen of its twenty-seven books (e.g., Matt. 10:19; Mark 13:14). Paul, a scholarly Jew and a member of the Sanhedrin, in becoming a Christian, did not modify his absolute confidence in the inspiration of the Old Testament. It always remained the Holy Scriptures with the same divine authority in establishing Christian truth as his own writings, which he knew were inspired (1 Cor. 2:13; 14:37; 1 Thess. 2:13). Paul quotes Scripture from Luke in the same breath as from Deuteronomy (1 Tim. 5:18; cf. Deut. 25:4; Luke 10:7). Peter classes Paul's writings with "the other Scriptures" (2 Pet. 3:15-16). The discourses of Peter, Stephen, and Paul in Acts are composed almost entirely of Old Testament quotations.

It is evident from this and many other passages that the writers of the New Testament were conscious that those who were instrumental in producing the Old Testament, as well as themselves, received revelations from God and considered themselves inspired of God to complete the Scriptures. They felt while writing that they were giving expression to the infallible truth of God through the operation of the Holy Spirit. This explains the absence of contradiction that would be natural, especially with writers so far removed from each other in point of time and circumstance.

Jesus Christ

To "bear witness unto the truth" was one object of Christ's coming into the world (John 18:37). But He did not speak from Himself; rather, His Father who sent Him gave Him a commandment regarding what He should say and what He should speak (John 12:49). In His farewell prayer Christ said, "I have given unto them the words which thou gavest me" (John 17:8). The following sections explain Christ's attitude toward the Scriptures.

He regarded them as authentic in their entirety. He showed this by quoting from the Pentateuch, Prophets, and Psalms (Luke 24:27).

He applied the whole Scripture to Himself. He used Isaiah 61:1 in the synagogue at Nazareth (Luke 4:16-21). He also reproached the Jews because, though they searched the Scriptures, they did not find Him, for, said He, "they are they which testify of me" (John 5:39).

He quoted from all the Scriptures as of equal authority. One word of the Bible, to Christ and to His opponents also, was sufficient to end any disagreement. His quotations from Deuteronomy silenced Satan

(Matt. 4:4, 7, 10). "What is written in the law?" He asked His critics. With that clear, no further arguments were needed. When some complained about the children singing His praises (Matt. 21:16), He merely replied, "Have ye never read, Out of the mouth of babes and sucklings thou hast perfected praise?" (cf. Ps. 8:2).

He upheld the verbal inspiration of the Scriptures. The Lord maintained strongly the inspiration of every word of the Scriptures: "Till heaven and earth pass, one jot or one tittle shall in no wise pass from the law, till all be fulfilled" (Matt. 5:18). The jot was the smallest Hebrew letter, while the tittle was a little projection distinguishing some letters. Not merely the words, but, according to the Lord, the very letters of the Bible were inspired.

He accepted the miracles of the Bible. Christ spoke of the Flood and the destruction of Sodom and Gomorrah (Luke 17:26-32) as people today might speak of the feats of the astronauts—as unquestioned facts. He alluded to the miraculous death of Lot's wife as a well-known catastrophe. He accepted Jonah's marvelous experiences (Matt. 12:40), as well as the book of Daniel with its miraculous happenings (Matt. 24:15).

SUMMARY

The doctrine of the inspiration of the Bible is of tremendous importance, for all Christian doctrines are developed from the Bible and rest upon it for authority. The term *inspiration* is defined as "God's power enabling man to accurately record the truth revealed."

Several theories of inspiration have been advocated.

The theory of *natural inspiration* identifies inspiration with a high order of human ability. Proponents of this view say that Bible writers were no more inspired than were secular writers. Holding this view discredits the Word of God.

Another view is *mechanical inspiration.* This view ignores human instrumentality in the preparation of the Scriptures and claims that the writers were like robots whom God used to write what He dictated. This view does not recognize the varied styles found in the Bible.

A third view is *partial inspiration*, which concludes that the Bible contains God's Word but that much of it is not God's Word, especially when it disagrees with current ideas of scientists. The obvious problem is, who determines what is and what is not inspired? This view leaves one with great uncertainty.

The fourth view is that held by the Christian church—*plenary inspiration*. Using 2 Timothy 3:16 this view claims that all Scripture is inspired by God. God so directed the biblical writers that even the words they used were inspired and accurate, making the entire record inerrant.

When God transmitted His Word to the biblical writers He used several methods. Some parts of the Bible were given as *divine utterances*. These sections are the exact reproductions of God's spoken words. Other sections are *divine dictation*. In these sections God put the very words into the Bible writers' mouths. A third method of recording the Bible could be termed *human expression*. This means that inspiration did not destroy the Scripture writers' individualities and literary styles. This accounts for the differences found in the Gospels. The Holy Spirit employed all the faculties of the biblical writers and worked through them.

The writers of both the Old and New Testaments claimed to be writing under direct guidance of the Holy Spirit. Jesus Christ also affirmed the inspiration of the Scriptures and even expressed that the object of His coming was to "bear witness unto the truth."

Christ's attitude toward the Scriptures is shown by the fact that He regarded them as entirely authentic, He applied them to Himself, He quoted from all as of equal authority, He upheld their verbal inspiration, and He accepted the miracles recorded in the Bible.

DISCUSSION QUESTIONS

1. Why is the authority of the Bible so essential?
2. Define and compare the terms *revelation, inspiration,* and *illumination.*
3. Define and refute the theories of natural inspiration, mechanical inspiration, and partial inspiration.
4. What is meant by plenary inspiration?
5. Why cannot inspiration be limited to the "thoughts" or "concepts" of the Scriptures?
6. Name or give examples of three important characteristics that express the nature of inspiration.
7. What are some of the claims for inspiration by Old and New Testament writers and the testimony of Christ?
8. How would you justify belief in the inspiration of the Bible to one who denies it?

RESOURCES

Hannah, John (ed). *Inerrancy and the Church.* Chicago: Moody Press, 1984.
Pache, Rene. *The Inspiration and Authority of Scripture.* Chicago: Moody Press, 1979.
Saucy, Robert L. *Is the Bible Reliable?* Wheaton, IL: Victor Books, 1983.

Chapter Two

CREATION AND FALL OF MAN

THE CREATION OF MAN

While Bible scholars differ in their interpretations of how and when God created the world, the Scriptures clearly affirm that God did create the world and placed man in it.

Man's Origin

The Bible says that God created man out of dust and gave him life (Gen. 2:7). This creative act took place completely separate from His creation of the animals. Man is infinitely more than a higher order of the animal kingdom. The biblical account of the divine touch contradicts the possibility of an animal origin or of man's evolving from a lower order of creation.

A DIRECT CREATIVE ACT

Not only in Genesis (5:2), but elsewhere in Scripture (e.g., Deut. 4:32; Ps. 100:3) it is taught that the human race originated by a separate creative act of God. This teaching separates man, even in his lowest condition, from the next lower order of creation. Evolution has no explanation for man's higher spiritual nature. The fact of man's supremacy over all other creatures would scarcely have been possible had he been merely one of them.

A SON OF GOD

Bible genealogies trace the human race back to Adam but are careful to note that the first man, like the angels, was a son of God (Luke 3:38). The Greeks were too proud and intelligent to claim an animal origin. When Paul quoted a Greek poet (Acts 17:28), he established common ground for Greek history and biblical fact and demonstrated that the two corresponded.

Man's Character

Man was made last of all the creatures. He could take no honor to himself as contributing toward the work of creation. And as the last of God's creative work he was honored and appointed ruler of the entire creation.

HIS MATERIAL NATURE

Man was made of the dust of the ground (Gen. 2:7a), an unlikely material for making a man. His body was formed from materials that the earth supplies. The Bible states what modern chemistry confirms, that all the elements of our physical structure are found in soil that covers the earth (Job 33:6). At its dissolution in death the body returns to its origin—"for dust thou art, and unto dust shalt thou return" (Gen. 3:19b); but the spirit returns to its origin—"unto God who gave it" (Eccles. 12:7).

HIS SPIRITUAL NATURE

The body was created, and then into it God breathed the breath of life (Gen. 2:7b; Job 33:4). This process was not followed with the members of the animal kingdom, but only with man. God put the breath of heaven into dust of the earth. The spirit dwells in the house of clay and is the life and support of it. The body would be worthless and useless without the spirit to enliven it. At death the body is committed to the grave, but into God's hands the spirit is committed, for it is from God's hands that it is received.

GOD'S IMAGE IN MAN

Genesis 1:27 says that God created man in His own image. Man was not made in the likeness of any creature that went before him, but in the likeness of his Creator. Yet between God and man there is an infinite distance. Christ alone is the image of God's person, having the same nature (John 14:9; Heb. 1:3). How then is man like God?

Personality: The divine breath gave man a soul as well as a spirit (1 Thess. 5:23; Heb. 4:12). Through his senses man has world-consciousness and through his spirit, God-consciousness. But it is through his soul that he possesses self-consciousness or personality. Personality consists of intellect, emotion, and will. Adam was not a primitive being, slowly groping toward articulate speech, but an intelligent, thinking individual able to provide a suitable name for every creature (Gen. 2:19). He also had the freedom to exercise the power of his will in moral and spiritual choices. Man could not lose this resemblance to his Creator and still be a man.

Morality: Man was created pure and upright. His nature conformed to the ideals of right human conduct. However, this phase of his resemblance to his Creator was forfeitable, and indeed man did lose it. Adam was created with tendencies toward God; since Adam's fall, people are born with tendencies away from God. When a person becomes "a new creature . . . in Christ" (2 Cor. 5:17), he is morally reinstated. He is invited to "put off the old man with his deeds" and to "put on the new man, which is renewed in knowledge after the image of him that created him" (Col. 3:9-10).

Man's Helpmate

In the beginning Adam was alone, belonging neither to the upper world of angels nor the lower world of animals. God acknowledged this fact when he said, "It is not good that man should be alone" (Gen. 2:18a). Therefore God graciously provided companionship for him.

Woman, as was man, was created by a special act of God (Gen. 2:21-22; 1 Tim. 2:13). However, she was not made of dust, but of man. Man was dust refined, but woman was dust twice refined, one step further from the earth. While Eve was created, Adam slept, not only so that the operation might be painless, but so that God alone might be author of the new creature.

Genesis describes the true relationship between man and woman (2:23-24). One is the complement of the other. The two together make a perfect unity (Matt. 19:4-6). Matthew Henry says: "The woman was formed out of man, not out of his head to rule over him, not out of his feet to be a doormat, but out of his side to be his equal."

Man's Dominion

Man is God's deputy or representative. He is ruler over the natural creation. His Maker assigned him this place of preeminence (Gen. 1:26-30; 2:19-20; Ps. 8:3-8).

HIS AUTHORITY

Many evidences provide a living witness to man's authority over nature. The constant advances of science characterizing our space age, such as orbital travel, global communication, and other technological developments, reflect the God-ordained power of man to harness the mysterious forces of nature.

HIS RESPONSIBILITY

In accepting authority over the Garden of Eden, Adam was given a responsibility. He was commanded "to dress it and to keep it" (Gen. 2:15). If the Hebrew word is here translated "preserve," as it is in a later chapter, it would suggest the possibility of someone contesting Adam's right to ownership. This makes it easier to understand why Satan should

try to gain control over Adam and Eve. When he found this inferior creature, Adam, over the kingdom that he desired to govern, Satan was
aroused to intense jealousy and hatred and sought any means to defeat
God and seize man's inheritance from him.

THE FALL OF MAN

In the story of Job we are admitted to the councils of heaven, and we hear
God giving Satan permission to test Job. Perhaps a similar scene had been
enacted before the fall of Adam, at which time Satan intimated that Adam
could not resist evil. He might have argued that a weakling who would
fall to temptation would not be a fit subject to take an angel's place as
ruler over the earth. As God later allowed Satan to try Job, He may also
have allowed him to test Adam.

The Temptation

Satan laid his plans carefully. He attacked Eve in Adam's absence, knowing that one would yield more easily than two. It is probable that he
tempted her near the tree. She had time for reflection and thought. He
was careful to conceal his true character as God's enemy. He did not begin
by telling of his own fall or by speaking boastfully of his own rebellion.
He pretended to be friendly toward Eve.

DOUBTING GOD'S GOODNESS

Satan spoke politely of God the Creator; yet by a sly question he suggested unkindness in the form of an unnecessary and unreasonable
restriction. He acted as if it were difficult to believe God could have
treated them so unkindly. He planted a doubt in Eve's mind as to the
fairness of God's dealing. This is evident from her reply. Although she
gave Satan a full account of the law that God had laid down, she made
certain changes in her statement, indicating she already suspected there
was some truth in Satan's inquiry. God had said, "Of every tree of the garden thou mayest freely eat" (Gen. 2:16-17), but in restating the divine
command (3:1-3), Eve left out the word "freely," thereby implying God's
strictness instead of his generosity.

She also added the words, "neither shall ye touch it," though God had
not required this. So she subtracted from God's permission and added
to His prohibition.

In the third place, she downplayed the penalty for disobedience. God
had said, "In the day that thou eatest thereof thou shalt surely die," but
Eve softened this to "lest ye die."

DENYING GOD'S TRUTHFULNESS

Satan, greatly encouraged by Eve's reply, saw she was already wavering and boldly declared that Adam and Eve would not surely die (Gen. 3:4). Then Eve gave a ready ear to Satan's lie.

The devil could do little then, and he can do little now, except as openings are made for him by those he tempts. It was Eve's initial unbelief, shown by her "lest ye die," that encouraged Satan's attack. He intimated that although God was not good enough to let Adam and Eve have full liberty in the garden, He was too good to put them to death for disobedience.

DISCOVERING GOD'S SECRETS

Satan appealed to Eve's curiosity and pride by insinuating that God was hiding something from her. He even led her to believe that God had made the prohibition for fear those human creatures might become His equal (Gen. 3:5). Satan had ruined himself by desiring to be like God (Isa. 14:14), and he sought to ruin Adam and Eve by infecting them with the same desire.

The Transgression

UNRESISTED IMPRESSION OF SIN

Satan used three avenues of approach and met with no opposition. Eve's first steps toward willful disobedience were in listening, looking, and lusting.

Eve lost ground just as soon as she began to argue with Satan (Gen. 3:2-3). If she had remembered God's goodness, she would have replied differently.

Satan next opened Eve's impressionable eyes to the forbidden fruit (Gen. 3:6a). Through the eye either fires of devotion or sparks of temptation are kindled.

The final appeal was to the heart. Eve had heard and seen, and now she coveted the enticing fruit that had been expressly forbidden (Gen. 3:6b). Had she been wholehearted in her love for God, she would have rejected the thought of displeasing Him. But Satan had already shaken her confidence in God's love.

UNRESTRAINED EXPRESSION OF SIN

To covet may be at first an inward sin only, but, unless resisted, it leads to outward expression. Here are three downward steps (Gen. 3:6c): touching, tasting, tempting.

After telling Satan that God had commanded that the tree should not even be touched, Eve came to believe that she would not surely die even if she picked this enticing fruit.

It was not enough to take the forbidden fruit into her hands; she must eat it to realize Satan's promise of an advance in knowledge. She felt she must have wisdom, and she must have it at all risks and without delay.

Eve no sooner fell than she became a tempter. Instead of consulting Adam before she took the fatal step or warning him after she had fallen, she enticed him to share her sin. But there was an hour of reckoning for the guilty pair.

The Tribunal

THE PROSECUTION

The disobedient subjects were then arraigned before the righteous Judge of heaven and earth (Gen. 3:9-11). In response to God's question, "Where art thou?" the trembling Adam did not confess his guilt, but he revealed it by his very fear and shame. Adam was afraid to appear before God because he was naked. Of the obviously guilty pair the Judge asked, "Who told thee that thou wast naked? Hast thou eaten of the tree, whereof I commanded thee that thou shouldest not eat?"

THE PLEA

The guilty pair had an opportunity to answer why they should not be punished for their sin. But instead of confessing guilt, Adam blamed Eve, and she blamed the serpent (Gen. 3:12-13).

Adam had not a word to say for himself. He blamed not only Eve, but God for his trouble. "The woman whom thou gavest to be with me, she gave me of the tree, and I did eat." God made no answer to this foolish excuse but turned to the woman: "What is this that thou hast done?"

The woman likewise refused to make an honest confession of guilt. "The serpent beguiled [deceived] me, and I did eat" was her answer. Admitting the subtlety and deceitfulness of Satan did not justify her in God's sight. Her excuse was no better than her husband's.

THE PUNISHMENTS

The Judge proceeded to pass sentence (Gen. 3:14-19).

Degradation fell upon the serpent itself. No other animal shows so sharp a contrast between its keen intellectual powers and its creeping, squirming degradation. The final doom was also pronounced upon

Satan, the instigator of the serpent's actions. Christ, the seed of the woman, would someday crush his head.

God predicted suffering for the woman. Pregnancy and childbirth would be painful. The woman would also be subordinate to her husband and would experience conflict with her husband in ways that she would not have if they hadn't sinned.

Physical hardships, painful toil, disappointing problems, and hard struggles were appointed as man's lot, who was also judged a guilty sinner. Formerly the soil had yielded its produce easily, freely, and in great abundance. Now the man would struggle to make it produce life's necessities.

Thorns and thistles would multiply until they became a burden to man and beast. Job 31:38-40 and Isaiah 7:23-24 refer to them as judgments, and our Lord spoke of them as injurious (Matt. 13:7).

In addition, Adam's sin caused sin to enter the human race, making all mankind guilty of sin.

SUMMARY

Only God knows exactly how and when the world was created. But He did create it and placed man in it. Man came into being by God's direct creative act, making man a high order of creation above the animal kingdom.

Man's character has a threefold nature—body, spirit, and soul. God formed man's body from dust. Man's spirit and soul came into being when God breathed into him the breath of life. The soul expresses itself in man's personality and morality.

Having no one with whom to share his life caused Adam to become lonely. God acknowledged this and provided woman to be his companion. Woman was also created by God. She was created from man while he slept, making God alone the Creator.

As God's representative, man was to rule over the animals and keep the garden where he lived.

But Satan contested man's right of ownership. Satan, taking the form of a serpent, tempted the woman. Satan caused the woman to doubt God's goodness, to deny God's truthfulness, and to try to discover the secrets of God. As a result the woman succumbed to the temptation and ate from the forbidden tree of the knowledge of good and evil. Then Adam did likewise.

God dealt out punishment on all the parties to this first sin. The serpent was cursed and made to crawl on his belly. Later, when Christ came, He would crush Satan's head. The woman was to bear pain in childbirth and be subordinate to the man. The man would have to toil long hours to gain life's necessities.

DISCUSSION QUESTIONS

1. React to the theory of evolution from your study of the Genesis account of creation.
2. What three characteristics can be observed in man's creation?
3. Why did Satan become jealous of man?
4. How does the setting of the first chapter of Job suggest a similar scene before the fall of Adam?
5. In what ways did Satan cast doubt on God's goodness?
6. How did Satan appeal to Eve's curiosity?
7. Describe the first three steps in Eve's willful disobedience.
8. Describe the three steps that completed her unrestrained expression of sin.
9. What excuse did Adam and Eve make for their sin?
10. Discuss the extent of the consequences of Adam's disobedience.

RESOURCES

Flynn, Leslie B. *What Is Man?* Wheaton, IL: Victor Books, 1983.

Youngblood, Ronald. *How It All Began.* Ventura, CA: Regal Books, 1980.

Chapter Three

FAITH AND REGENERATION

FAITH

The King James Version defines faith in Hebrews 11:1 as "the *substance* of things hoped for, the *evidence* of things not seen" (italics added). The New American Standard Bible says in the same verse, "Now faith is the *assurance* of things hoped for, the conviction of things not seen" (italics added).

Faith is belief based on facts. The Gospel is a statement of definite, historical facts that the Old Testament saints were confident would occur and that the New Testament saints believed had occurred. "I declare unto you the gospel which I preached unto you," said Paul; and then he made plain exactly what the Gospel is: "how that Christ died for our sins according to the scriptures; and that he was buried, and that he rose again the third day according to the scriptures" (1 Cor. 15:1-4). Here are three tremendous facts: the substitutionary death of Christ, His burial, and His resurrection.

But faith is more than a recognition of facts. A person may know all about Christ as revealed in the Bible, may even believe God's Word to be true, and yet not have real faith in Christ as his personal Savior. Agreement by the mind is not the same as surrender of the heart. Satan and the fallen angels believe in God to the extent that they tremble for fear of Him (Jas. 2:19). Faith not only accepts but also believes and applies the facts. Faith involves the affections and the will as well as the intellect. Faith harmonizes the will and the understanding.

Faith is "the conviction of things not seen." Faith enables the seeking soul to penetrate into the spiritual realm. Faith is the source of all spiritual achievement. "By it the men of old gained approval" (Heb. 11:2, NASB). Abel, Enoch, Noah, Abraham, Isaac, Jacob, and many others have their names inscribed in the Bible's hall of fame, not because of their wealth or wisdom or worldly achievements, but because of their faith. Faith is the supreme requirement for heaven's favor. "Without faith it is impossible to please him: for he that cometh to God must believe that he is, and that he is a rewarder of them that diligently seek him" (Heb. 11:6).

Saving Faith

Adam's sin brought death to the human race. "Dust thou art, and unto dust shalt thou return" (Gen. 3:19) was the divine decree issued to the first parents. The all-important question that every person must ask is, "If a man die, shall he live again?" (Job 14:14). People may want one thing today and another tomorrow, but at the time of death the one thing they want above everything else is life, which can be had only through Christ. "I am come that they might have life" (John 10:10).

Saving faith produces salvation from the penalty of sin (John 3:16-18); it is belief in the only Savior appointed for this purpose. Without faith in Christ, a person will be deprived of heaven's happiness through eternity (John 3:36). He or she must share forever the punishment that has been prepared for the devil and his angels (Matt. 25:41).

Those with saving faith believe with the heart (Acts 16:31) and confess with the mouth (Matt. 10:32). With the heart there is recognition that the Lord Jesus is the sinner's substitute, and with the mouth there is confession not only of a hopeless condition, but of the Lord Jesus Christ as personal Savior (Rom. 10:8-11).

Upon Calvary's three crosses hung three representatives of the human race (Luke 23:39-43). The two malefactors were alike in their sin. They were alike in their condemnation. But in their last moments one cruelly mocked the Lord and called Him an impostor, unable to save Himself and these guilty thieves, while the other rebuked his companion's blasphemy and then took the necessary steps for salvation. He recognized the justice and judgment of God, admitted his own guilt, confessed the Savior, and asked for salvation. Here was a man who in his dying breath had faith enough to recognize Jesus as King. No wonder the Lord said to him, "Today shalt thou be with me in paradise" (Luke 23:43).

Living Faith

Faith is required not only for preservation from the *penalty* of sin but also for deliverance from the *power* of sin. When people once understand the love of God as expressed in Jesus Christ, they are not to continue in sin. How then are they to persevere when they are tempted?

God uses temptation to test faith. Not that God tempts people, for God is not the author of evil (Jas. 1:13), but He allows Satan to do so.

God *tests*, but Satan *tempts*. Moreover, Satan's temptations can be recognized, for they are common to all people; and they can be resisted, for a way of escape has been promised (1 Cor. 10:13). Believers are to rejoice in the midst of temptation since it is proof of God's loving discipline (Jas. 1:2-3).

The only one who can deliver us from temptation is the Lord Jesus Christ (Heb. 2:18; 2 Pet. 2:9), who is "the author and finisher of our faith" (Heb. 12:2). He was tempted in all points as we are and yet was without sin. Faith in His victory and His power is the shield with which we are "able to quench all the fiery darts of the wicked [one]" (Eph. 6:16).

Working Faith

Sinners are saved by faith, not by works; but it is by works that they demonstrate and prove their faith. Christians are God's "workmanship, created in Christ Jesus unto good works, which God hath before ordained that we should walk in them" (Eph. 2:10). Though not created in Christ Jesus *by* good works, believers are created *unto* or *for* good works (Titus 2:14). Works do not justify people, but justified people work.

Work is the fruit of faith. An inactive Christian life is empty and unfruitful. Work is not the foundation but the completion of faith. James is called the apostle of works, but he does not minimize the importance of faith (2:14-26). True faith will express itself in actions. James teaches that where there are no good works, there is not true religion, and a faith that is not producing good works is of no value. Actions must be regarded as the evidence of a justified person.

REGENERATION

Saving faith and regeneration are inseparable. The moment people believe in Christ, they are born of God. The weakness of their faith may make them unaware of the change, just as newborn infants know little or nothing about themselves. But where there is saving faith, there is always new birth; and where there is no faith, there is no regeneration.

Necessity of the New Birth
MANKIND'S DEPRAVITY

The fall of Adam becomes tremendously more important when we discover it was *our* fall, for the entire human race has inherited Adam's sinful nature (Jer. 17:9). As David, the man after God's own heart, confessed, "I was shapen in iniquity" (Ps. 51:5). Paul put it even stronger when he said that "the carnal mind is enmity against God" (Rom. 8:7). It is not only corrupt, but corruption. It is not only wicked, but wickedness itself (Rom. 7:18).

GOD'S HOLINESS

When Adam and Eve lost their original righteousness, they at once forfeited communion with their Creator (Hab. 1:13). No one has ever been admitted to heaven in his sins. No one can see God without a pure heart (Matt. 5:8). No one can come into his sacred presence unless he is partaker of the divine nature (2 Pet. 1:4). God's holiness requires holiness in His children.

It is only when people begin to understand something of the unchangeably holy nature of God that they come to realize how absolutely unfitted they are in their natural condition to have fellowship with Him.

CERTAINTY OF DEATH

Everyone must die (Rom. 5:12; 7:5). As the Scriptures point out, one of the direct consequences of sin is universal death. Between Genesis 1, which records the creation of Adam, and Genesis 3, which records his death, stands the fall of man and the entrance of sin.

There is nothing that people can do to overcome death. In spite of their scientific advances, they still die.

God, however, has made provision for this human predicament. The whole story is presented simply and wonderfully in the familiar verse John 3:16. Everlasting life is given to those who accept the offer of God's love shown in Jesus Christ. The presentation in Romans 5 notes that while Adam brought death upon the human race, Jesus Christ brought life. Another familiar reference, Romans 6:23, pictures clearly this contrast between death and life.

Nature of the New Birth

Exactly when the new birth takes place cannot be told any more than the exact moment that darkness blends into dawn can be identified. Just how the new birth takes place is impossible to explain (John 3:7-8), but the Bible says it is as instantaneous as all of God's works of creation. "He spake, and it was done" (Ps. 33:9). But although it is not known when and how, it is sure that the new birth has taken place by the evidences that accompany this miracle.

It is possible for people to improve their condition to such an extent that they may be deceived into believing they have experienced regeneration. Thousands of good people have never been born again and are still "dead in trespasses and sins" (Eph. 2:1). It is well, therefore, to know the nature of regeneration.

MORE THAN NATURAL DESCENT

The Jews were God's chosen people, but to be born of Hebrew parents was no guarantee of salvation. Esau was a child of the covenant, but he sold his birthright for a single meal (Heb. 12:16-17). Nadab and Abihu were the sons of the high priest, but they were so godless that they were destroyed by fire (Lev. 10:1-2).

The blessing of being born into a godly Christian family does not automatically grant salvation. Regeneration is not the result of human birth or earthly relationship.

MORE THAN HUMAN DECISION

The new birth is not self-reformation, though many would like to think so. Education and enlightenment will not make sinners holy. The meanest kind of scoundrel is an educated scoundrel, and the most detestable criminal is the enlightened hypocrite. Joash was well educated by Jehoiada, the high priest, but as soon as his faithful instructor died, he fell into evil ways (2 Chron. 24:2, 17-18). Saul of Tarsus was also well-educated, but that did not keep him from persecuting the church (Phil. 3:4-6).

MORE THAN HUMAN DETERMINATION

As much as Christian parents desire and urge their children to experience the new birth, regeneration comes only from God. Christian parents who know the Lord and desire their children to have the same experience should not pressure their offspring into making an early decision. Far better it is to obey God's command to "bring them up in the nurture and admonition of the Lord" (Eph. 6:4) and to take the Lord at His word seen in Proverbs 22:6, "Train up a child in the way he should go: and when he is old, he will not depart from it." Exposure to Christianity as living and working faith, constant prayer, and trust in God must take the place of human determination.

BEING BORN OF GOD

Regeneration starts with God and ends with God. The faith that justifies is the work of God, by which the old nature is crucified and believers are made into the likeness of Christ (Eph. 2:1, 4-5), thus becoming new creatures and children of God. The new birth is a new creation. Believers are born from above, not of corruptible seed, but of incorruptible. The new birth is the supernatural work of the Holy Spirit (John 3:5).

Nobility of the New Birth

Adam was not a child born of natural descent, nor of human decision or determination, but of God. A restored or regenerated son is as marvelous a creation as Adam. There is nothing higher than being admitted to sonship with God.

PARTAKERS OF THE DIVINE NATURE (2 PET. 1:4)

Unregenerated people are intellectually blind to spiritual privileges and corrupt in their affections. In the new birth, God imparts His own wise and holy nature, a nature that thinks as God thinks, feels as God feels, wills as God wills.

HUMAN BODIES BECOME TEMPLES OF THE HOLY SPIRIT (1 COR. 6:19)

It is almost unbelievable that the Holy Spirit condescends to dwell with people. And yet we know that our Lord's parting gift to His disciples was the abiding presence of the third Person of the Trinity. Since Pentecost He has not only been the governor and director of the church, but the personal companion of each individual member.

REGENERATED PEOPLE CAN OVERCOME THE WORLD (1 JOHN 5:4)

Real Christians on their way to heaven have a challenge to fulfill: They must overcome the world because the world is under Satan's dominion. As its prince and ruler, he finds temptations suited to everyone. The smile of the world and hope of its favor lure many into becoming traitors to God; the fear of its frown keeps many from confessing Christ. But Christians lose their love for the world and the things of the world and confess that they are pilgrims and strangers on this earth, looking for a city whose builder and maker is God.

REGENERATED PEOPLE BECOME SIN-CONQUERORS (1 JOHN 3:9)

Being born again does not mean that people have already attained perfection. Sin is still present, but it no longer has power over them. The new nature imparted in regeneration makes the continuous practice of sin impossible. To live in sin is contrary to the new nature of which they have been made partakers. As the whole nature of God hates sin, so those who are partakers of the divine nature come likewise to turn from and hate evil.

REGENERATED PEOPLE LOVE OTHERS (1 JOHN 3:14; 4:7)

Love is the atmosphere of heaven. God never said, "Thou shalt not" to the angels because they always love Him with all their being. People who have experienced the second birth love their enemies as well as their friends and thus prove that they are partakers of the divine nature. "See how those Christians love" was the comment of observers on the character of the early church members.

SUMMARY

Faith and regeneration are God's way for mankind to overcome the sinful nature that they inherit from Adam.

Faith is belief based on facts. There are three types of faith—saving, living, and working.

Saving faith is the recognition of salvation from the penalty of sin. In order for people to acquire saving faith, they must first recognize the justice and judgment of God. Second, they must admit their guilt. And third, they must confess belief in Christ as the Savior before others.

Faith is needed not only to save from death, but also to live the Christian life. *Living faith* delivers the believer from the power of sin. Satan's temptations test our faith. In times of testing the believer needs to draw closer to God, and God will provide the strength needed to stand up to any temptation.

Working faith is the outward manifestation of living faith. Working faith expresses itself not so much in words but in actions. Works do not justify people, but justified people work.

Saving faith and regeneration are inseparable. Where there is faith there is always regeneration.

Regeneration (the new birth) is necessary because it is demanded by mankind's depravity, God's holiness, and the certainty of death.

John 1:13 explains the nature of the new birth. It is more than natural descent, human decision, or human determination. It is being born of God. Regeneration is the supernatural work of the Holy Spirit.

Regenerated people become partakers of the divine nature, have bodies that are temples of the Holy Spirit, are able to overcome and conquer the powers of sin and the world, and love others.

DISCUSSION QUESTIONS

1. What is the biblical definition of faith?
2. Define saving faith.
3. How is saving faith illustrated in the case of the penitent thief on the cross at Calvary?
4. Give an illustration of living faith.
5. Define working faith.
6. What is the relationship between faith and regeneration?
7. Why is the new birth necessary?
8. What is meant by the depravity of mankind?
9. Using John 1:13, explain the nature of the new birth.
10. How have people tried to save themselves?
11. In what ways is a Christian as marvelous a creation as Adam?
12. What conquests are made possible for regenerated people?
13. How would you explain the new birth to an unsaved person?
14. How can a person experience salvation in Christ?

RESOURCES

Chafer, Lewis S. *Salvation*. Grand Rapids, MI: Zondervan, 1972.

Ryrie, Charles C. *A Survey of Bible Doctrine*. Chicago: Moody Press, 1972.

Chapter Four

JUSTIFICATION
AND ADOPTION

JUSTIFICATION

Justification is a legal term implying a clearing of one's name, the winning of a favorable verdict, whether it be in a court of law, of public opinion, or of conscience. God's justification is not for the righteous, but for the wicked. Hence justification is the judicial act of God whereby guilty sinners, who put their faith in Jesus Christ as Savior and Lord, are declared righteous in His eyes and are freed from guilt and punishment.

The Process of Justification

The process of justification is simple enough to all who understand and appreciate God's grace. But mankind's sinful nature makes it difficult to realize the extent of God's love and mercy or to accept His unmerited favor.

The process of justification includes the forgiveness of sin and the application of Christ's righteousness and is conditional upon faith.

Passages in Scripture that declare God's willingness to forgive sin and remove the death penalty include Psalm 130:4; Micah 7:18-19; Acts 13:38-39; Romans 8:1, 33-34; and Colossians 2:13-14.

Everyone has sinned. All sin offends God. His whole nature is turned against it. If all the sins of a person's life were recorded, they would make an almost endless list, for "There is none righteous, no, not one" (Rom. 3:10).

It is God who justifies. People cannot justify themselves. Only because of Christ's atoning death on the cross can God cleanse sinners and justify them completely. How marvelous that God who intensely hates sin can so greatly love the sinner. Justification is far more than pardon. Sinners desperately need to be released from their guilt to save them from the judgment of a holy and righteous God. The forgiven sinner receives more benefit than even a discharged criminal. The righteousness of Jesus Christ, God's beloved Son, is credited to his account (Rom. 3:22; 5:17-21).

A good illustration of this principle is found in Paul's letter to Philemon in Colosse concerning Onesimus, Philemon's runaway slave. Onesimus had stolen some of his master's money and fled to Rome where he wasted it. But while Onesimus was able to hide from his master in the great city, he could not get away from God. Under Paul's preaching, he was converted. Repentant of his crime, Onesimus prepared to go back and make amends to his master. He carried with him an important letter from Paul to Philemon. Paul wrote of the great change that had taken place in Onesimus and made the following request: "But if he has wronged you in any way or owes you anything, charge that to my account" (Philem. 18, NASB).

God accepts the believer through Christ; and in every case where the believer has wronged God, Christ has sustained the guilt and penalty (1 Cor. 1:30). What the believer owes God in complete obedience, but could never pay, Christ has paid for him.

Saving faith is both a condition of regeneration and of justification. Paul uses the life of Abraham as an illustration of justification by faith (Rom. 4). He states that righteousness was applied, counted, imputed to the patriarch without works. Abraham never questioned the promises of God, remote and seemingly impossible as they must have seemed. He was "fully persuaded" that whatever God promised He would do (v. 21). It is this kind of trust in God that the believer must have in order to be justified.

Justification is the free gift of God (1 Cor. 6:11). It is given *"freely* by his grace" (Rom. 3:24). God "hath raised us up together, and made us sit together in heavenly places in Christ Jesus: that in the ages to come he might show the exceeding riches of his grace in his kindness toward us through Christ Jesus" (Eph. 2:6-7).

The only way a righteous and just God could forgive sin was to provide a sinless substitute (Isa. 53:11). To overlook sin would cancel His holiness and bring moral chaos into the world. Only by the death of the perfect Son of God could the penalty be paid for all mankind (Rom. 5:9; 2 Cor. 5:21). The Old Testament sacrifices foreshadowed the supreme sacrifice to come, for "without shedding of blood is no remission" of sin (Heb. 9:22-28; 1 John 1:7).

Marvels of Justification

God's justification means more than pardon. It provides salvation and security and includes peace, joy, and eternal glory.

The enmity between sinners and God is ended by the cross. The moment sinners believe in Christ, they are justified and have *peace with God*. This is not a mere truce or even an armistice, but a permanent and abiding relationship.

The *joy* of justification springs from the assured hope of a glorious future and is distinctly the Christian's heritage. In contrast, "no hope" is the characteristic description of those without Christ. Of all people, believers should be the most happy and joyful. They are at peace with God and will enjoy Him forever.

"In the world ye shall have tribulation" (John 16:33), the Lord told His disciples, and His purpose is understood by those who have been justified. Realizing their sonship changes believers' attitudes toward suffering. The justified know "that the sufferings of this present time are not worthy to be compared with the *glory* which shall be revealed in us" (Rom. 8:18, italics added).

Christ in His farewell prayer asked that the disciples might be with Him to be partakers of His glory (John 17:22-24). Nothing can compare with the amazing grace of Jesus the Lord who consented to allow people to share His glory.

ADOPTION

Adoption means the "placing of a son." It is a Roman word, for adoption was little known among the Jews. It means the taking voluntarily of a child of other parents to be one's own child, bestowing on him all the advantages of a child by birth. It is used of the believer when the question of rights, privileges, and inheritance are involved. God's adoption of believers into His own family shows His grace and gives believers a new status. They are not slaves but sons, possessing all the rights of children as well as an inheritance from the Father.

Participants of Adoption

THE NATION ISRAEL

"Who are Israelites, to whom pertaineth the adoption," said Paul (Rom. 9:4). Comparing this with Deuteronomy 14:2 and Isaiah 43:1, it is evident that the reference is to Israel's being the chosen people of God. "I have redeemed thee, I have called thee by thy name; thou art mine," the Lord said to Israel.

God's marvelous protecting and delivering power was exercised over Israel. To them His precious promises were given. They were His children by His own choice. But they chose otherwise. They turned against God as their Father, completing their rejection in refusing the promised Redeemer, the very Son of God.

BELIEVERS

The loving heart of God still yearned for a people of His own on whom He might shower the abundance of His grace. Thus God opened the door to the Gentiles. "But as many as received him, to them gave he power to become the sons of God, even to them that believe on his name" (John 1:12). Israel was God's son, but now under the Gospel individual believers, either Jews or Gentiles, receive the adoption of sons.

Adoption gives a godly nature (Gal. 4:6): All who are adopted into the family of God partake of His nature, for He desires that all His children resemble Him.

Adoption gives equal rights to all sons (Gal. 4:7): All God's children are heirs. In some countries children do not share their father's estate equally unless he so wills; the eldest son is the heir. In the family of God all the children are declared joint-heirs with Christ, the first-born (Rom. 8:17).

Adoption brings fellowship (2 Cor. 6:17-18): Adoption involves the fellowship of Father and child. Adoption is an eternal agreement; only as Christians separate themselves from sin, setting their affections on things above, can they know the fellowship of Father and child.

Time of Adoption

When does adoption into the family of heaven take place? Adoption is a past, present, and future act.

ETERNAL IN GOD'S PLAN

Christ's sacrificial death and the adoption of believers were planned by God ages before they actually happened. Not only did God, before the foundation of the world, choose to have a heavenly family of earthborn mortals, but He knew which individuals would be adopted (Eph. 1:4-5).

RECEIVED WHEN ONE BELIEVES

The actual act of adoption cannot take place for the individual until he is born again—that is, until he believes fully in Jesus Christ for salvation. A holy God cannot receive into His family an unrepentant child. However, adoption takes place the moment one believes in Christ. Sonship is the *present* possession of the believer (Gal. 3:26; 1 John 3:2).

But how can God's predestination of those to be adopted (Eph. 1:5) be reconciled with man's free will to determine his adoption (John 1:12)?

Suppose that over the door of a great building is written, WHOSOEVER WILL, LET HIM COME IN. A person accepts the invitation and enters. But after he is inside, he sees on the other side of the door, PREDESTINED TO BE ADOPTED. He is satisfied. He finds no fault with either inscription. An unbeliever cannot understand adoption. His first concern is salvation, but once he accepts God's gracious plan, he learns that he has not only been regenerated and justified, but adopted into the family of God.

COMPLETED AT THE LORD'S RETURN

The full revelation of a believer's status as a son of God is reserved for a future day (Eph. 1:5, 10-11). Here in this world Christians are not accepted as the sons of the mighty God, but someday they will appear with Jesus Christ and will be like Him (Col. 3:4; 1 John 3:1-2).

Results of Adoption
NO LONGER UNDER TUTORS OR BONDAGE

"But after that faith is come, we are no longer under a schoolmaster" (Gal. 3:25). The Greek word translated "schoolmaster" means a trusted slave who cared for a child until he was twelve. He kept him from physical and moral evil and accompanied him constantly. He gave him commands and prohibitions and limited his freedom. All this was done to train the child for adult responsibilities. Thus the law was meant to lead people to Christ and to show them their sin and condemnation, in order that they might recognize their need of a Redeemer. This purpose being accomplished, people are no longer under the law but are adopted as adult sons when they are born again.

Israel was placed under the law and thus was in constant bondage and fear through a lack of perfect obedience. Jehovah was teaching a sinful people His holiness, and to draw near to Him was possible only by sacrifice. But when Christ came, all was different.

BUT NOW "SONS OF GOD"

"And if children, then heirs; heirs of God, and joint-heirs with Christ" (Rom. 8:17). If a man is really a child of God, he becomes God's heir. When children inherit their parents' wealth, it is because they were born into their parents' family. It is not because they do anything. Their parents bestow the inheritance on them. The young ruler said, "What shall I do to inherit . . . ?" (Luke 18:18). This is a contradiction in itself! Ages and ages of ever-increasing blessings are promised to believers as "joint-heirs."

Blessings of Adoption

A HEAVENLY FAMILY

Adoption into the family of heaven provides a family name, family likeness, and family love.

How can anyone be like God? It seems impossible for a human creature, but to be like God is to be like Christ, who is "the express image
of his person" (Heb. 1:3). Christ is God, expressing Himself in language
that humans can understand. Christ is the great pattern for heaven's family. To be imitators of our Lord Jesus Christ in the true biblical sense is
to reveal the characteristics of the heavenly family.

Christians cannot pray "our Father" and then despise their brethren.
Family love demands that they live and act as brothers and sisters should.
They must, like Christ, love those who differ from them in language
and custom, even those who do not yet know their Father (John 13:35;
Rom. 5:5; 1 John 3:14).

A HEAVENLY FATHER

Christ taught His followers to pray, "Our Father which art in heaven"
in order that they might understand and appropriate God's provision,
comfort, and correction. Since God is Christians' Father, He hears and
answers their prayers and provides for all their needs (Matt. 7:11).

"Like as a father pitieth his children, so the LORD pitieth them that
fear him" (Ps. 103:13). With His pity goes His perfect comfort: "I, even
I, am he that comforteth you" (Isa. 51:12). At best an earthly father's consolation can only be temporary. Grief and sorrow cannot be avoided,
but "the God of all comfort . . . comforteth us" (2 Cor. 1:3-4).

If Christ, God's only Son, suffered that believers might be adopted
into the family of heaven, what better treatment could be expected by
adopted sons? "The servant is not greater than his lord" (John 15:20).
Why should Christians expect that God will nourish His adopted sons
with less love and less rigorous discipline than He did His only begotten Son? "As many as I love, I rebuke and chasten," God says (Rev. 3:19;
cf. Heb. 12:5-11), and He constantly corrects His beloved children for
their own good.

A HEAVENLY INHERITANCE

Since Christians are the adopted children of God, heaven is their inheritance. This legacy that the heavenly Father bestows as the proof of His
love is incorruptible and undefiled. The inheritance will not perish as

do earthly fortunes. It is an everlasting possession that neither moth nor rust can corrupt nor thieves steal.

The inheritance will lose none of its brilliance and splendor. The crown of glory, though worn for millions of ages, will not be dimmed. The golden streets will lose none of their luster. God's children will never grow weary of heaven.

SUMMARY

Justification is an act of God whereby guilty sinners, who put their faith in Christ as Savior and Lord, are declared righteous in His eyes and are freed from guilt and punishment.

The process of justification unfolds in three steps. The first is the forgiving of sin. Because everyone has sinned, everyone needs God's forgiveness. The second step is the application of Christ's righteousness. Justification is more than pardon. When sinners accept God's forgiveness, they discover that the righteousness of Jesus Christ is credited to their account. Finally, the process of justification is conditioned upon faith. When sinners are justified, they become fully persuaded that whatsoever God promised, He will do. They accept it as a free gift of God through the shedding of Christ's blood.

When sinners are justified, they receive many blessings. Among these are peace with God, joy, and title to eternal glory. They are adopted into the family of God with full rights and privileges as sons and daughters.

The participants of adoption in the Old Testament were the Israelites (and Gentiles who came to God through the Jewish religion). But when the Jews rejected Christ, God opened the way for everyone who believes.

From the beginning God planned this adoption. He planned that it would take place at the time the individual believes in Christ for salvation. However, the full revelation of the status of adoption will not be complete until Christ returns, at which time believers will be made like Him.

When believers are adopted into God's family, they are no longer under the law but are adopted as sons. They no longer have the bondage of fear for not keeping the law perfectly, but they are now sons of God and joint-heirs with Christ.

When believers are adopted by God, they are part of the heavenly family. They take on God's family name and His family likeness and share His family love. As children of God Christians are recipients of His fatherly provision, comfort, and correction. And finally, Christians have a heavenly inheritance. As proof of His love, the heavenly Father bestows

on His children an incorruptible, undefiled, and unfading inheritance—
heaven.

DISCUSSION QUESTIONS

1. What does justification mean as related to the sinner's position before God?
2. Describe the process whereby a sinner is justified.
3. What is meant by the application of Christ's righteousness?
4. How is faith related to justification?
5. What is meant by adoption in relationship to the believer?
6. What benefits are conferred in the adoption of believers?
7. How is adoption related to the past, present, and future?
8. Write your own definitions of *justification* and *adoption*.

RESOURCES

Henry, Carl F. H., ed. *Fundamentals of the Faith*. Grand Rapids, MI: Zondervan, 1969, Chapter 9.

Ryrie, Charles C. *A Survey of Bible Doctrine*. Chicago: Moody Press, 1972, Chapter 7.

Chapter Five

WORSHIP
AND PRAYER

WORSHIP

An important function of the church is the public worship service. Family members also gather together daily for family worship. Many individuals set aside time each day for private worship. What is worship? Reading the Word of God, listening to a sermon, praying, and singing are contributing factors to worship, but they can be done without worshiping.

The root of the word translated "worship" in the Old Testament means "to bow down." However, worship is more than a physical act or intellectual exercise. Worship, as used in the Bible, is concentrating on God and thinking about His power and majesty, thus turning attention away from oneself. Worship is a spiritual activity. "God is a Spirit: and they that worship him must worship him in spirit and in truth" (John 4:24).

The need for worship is as natural as the need for protection and love. People worship a variety of things in an attempt to fill this need. But only when the focus of worship is God can this desire be fulfilled.

The Object of Worship
GOD

It is evident from the very first of the Ten Commandments that men worship other gods (Exod. 20:3). Israel, the highly favored nation to whom God revealed His majesty and His might, was forbidden to substitute other objects of worship (cf. Matt. 4:10). However, despite the solemn warning that any Israelite who worshiped the sun, moon, or host of heaven was to be stoned to death (Deut. 17:2-5), sun worship prevailed among God's chosen people again and again.

The nations surrounding Israel worshiped many gods. The sun, the most prominent and powerful agent in nature, was worshiped throughout the nations of the ancient world. The Arabians appeared to have paid direct homage to it without the intervention of any statue or symbol (Job 31:26-28). In Egypt the sun was worshiped under the title of Ra. Baal of the Phoenicians, Molech of the Ammonites, Hadad of the Syrians, and Bel of the Babylonians were also deities of the sun.

Not only were the Israelites forbidden to substitute the works of creation for the Creator, and this included men and angels (see Rev. 22:8-9), but they were not permitted to make an image or likeness of God for an object of worship. This is the purpose of the second commandment.

Many people today who may not bow down to idols nevertheless find that their worship is not acceptable because they have permitted other objects to rob God of the love and affection that rightly belong to Him. One writer named nine gods that people worship: gold, fashion, fame, ease, intellect, travel, chance, passion, and drink. When any of these or other things dominate a life, they are in effect other gods; and when they occupy the mind during the worship of God, the worshiper is not fully occupied with God.

CHRIST

Because Jesus is God, He accepts worship (Matt. 14:33; 28:17; John 9:38). When men sought to worship Peter, Paul, and Barnabas, they became angry (Acts 10:25-26; 14:11-15). Compare their reaction with the Lord's acceptance of worship (in addition to the references above Luke 5:8; 24:52). Peter and Thomas openly testified to Christ's deity (Matt. 16:16; John 20:28). And Christ, because He is God, accepted these testimonies. Christ said, "all men should honour the Son, even as they honour the Father" (John 5:23; cf. 10:30). This implies a demand for worship.

Paul in his epistles makes it plain that "at the name of Jesus every knee should bow, of things in heaven, and things in earth, and things under the earth; and that every tongue should confess that Jesus Christ is Lord" (Phil. 2:10).

Acceptable Worship

God is the omnipotent, omniscient, omnipresent one, and the believer's worship must be pleasing to Him, and thus *never* taken lightly or done carelessly. In order for worship to be acceptable, it must be in the name of Christ, guided by the Holy Spirit, and in conformity with the Word of God.

The Christian can pray to and worship God directly only because of Christ's death and resurrection (Heb. 9:7, 14). The veil of the temple, which shut out all but the high priest from the Holy of Holies, the most holy place, was torn from top to bottom at the crucifixion of the Lord. Christ opened the way into the most holy presence of God, so that the believer may now enter and worship.

True worship, which is acceptable to God, is that which the Spirit inspires. "They that are in the flesh cannot please God" (Rom. 8:8). God is seeking worshipers who worship in the Spirit and have "no confidence in the flesh" (Phil. 3:3). To please God in worship, the Christian must turn his eyes from himself and ask the Holy Spirit to teach him and to "help[eth] [his] infirmities" (Rom. 8:26-27).

God does not accept a pretended worship. It is possible to bow the head and even the body without bowing the soul in reverence before God. The true worshiper approaches God with a desire to glorify Him and enjoy Him. He comes without showiness and pride, but with sincerity and an offering of gratitude and prayer (John 4:24).

Response to Worship

True worship creates response in the worshiper. As the face of Moses shone after his communion with God (Exod. 34:29-30), so the radiance of heaven will be manifest in the life of the true worshiper. In fact, there is no higher, deeper, or purer joy than that which springs from the adoring contemplation of God. Such joy fills the soul as the Christian bows in worship, occupied and satisfied with God. It was the one thing David desired above everything else (Ps. 27:4) and prompted him to write, "In thy presence is fulness of joy" (Ps. 16:11).

PRAYER

The reading of God's Word and prayer occupy an important place in a service of worship. When a believer reads the Bible, God is speaking to him; when he prays, he talks to God. God has provided His Word; His child must read and study it to hear His voice. He has provided prayer; His child must communicate with Him through prayer to understand and apply His Word.

Reasons for Prayer

From one of the oldest books in the Bible comes the question, "What profit should we have, if we pray unto him?" (Job 21:15). God can work without the believer's prayers, and often does, but He prefers to have the Christian cooperate with Him in carrying out His plans. "We are laborers together with God," "true yokefellow[s]", "fellow laborers" (1 Cor. 3:9; Phil. 4:3).

There are many reasons why believers pray.

GOD'S DESIRE (LUKE 18:1; EPH. 6:18)

God wants the believer to be in constant fellowship with Him. Any situation and any request can be brought to Him at any time. God promises, "If ye shall ask any thing in my name, I will do it" (John 14:14). God works as the believer prays. Through prayers God moves the hearts of men, breaks down barriers, reveals pathways, supplies needs. Both the assurances in God's Word and the evidences of answered prayer guarantee His desire for and use of prayers.

BELIEVERS' NEEDS AND DESIRES (PS. 40:17; HEB. 4:16; 1 PET. 5:7)

Only God can supply all the believer's needs. He gives exceeding abundantly above all that the believer asks or thinks (Eph. 3:20). Individual needs are not the only reason for the Christian to pray. The harvest is great, but the laborers few; therefore he prays for the needs of the whole world (Luke 10:2). All men need to be saved; therefore he prays for all men (1 Tim. 2:1-4). The church of Christ needs continual support; therefore he prays for all believers (Eph. 6:18). Only God can fulfill desires. Where there is delight in God's will, He will give the desires of the heart (Ps. 37:4).

SPIRITUAL POWER (MATT. 6:13; 26:41)

"The spirit indeed is willing, but the flesh is weak." The Christian is continually tempted by the world—the enemy around him; by the flesh— the enemy in him; by the devil—the enemy beside him. Many evil desires cannot be overcome in one's own strength. But God has provided prayer through which the Christian communicates with Him and receives strength to withstand temptation.

SATAN'S DEFEAT (EPH. 6:11-12; JAS. 4:7-8)

Prayer is not only a calling on God, but a conflict with Satan. To resist Satan's attacks, the believer must draw closer to God in prayer.

Requirements for Prayer

AWARENESS OF A RELATIONSHIP TO GOD (1 JOHN 1:9)

The privilege of prayer is only for those who know Christ as their Savior and have the awareness that their sins are forgiven. But even the child of God may have his prayers hindered because of unconfessed sin (Ps. 66:18). If so, he has the blessed privilege of confessing that sin to Him who is faithful and just to forgive him and cleanse him from all unrighteousness (1 John 1:9). Prayer enables the believer to see what is wrong; prayer adjusts the soul.

It is not always some flagrant sin that prevents real communion with God. More often it is little hindrances that mar fellowship with God and make prayer ineffectual. It is the "little foxes," says Solomon, that "spoil the vines" (Song 2:15).

There must be perfect union between the Lord and His child. The true Christian abides in and obeys Him. An answer to prayer is conditioned on the believer's obedience. He must not knowingly disobey the revealed will of God, but instead actively strive to carry out Christ's commands.

A RIGHT ATTITUDE (JER. 29:13; JAS. 5:16B)

It is the "effectual fervent prayer" that "availeth much." To pray with "all your heart" is to put forth all spiritual energy in prayer, remembering that the devil would prevent the answers to prayers if possible. Charles Finney said, "Prevailing, or effectual, prayer attains the blessing that it seeks. It is that prayer that effectually moves God. The very idea of effectual prayer is that it effects its object."

"Praying Hyde," the missionary whose prayer life stirred all India, found that the obstacle preventing a prayer being answered was the lack of praise. He would then confess this as a sin and ask for forgiveness and for the spirit of praise. As he praised God for souls, the souls always came. Along with telling God needs and desires, the Christian must not neglect to praise and thank Him.

PRAYING WITHOUT CEASING (1 THESS. 5:17; ROM. 12:12)

It is as possible to "pray without ceasing" as it is to breathe without ceasing.

The soul needs stated times of prayer each day. This "quiet time" fills the soul with spiritual power and blessing, leading to a continual spirit of prayer and fellowship with God. The Christian's ability to stay with God in his or her quiet time measures his or her ability to walk with God at all other times.

The word for "ejaculatory" prayer comes from the word *jaculum*, a dart or arrow, and fittingly describes prayer that "darts" up to God at any time. Short emergency prayers owe their point and efficiency to the longer prayers that have preceded them. Thus prayer is both an act and an attitude.

ACCORDING TO GOD'S WILL (1 JOHN 5:14)

All prayer is based on God's revelation of Himself and His will. His promises encourage and His commands motivate the believer to pray, but His will sets the necessary limit of prayer. The believer asks in faith lest he be like a tossed wave (Heb. 11:6; Jas. 1:6); he prays in submission to God's will lest he ask amiss (Jas. 4:3). A will wholly yielded to God is able to say, "Not my will, but Yours be done."

Prayer in fleshly strength will produce fleshly results, for "that which is born of the flesh is flesh" (John 3:6). God is the only giver of life. The highest function of the believer is to be a transmitter of the life of God to others. This is accomplished through prayer. Prayer connects one with the source of life and power.

Responsibility to Pray

For the Christian to cease to pray is sin (1 Sam. 12:23). God has made the believer responsible for bringing things to pass through prayer. He or she who has great gaps in his or her prayer life will have no sense of urgency or power in prayer. God would have him or her bring "into captivity every thought to the obedience of Christ" (2 Cor. 10:5). Some will say, "What a price to pay!" But consider what such a price purchases!

SUMMARY

Worship means to concentrate on God, to think about His power and majesty. It is a spiritual act, and the need to worship can only be fulfilled when the believer worships God as He has commanded. Objects or people must never take His place. Christ, as God, accepts worship, and one day the entire universe will recognize Him as Lord and will bow before Him.

The Christian should not worship carelessly. True worship is in the name of Christ, guided by the Holy Spirit, and conformed to God's Word. It creates a response of pure joy because the worshiper is satisfied and occupied with God alone.

When the Christian reads the Bible, God speaks to him. When he or she prays, he or she talks to God. Prayer is vital for the believer. God desires prayer and works through it; the believer expresses his or her needs and desires in prayer; spiritual power is received, and Satan is defeated by prayer.

The Christian must allow God's Holy Spirit to direct him or her when he or she prays. Unconfessed sin will hinder prayers; so the believer must confess sins and be conscious of forgiveness. In striving to serve Christ, the believer is in union with Him—abiding and obeying. This abiding calls for continual prayer. In addition to stated times of prayer in which the soul is filled with spiritual power, the Christian must be in communication constantly. Effective prayers are made with all the heart, filled with praise and thanks, and spoken in accordance with God's will.

For the Christian, it is a sin not to pray. Prayer is a responsibility and a blessing from God.

DISCUSSION QUESTIONS

1. What is true worship?
2. Why do you think many people are careless in worship?
3. What three things are required to make our worship acceptable and why?
4. How does the Holy Spirit guide in worship?
5. How are God's Word and prayer related?
6. Explain how our prayers are hindered.
7. How can the Christian pray without ceasing?
8. Why should praise and thanksgiving be included in prayer?
9. Since God knows all our needs before we ask Him, why should we pray?
10. What is the relationship of true worship and prayer?

RESOURCES

Gibbs, Alfred P. *Worship, the Christian's Highest Occupation.* Kansas City, KS: Walterick Publishers, n.d.

Lavender, John Allan. *Why Prayers Are Unanswered.* Wheaton, IL: Tyndale House, 1981.

Chapter Six

ORIGIN AND PURPOSE OF THE CHURCH

THE ENGLISH WORD *church* is a translation of the Greek word *ecclesia*. It means "the called-out." The members of the church are called out from the old creation into the new (2 Cor. 5:17). Though they are *in* the world, they are not *of* the world. The Father has given them to the Son out of the world (John 17:6, 11, 14, 16). They are Christ's body of believers.

The church is more than an organization—it is an organism. An organization is a body of persons enlisted together for united action. An organism is a body having life within itself, with mutually dependent parts, all functioning toward a common purpose. The purpose for the church is the spread of the Gospel to all men.

The church has a record of service through the ages. The way in which it has expanded, from its small beginnings in a remote Roman province into a great world institution, gives it a historical perspective unequaled by any international organization. Medieval history largely centered around the church, which was the great factor in the civilization of Europe. Modern history centers on international and interracial relations and has followed in the wake of the worldwide missionary movement of the church. The church is responsible for the founding of many benevolent services including orphanages, homes for senior citizens, and youth programs. The education of the masses began with the church. True, these movements have not all maintained their original Christian standards, but they were started by men of God and have been used by God for good.

ORIGIN OF THE CHURCH

The church is a New Testament institution that had its birth with the outpouring of the Holy Spirit at Pentecost, but its conception was long before that.

Originated with God

The church originated in the mind of God and is an important part of His program for the earth. The importance of the church is recognized by the fact that its program was determined and its members chosen "before the foundation of the world" (Eph. 1:4). There is no room here for chance or uncertainty. God's plans are complete and His purposes definite.

God the Father is the author of the salvation that the church proclaims. Christians can do nothing to earn God's grace. Their possession of "all spiritual blessings in heavenly places" is not because of what they have done. God Himself chose the members of the church, predestined them to be conformed to the image of His Son, and accepted them in Christ (Eph. 1:3-6).

The members of the church are redeemed by the Son of God. The death and resurrection of Christ provide access to God and show God's plan to unite the entire universe in Christ (Eph. 1:7-11).

But God's record concerning Christ cannot be believed without trusting in Him. Faith comes by hearing the truth of the Gospel, and God honors the faith of the members of the church by sealing them with His Holy Spirit. "In whom also after that ye believed, ye were sealed with that holy Spirit of promise, which is the earnest of our inheritance" (Eph. 1:13-14).

Announced by Christ

The first mention of the church in the New Testament is in Matthew 16:16-19, but no supremacy was here given to Peter, for a comparison of these verses with other Scriptures (Matt. 18:15-20; John 20:19-23) clearly reveals that the same privilege of binding and loosing was given to other disciples, and to the whole church. The rock upon which the church was to be built was the Lord Jesus Christ, who is "the chief corner stone" (Eph. 2:20). "Other foundation can no man lay than that is laid, which is Jesus Christ" (1 Cor. 3:11).

FOUNDING OF THE CHURCH

The church had its first converts on the day of Pentecost (Acts 2). Pentecost was known as the Feast of Weeks, and the Jewish law required the attendance of all males at the celebration in the temple (Exod. 23:14-17; 34:22). Jerusalem was the central gathering place for the Jews, not only those of Palestine, but also those from the whole Roman Empire. This explains the presence of the vast multitudes, and especially the people from other lands. Although born and brought up in other countries, the Jews remained faithful to their laws and strict observance of them; consequently, thousands had come to Jerusalem for this feast. These Jews heard the apostles speak in the language of those countries from which they had come. As representatives from foreign lands, they were in reality the first missionaries of the church whose members Christ commissioned to preach the Gospel "unto the uttermost part of the earth" (Acts 1:8).

The men and women who became the first members of the church all came from the Jewish faith. They were, however, divided into three classes: Hebrews, Hellenists, and proselytes.

The Hebrews were those whose ancestors had lived in Palestine. In their synagogues they read the Hebrew Scriptures faithfully and interpreted them sentence by sentence into Aramaic, which was the common language. The Hellenists were Grecian Jews whose homes, if not ancestry, were in foreign lands. After the conquest of the Orient by Alexander the Great, Greek became the leading language of the world, and on this account Jews of foreign ancestry were called Grecians or Hellenists. They represented the most educated and most prosperous branch of the Jewish people. Proselytes were Gentiles who had accepted the Jewish faith. Although a minority among Jewish people, they were found in many synagogues in the Roman Empire.

PURPOSE OF THE CHURCH

The world is filled with a variety of nations and languages, but God divides all into three great groups of people—Israel, the Gentiles, and the church (1 Cor. 10:32). Israel had three main purposes in God's redemptive plan. Israel was to be entrusted with the Scriptures (God's Word), a channel to introduce the world's Redeemer, a witness to the world.

The study of the Old Testament reveals that while Israel realized the first two purposes for which the nation was set apart, she failed in the third. The New Testament introduces the church, whose members were commissioned as witnesses of God's plan of salvation to both Jews and Gentiles. But that is not the only mission with which the church has been entrusted.

A Revealed Mystery

The Greek word sometimes translated "mystery" occurs twenty-seven times in the New Testament, with about half of these referring to the church. In the New Testament this term means a revealed secret or a divine truth once hidden but now disclosed. ". . . according to the revelation of the mystery which was kept secret since the world began, but now is made manifest" (Rom. 16:25-26).

The church was "hid in God" (Eph. 3:9) from the beginning of the world. Not even the angels or the prophets knew of the church or its vital part in God's plan.

What had been concealed from angels and prophets was revealed to Paul to record. The mystery "hid in God" was the divine purpose to make of Jew and Gentile a new creation, the body of Christ, formed by the baptism of the Holy Spirit, in which the earthly distinction of Jew and Gentile would disappear (1 Cor. 12:12-13; Col. 3:10-11).

That the Gentiles were to be saved was no mystery. Those who had the Old Testament realized that Christ was to come for the salvation of both Jew and Gentile. This was plainly foretold (Isa. 42:6; 49:6; cf. Rom. 9:24-33). But never had there been such a marvelous announcement as this: "Christ in you, the hope of glory" (Col. 1:27). The unfolded mystery was that Christ should gather *out* a people, live *in* them, and work *through* them.

The Body of Christ

The church had its beginning at Pentecost when the believers were all assembled according to divine directions (Acts 1:4). Christ was at the right hand of God, but He sent the Holy Spirit to dwell in each believer. The Holy Spirit united the believers to Christ and also to one another, and thus the body, the church, was born (Rom. 12:4-5; 1 Cor. 12:12-27).

This body of Christ has been formed "to the praise of the glory of his grace, wherein he hath made us accepted in the beloved" (Eph. 1:6). Christ as the Head is united by the closest spiritual ties with the members of His body. One spirit of love unites believers in complete fellowship. Christ is not only Lord *over* us, but He is also dwelling *in* us as members of His body. The relation between Christ and the church is not only to be that of King and subject, but one of husband and wife, a relationship of perfect intimacy and spiritual union. We have been called to the *fellowship* of God's Son (Eph. 3:14-19; Col. 1:12-18).

This body of Christ has work to do on earth. Certain officers are to be chosen by the church "for the perfecting of the saints, for the work of the ministry, for the edifying of the body of Christ" (Eph. 4:12). The object of this general ministry on the part of every member is the building up of the body of Christ, the increase of its membership, the completing of it as an organism (Eph. 4:15-16).

The Bride of Christ

The membership of the church must be completed before the Son of Man can come in His glory (Rev. 19:7; cf. 2 Cor. 11:2). Christians labor for the completion of the church, for when this object is gained, the Lord will return. The bridegroom will have His bride, the church, which will be presented and united to Him.

The church will be with Christ in heaven, for God has "made us sit together in heavenly places in Christ Jesus: That in the ages to come he might show the exceeding riches of his grace in his kindness toward us through Christ Jesus" (Eph. 2:6-7). The union between Christ and his church is divine and will continue eternally.

SUMMARY

The word *church* means "the called-out." The members of the church are called *out of* the world to be Christ's body and His messengers *in* the world.

Originating in the mind of God, the church was determined before the foundation of the world. God the Father originated the plan; God the Son died for the salvation of believers; and God the Holy Spirit sealed believers and revealed truth. Hence, all three persons of the Trinity took part in the birth and growth of the church. Christ Himself announced the first church.

The church was born on the day of Pentecost. Jews from all over the Roman Empire were gathered in Jerusalem for the Feast of Weeks, and on that day the Holy Spirit spoke through the small group of believers in the languages of the many foreigners. The Jews who were converted went back to their homelands to spread the news. Three major groups became members of the first church: Hebrews—Jews in Palestine who spoke Aramaic; Hellenists—Jews of foreign ancestry who lived in Palestine and in other lands; proselytes—Gentile converts to the Jewish faith.

At last called into existence to witness to God's salvation, the church had been a mystery, a secret "hid in God" from the world's beginning. Neither the angels nor the prophets knew of the divine plan to draw both Jews and Gentiles together into one body with Christ as the Head. In addition, the Holy Spirit would dwell in all believers, uniting them with God and with one another.

When the membership of the church is completed, Christ will unite the church with Himself, as the bride to the bridegroom. Believers will be with Him in heaven, glorifying him eternally.

DISCUSSION QUESTIONS

1. Explain the meaning of the word *church*.
2. What is the origin of the church?

3. According to Matthew 16:18, what was the rock on which Christ said He would build His church?
4. Why were so many nations represented in Jerusalem at Pentecost?
5. Describe the three classes that were members of the first church.
6. Why was the church called into existence?
7. What is meant by the word *mystery* in the New Testament?
8. Explain the mystery of the church as it was revealed to Paul.
9. Describe the church as the body of Christ.
10. Describe the church as the bride of Christ.

RESOURCES

Beyer, Douglas. *Basic Beliefs of Christians.* Valley Forge, PA: Judson Press, 1981, Chapter 9.

Demaray, Donald E. *Basic Beliefs.* Grand Rapids, MI: Baker Book House, 1958, Chapter 8.

Dowley, Tim, ed. *Eerdmans' Handbook to the History of Christianity.* Grand Rapids, MI: Wm. B. Eerdmans, 1977.

Shelley, Bruce L. *What Is the Church? God's People.* Wheaton, IL: Victor Books, 1983.

Chapter Seven

GROWTH, CHARACTER, AND ORGANIZATION OF THE CHURCH

GROWTH OF THE CHURCH

The Christian church was founded on the day of Pentecost (Acts 2:1ff.), when the Holy Spirit moved in a wonderful way in the hearts of men. The marvelous events that followed and that form the account of the earliest history of the church are, in reality, the acts of the Holy Spirit (Acts 4:31; 5:32; 13:2; 16:6).

The Message

The church held three fundamental beliefs.

JESUS IS MESSIAH (ACTS 2:36; 5:31; 17:3)

All the disciples gave witness that Jesus of Nazareth was the long-expected Messiah of Israel who died, rose again, and is exalted at God's right hand. Each member of the church was expected to give personal loyalty, reverence, and obedience to Him as Savior.

JESUS ROSE FROM THE DEAD (ACTS 4:33; 13:33; 17:31)

The resurrection was proclaimed not only as proof of Christ's deity, but also as evidence that God had accepted His atonement for sin and appointed Him to judge the world in righteousness.

JESUS WILL RETURN (ACTS 1:11; 15:16)

The disciples believed and taught that Jesus had ascended to heaven and would come back to earth and reign. This blessed hope supported the believers in the midst of great need, danger, and persecution.

The Method (Acts 1:8, 22; 5:32; 10:39; 13:31)

The method of the church through which the world was to be won was the witnessing of its members. As the numbers were multiplied, the witnesses multiplied, for every member felt his or her responsibility for actively furthering the work. This universal testimony was a powerful influence in the rapid increase of the church.

However, the building process is not merely the addition of numbers. The early church also built up its members by teaching them in a continual program of Christian education. The disciples literally obeyed the Lord's great commission to "go" and "teach" (Matt. 28:18-20). The word "teach" is found twice in our Lord's farewell address, and the instruction in teaching was "to observe all things whatsoever I have commanded you."

The Movement (Acts 4:4; 5:14; 6:7; 9:31; 11:21; 14:1; 16:5; 17:4)

There were daily additions to the number of believers, and only a short time after the day of Pentecost the number reached five thousand. At the end of the first century Pliny told the Emperor Trajan, "So many believe in Christ that the temples of pagan worship are deserted." At the end of the third century there were no less than five million believers. By the tenth century there were fifty million members, and at the opening of the nineteenth century approximately two hundred million professed Christ.

The classic history of ancient Rome is given by Edward Gibbon in *Decline and Fall of the Roman Empire*, written in the eighteenth century by a scholar who was distinctly antagonistic to Christianity. Gibbon named four distinct reasons why Christianity grew so rapidly in the ancient world.

ENTHUSIASM

The Christians believed and applied the teachings of Jesus and refused to compromise with any pagan religion or secular code.

DOCTRINE OF FUTURE LIFE

Christians have a hope of future glory that cannot be understood by human intellect. The early Christians held this hope and shared it with certainty.

MIRACULOUS POWER

"With great power gave the apostles witness" (Acts 4:33). Marvelous miracles worked by the disciples demonstrated the truth of their teaching.

PURE MORALS

The believers would not compromise with pagan immoralities. They abandoned sins when they became Christians, lived exemplary lives, and exhibited a standard of virtue unknown to the ancient world. The early Christians exhibited what Paul calls "the mystery of godliness" (1 Tim. 3:16). Their aim was to be like Christ in all areas of life.

CHARACTERISTICS OF THE CHURCH

Today there are vast differences in the characteristics of an average church. In every local assembly there may be both saved and unsaved members. The characteristics of any local church are the total of the characteristics of its members. The early Christians were:

United *(Acts 2:44; 4:32; Eph. 4:1-7)*

"All that believed were together, and had all things common." The Christians united not only as a church, but as a family. Many Jewish converts were ostracized by their families and friends; so the Christians helped and encouraged one another. Their mutual faith in the Messiah bound them together as a group. And the Holy Spirit worked mightily as a result of their unity.

Steadfast *(Acts 2:42; Eph. 4:14-16)*

Their doctrine did not turn aside from facts to fables. They remained steadfast in their belief in God's Word and the apostles' teaching.

They recognized their vital need for *fellowship* and remained steadfast in it. If the members had stopped to criticize, no doubt they would have found faults in each other. Instead, they were quick to see their own failures, but slow to criticize others.

Christ was the substance of their sermons and the center of their worship. The institution of the *Lord's Supper* and of *baptism* represented the work of grace in the hearts of the early believers, and they remained steadfast in observing these.

The believers continued steadfast in *prayer*, praying "with one accord," together, in agreement (Acts 1:14). The early church realized the power in prayer and God's faithfulness to answer.

Charitable *(Acts 2:45; 4:34-35; Eph. 4:28)*

They "sold their possessions and goods, and parted them to all men, as every man had need." The members gave spontaneously. Their love for Christ and their desire to spread the Gospel were so great that they saw their material possessions as gifts from God to be used for Him. Their sharing came as the result of Christian affection and faith, not by legislated direction or force. Their charity was a wonderful testimony of the love of Christ in their lives. Those who looked on the scene could well comment, "See how those Christians love."

Joyful (Acts 2:46-47; Eph. 5:18-21)

They continued "daily with one accord in the temple . . . with gladness and singleness of heart." It was this "singleness of heart" that gave them joy. They were not divided between Christ and the world, but being wholly the Lord's, they rejoiced in Him and were full of His joy.

Successful (Acts 2:41, 47; 5:14; 6:7; 13:44; 16:5; 17:6; 18:8)

For the first two centuries the church spread like a wildfire of such vast proportions that the whole world was "turned . . . upside down."

The early church had *favor with God*, and its members were added to the Lord and by the Lord. Frequently today only the names of members are added to churches. These names increase the numbers, but not the churches' strength. When the Lord adds to the church, the members are united, steadfast, charitable, joyful. As a result, their presence makes the church successful.

It is remarkable that in spite of opposition and persecution from rulers and governments, the early church also had *favor with men*. The sincerity and joy of these first Christians could not fail to impress the men of the world.

ORGANIZATION OF THE CHURCH

That there were organized churches in the first century is clear from the fact that Paul addressed many of his epistles to groups in different localities. The first letter to the church at Corinth shows that certain forms of service were recognized (1 Cor. 12:4-11). Paul's later epistles to Timothy and Titus contain directions for a well-organized congregation of believers. Local administration by recognized officers and the presence of the Council at Jerusalem (Acts 15) indicate an established order in the developing church.

Officers

In the beginning of the church, there was no clergy. This and other offices were created as the need arose. Just as kings, judges, and generals came into existence to meet the needs of civil society, so the clergy developed to meet the needs and responsibilities of the growing church.

ELDERS (ACTS 11:29-30; 14:23; 20:17; 1 TIM. 3:1FF.; 5:17; TITUS 1:5)

While the institution of the office of elder is not definitely stated in Scripture, it was so well known and understood that it is believed to have been the familiar mode of governing the Jewish synagogues (Matt. 15:2; 21:23; 26:57), which in turn grew out of the organization of Israel (Exod. 19:7; 24:1; Josh. 23:2). The name originally suggested advanced years but came to signify the office for which one was especially fitted by wisdom and maturity of age. A similar honor was conferred by the Romans on their senators, or old men, who composed their governing body. That the officers of the early church bore this familiar title is in itself suggestive of the fact that they performed the well-known duties of rule and government.

The apostles were called elders (1 Pet. 5:1), but as their number was limited to those who had seen the Lord Jesus after His resurrection (Acts 1:21-22), they soon passed off the scene. Hence their leadership was temporal.

The elders were also called bishops or overseers (Titus 1:5, 7). The former was a name more familiar to the Jewish convert, but the latter to the Gentile, to whom it suggested government, for the term was already common under Roman rule.

The elders were often designated pastors (Eph. 4:11) to emphasize the fact that they were the divinely appointed shepherds who were to "feed the flock of God" (1 Pet. 5:2). They were, therefore, the appointed teachers and spiritual guides in the early Christian church.

DEACONS (ACTS 6:1-6; PHIL. 1:1; 1 TIM. 3:8FF.)

The office of deacon began with the appointment of Philip and Stephen and five fellow laborers. The office was primarily created to relieve the apostles of various menial tasks in order that they might give themselves wholly to prayer and the ministry of the Word. The duties of deacons did not include preaching and teaching; nevertheless they were among the first preachers of the Gospel (Acts 6:8-10; 8:5). In like manner they were the first evangelists, because their specific duties sent them to the homes of the poor. They constructed the framework of the institutions of charity in the church. In comparison with the number of elders, the deacons were few, but this magnified rather than minimized their office.

Qualifications

Great care was exercised in the selection of elders. The qualifications for this important office are listed in 1 Timothy 3:1-7. The elder was to be blameless and of good reputation. He was to prove his capacity for governing the church by first showing his ability to rule his own home.

Furthermore, he was to be sober, discreet in mind, orderly in conduct, hospitable, and able to teach. He was not to be quarrelsome, greedy, or a recent convert who could be blinded by pride.

Similarly, 1 Timothy 3:8-13 describes the qualifications for deacons. The deacon, like the elder, was to be a husband of one wife (who herself was to be serious, truthful, sober, and faithful in all things) and a father known to be capable of managing his children and of ruling his own house well. As he was to be selected from the younger men, he was to serve first on probation, and when fully approved, appointed to his office.

Responsibilities

In the early church there was no distinction between elders, bishops, and pastors as there is today. Even the office of deacon was not always limited to the care of the poor but frequently included the responsibilities assigned to the elders, as in the case of Stephen and Philip. However, the responsibilities administered by these officers were divided into three distinctive tasks.

EVANGELIZING

The evangelist planted the church. He was the missionary and extension worker. The apostles served in this capacity. Paul, the only apostle of whose work we have a detailed account, traveled from one place to another. His chief object was "to preach the gospel, not where Christ was named" (Rom. 15:20), and his epistles suggest a long list of churches that he planted.

SHEPHERDING

The pastor shepherded or governed the church. He was ordained in every church that the apostles founded and carried on the work the evangelist had begun. This work included supervising, preaching, and visiting.

Christ summed up such *supervising* when He spoke of assigning "to every man his work" (Mark 13:34) and assigning the task to "each according to his own ability" (Matt. 25:15, NASB). The unparalleled success of the early church was due largely to the fact that every member was an active participant. The apostles realized that Christ established the church for the development of workmen as much as for the accomplishment of work (Eph. 2:10).

Paul speaks of *preaching* in 2 Timothy 4:2 and Titus 2:1. Timothy was the pastor of the church at Ephesus, and Titus of the church at Crete.

Paul's epistles to these two young men say much concerning their pastoral duties, especially the content of their preaching.

Visiting church members, especially when they were in sickness or in sorrow, was a particular duty of the pastor. As the shepherd of the flock, he was to minister to the weak and the helpless, the poor and the needy.

TEACHING

The teacher edified, or built up, the church. Teaching was more common than preaching in the early church. While John the Baptist was a preacher, Christ was a teacher. Sixty out of ninety times that Jesus was addressed, He was called "teacher." And He commissioned His followers to teach as well as to preach (Matt. 28:19-20). While the words for "preaching" are found about 150 times in Scripture, those for "teaching" are mentioned about 250 times. The early church saw the vital importance of continually teaching its members from the Word of God.

SUMMARY

The Christian church was formed on the day of Pentecost, and the Holy Spirit has acted in its continued spread and growth. Holding three fundamental beliefs—that Jesus is Messiah, rose again, and will return—the church grew in numbers by witnessing, and the members grew from the continual teaching they received.

Christianity spread rapidly. Gibbon suggests four main reasons: enthusiasm, doctrine of the future life, miraculous power, and pure morals. The believers were united, steadfast, charitable, joyful, and successful. These factors stood out in sharp contrast to the paganism surrounding the church.

After its birth at Pentecost, the church soon became well organized. Offices were created as the need arose to meet the responsibilities of the growing church.

The office of *elder* may have grown from a similar office in the Jewish synagogues, and perhaps from the senators within the Roman government. It suggested the wisdom and maturity of advanced years. The apostles were called elders. Bishops, overseers, and pastors were other names for this office.

Deacons took over various menial tasks to allow the apostles to concentrate on prayer and the ministry of the Word. Stephen and Philip, two of the first deacons, were preachers as well as evangelists. This office formed the framework for the institutions of charity in the church.

Qualifications for each office are described in 1 Timothy 3. Their duties included evangelizing, shepherding, and teaching.

DISCUSSION QUESTIONS

1. Describe the three fundamental beliefs of the early church.
2. Describe the two methods of growth in the early church.
3. Why did Christianity spread so rapidly?
4. Explain the importance of the five characteristics of the early church.
5. In light of these characteristics, compare the early church with the church of today.
6. Distinguish between the elders and deacons.
7. Why did Paul write so specifically concerning qualifications?
8. Describe the three major duties of the church officers.

RESOURCES

Shelley, Bruce L. *What Is the Church? God's People.* Wheaton, IL: Victor Books, 1983.

Werning, Waldo J. *Vision and Strategy for Church Growth.* Grand Rapids, MI: Baker Book House, 1983.

Chapter Eight

ANGELS

THE BIBLE CONTAINS many passages about angels. Yet there is a tragic and widespread ignorance, even among Christians, concerning the Bible's doctrine of angels. Because of this ignorance, distorted pictures and varied superstitions have corrupted the doctrine concerning these spirit beings. The Bible has much to say about the origin, nature, and ministry of angels.

CREATION OF ANGELS

Angels have not always existed. They had a beginning. They were created by a divine command (Neh. 9:6; Col. 1:16).

Number and Rank (Job 25:3; Matt. 26:53; 1 Thess. 4:16; Heb. 12:22; 1 Pet. 3:22; Rev. 5:11)

Such expressions as "ten thousand times ten thousands," "a multitude of the heavenly hosts," and "myriads of angels" suggest that their numbers are beyond human calculation, if not comprehension.

There are various grades or ranks of angels, having different positions and capacities. Although God created them similar enough for us to recognize their divine origin, He manifested a variety among these beings. Angels are called powers, archangels, seraphim, cherubim, and celestial armies of the Most High.

Superior to Humans (2 Kings 19:35; Ps. 8:4-5; Luke 20:36; Acts 5:19)

Humans were created lower than the angels. Angels are invisible and immortal and moreover are not confined to this earth like people are. Angels are spirits created apart from their habitations. God gave heaven to the angels for a home, but "the earth hath he given to the children of men" (Ps. 115:16). Further contrasts will be observed between the character of the angels and that of humans.

Subordinate to God (Eph. 1:20-21; Col. 2:18; Heb. 1:6-8, 13; Rev. 19:10; 22:8-9)

Great as may be their superiority to humans, angels are vastly inferior to God. The theme of Hebrews 1 is the superiority of Jesus Christ to angels. He "was made flesh, and dwelt among us" (John 1:14) and thus became "a little lower than the angels" (Ps. 8:5). Yet when He returned to heaven He was set at the right hand of God, "far above all principality, and power, and might, and dominion" (Eph. 1:21).

Angels never permitted people to worship them. One of the principal reasons for the writing of the Epistle to the Colossians was to correct the prevailing practice of angel worship, which some of the early Christians had taken over from the pagans, a practice that proves that the ancient world believed in angel worship.

CHARACTERISTICS OF ANGELS

Holy (Matt. 25:31; Luke 9:26; Acts 10:22; Rev. 14:10)

Angels in their unfallen state are completely pure. They are in a state of established and superior holiness and are not tempted with evil. Their refusal to receive worship from humans is evidence of this. Their whole nature abhors that which is evil. Their moral perfection is shown by such biblical phrases as "holy angels" and "the elect angels."

Angels are glorious beings. In only a few passages is their appearance to people accompanied by a description of their personality. It is interesting to note that Christ, in speaking of His return, refers to the glory of the angels as well as to His own (Luke 9:26).

Intelligent (2 Sam. 14:20; 1 Cor. 13:1; Gal. 1:8)

Both the Old and New Testaments contain high estimates of the wisdom of angels. The scholarly Paul acknowledged their superior intelligence. However, they are not omniscient, as is God. We read that the church was just as much a mystery to the angels as to the Old Testament prophets (1 Pet. 1:12) and that the hour of the Lord's return is unknown to them, as it is to us (Mark 13:32).

Mighty and Powerful (Ps. 103:20; 2 Thess. 1:7)

Not only do they "excel in strength," but also they are spoken of as "mighty." In Revelation, angels are attributed with carrying out various judgments that affect millions of people. However, while mighty, they are not almighty, and are in subjection to God (1 Pet. 3:22).

Undoubtedly angels can move more swiftly than light (186,000 miles per second). Perhaps they move as rapidly as thought. Daniel was told that at the beginning of his prayer, the angel Gabriel was commissioned to fly swiftly, that he might be with him at the close (Dan. 9:20-23).

Humble and Obedient (Isa. 6:2; 2 Pet. 2:11; Jude 9)

The seraphim that Isaiah saw were a high order of angels, but they humbly covered their faces in the presence of the Lord. Michael, an archangel, when contending with an angel of greater authority, showed humility by calling on God to rebuke him.

The fact that the Lord taught His disciples to pray that His will be done on earth as it is in heaven indicates that all in heaven are obedient. And this obedience is prompted by love. Because the holy angels love God, they obey Him.

MINISTRY OF ANGELS

Angels are perfect in character. Every angel renders consecrated service of praise to God (Ps. 148:2). Angels are at the same time both worshipers of God and servants of men (Heb. 1:14). The Lord set forth this truth when He said that the angels of children ever behold the face of the Father in heaven (Matt. 18:10).

Guidance (Luke 2:10-12; Acts 8:26; 10:3, 7-8)

Angels sometimes appeared to God's people to announce His plan for their lives or to direct the work He had for them to do. It is of particular interest to note that angels are deeply interested in Christians' work. In the cases of Peter and Cornelius, an angel guided a Christian worker to the sinner and the sinner to the Christian worker. Angels watch over the relationships of believers with nonbelievers. They rejoice each time a sinner repents and returns to God (Luke 15:10).

Comfort (Matt. 4:11; Luke 22:43)

The angels' ministry of comfort is evident in the lives of Hagar, Elijah, and Paul: Hagar when she first fled from Sarai (Gen. 16:7-12), Elijah when he ran into the wilderness to escape Jezebel's wrath (1 Kings 19:2-8), and Paul when he was shipwrecked (Acts 27:23-24).

Spurgeon said: "It is my firm belief that angels are often employed by God to throw into the hearts of His people comforting thoughts. Angels came and ministered unto Jesus, and I doubt not that they minister unto us. Few of us have enough belief in the existence of angels."

Protection (Ps. 91:11; Isa. 63:9)

Angels fulfill a protective ministry over God's people. Angels are also shown as protectors of the nation of Israel (Exod. 14:19; 23:20) and of Daniel (Dan. 6:22).

These portions of Scripture indicate God's great love. What greater blessing can the believer receive than protection from danger by God's angels.

Deliverance (Ps. 34:7)

Several times it was evident that angels delivered the apostles from persecution during their ministry.

When the Jews imprisoned Peter and some of the other apostles, an angel came by night, opened the jail doors, and led them out (Acts 5:17-20).

Later, when Herod imprisoned Peter intending to kill him, an angel appeared in Peter's cell, woke him, broke his chains, and freed him (Acts 12:6-9).

Prison walls, iron gates, and the guard of four soldiers could not prevent angels from rescuing the seemingly doomed apostles.

Judgment (2 Thess. 1:7-9)

Several accounts in the Bible tell of the angels' ministry of judgment.

In Genesis 19, God's judgment on wicked Sodom and Gomorrah was executed by two angels.

David had a choice of three penalties for his sinful pride in numbering the people in order to estimate the strength of his armies. In choosing plague rather than famine or defeat, he threw himself on the mercy of God and of the angel that executed the decree (2 Sam. 24:15-16).

The Assyrian army seemed unconquerable. City after city had fallen before the victorious armies of that rising world power. Jerusalem appeared doomed. But that night when the city was in despair, Hezekiah prayed, and an angel slew 185,000 of the enemy (2 Kings 19:35).

CORRUPTION OF ANGELS

The study of the holy and righteous character of God makes it impossible to believe that He would have created anything that was essentially and originally evil. The study of man shows that he was created perfect, but by an act of willful disobedience he corrupted his nature and became sinful. The same is true of the fallen angels. They were not created thus. Peter says that they "sinned" (2 Pet. 2:4), while Jude declares that they "did not keep their positions of authority but abandoned their own home" (Jude 6, NIV).

It is not easy to discover all of God's dealings with these majestic creatures with whom He has surrounded Himself as partakers of His holiness and participants in His glory. From widely scattered implications, however, the events that might have taken place can be pieced together.

The Anointed Cherub (Ezek. 28:14ff.)

"Cherub" is the highest rank in the angelic world. A study of the word *cherubim* (plural of *cherub*) as presented in Scripture, though not always translated with that word (Ezek. 1:5-14; 10:8-22; Rev. 4:6-11; 5:11-14), intimates that this superior rank of God's creatures sat nearest to God's throne and led the worship of the entire universe. The use of the word "anointed" in Ezekiel 28 would indicate that Lucifer was the chief of the cherubim, a position to which he was specially appointed by God.

Rebellion

Scripture tells the cause of Lucifer's unrest, dissatisfaction, and final rebellion. The glory of his position and the magnificence of his person were more than he could bear. Pride ruled his heart and overwhelmed him (1 Tim. 3:6). His heart was lifted up because of his beauty, and his wisdom was corrupted by reason of his brightness. Like Absalom, the handsome son of David (2 Sam. 15:2-6), he sought, by stealing the hearts of the unstable in the kingdom, to occupy the seat of royalty.

How graphically Isaiah describes the ambition of this haughty monarch, Lucifer! For while the prophet refers to the king of Babylon, he also describes the powerful and prosperous Lucifer who aspired to be God (Isa. 14:12-14; cf. Acts 12:21-23).

When Lucifer imagined that he might be God, rebellion ruled his heart, and he plotted against Him to whom he had formerly been loyal and obedient. Then, doubtless, dissatisfaction appeared among the angels, which only strengthened him in defiance and disobedience.

Defeat

Lucifer's rebellion was unsuccessful, as God foreknew. The result of this conflict between heavenly forces was defeat for Satan and his followers. They "prevailed not; neither was their place found any more in heaven" (Rev. 12:8). The results of that overthrow included Satan's loss of position and the appointment of a successor to fill the vacated place in heaven.

The rebels of heaven were dealt with speedily and severely. "God spared not the angels that sinned, but cast them down to hell" (2 Pet. 2:4). Though they were very great and very powerful, God did not spare them. Even their vast numbers made no difference. There was no delay. Punishment followed hard upon the crime (Isa. 14:15; Ezek. 28:17).

Since pride was the cause of the first terrible misdeed that marred the holiness and happiness of heaven, God in His omniscience formulated a penalty in just proportion to the transgression. The sin of pride was punished by an exhibition of grace. A subordinate race was created and placed on the earth. God saw fit to ordain strength out of far weaker and lowlier creatures (Gen. 1:26-28; Ps. 8:2-5).

We will say more about Satan in the next chapter of this book.

SUMMARY

The subject of angels is not well known even among Christians. As a result, many misconceptions and superstitions have distorted this doctrine. But the Bible has much to say about angels.

Angels are created beings. They have various ranks and are referred to in Scripture by many words. Angels are superior to humans, yet subordinate to God.

The Bible has much to say about the characteristics of angels. They are holy, intelligent, mighty and powerful, humble and obedient.

Angels have a varied ministry and purpose. They carry on a ministry of guidance, comfort, protection, deliverance, and judgment.

Angels, like humans, were created perfect and, also like humans, by an act of willful disobedience became corrupt. The Bible says that Lucifer, the chief of the angels, rebelled against God and sought to be God. Lucifer (subsequently called Satan) was unsuccessful, lost his position of authority, and was punished and thrown out of heaven.

DISCUSSION QUESTIONS

1. Why is there such widespread ignorance about angels?
2. What does the Bible tell us about the number and rank of the angels?
3. Give references showing angels' position in relation to mankind and to God.
4. List the characteristics of the angels.
5. When and where have angels served in the ministry of guidance?
6. Name some Bible characters who were protected by angels.
7. List some occasions when angels have ministered deliverance.
8. What led to Lucifer's rebellion and defeat?
9. What happened as a result of Satan's defeat?
10. Discuss the position and service of angels since Bible times.

RESOURCES

Beyer, Douglas. *Basic Beliefs of Christians.* Valley Forge, PA: Judson Press, 1981, Chapter 6.

Dickason, C. Fred. *Angels: Elect and Evil.* Chicago: Moody Press, 1975.

Ryrie, Charles C. *A Survey of Bible Doctrine.* Chicago: Moody Press, 1972, Chapter 5.

Chapter Nine

CHARACTER, WORK, AND WORSHIP OF SATAN

SATAN HAS ALREADY been conquered by Christ's death and resurrection; however, he is still present as ruler of this world. Previous chapters treated Satan's former position as God's anointed angel, his fall, and his temptation of the first humans. The character of Satan, his further work on earth, and the reality that he is worshiped will now be considered.

THE CHARACTER OF SATAN

Multiple Scripture passages leave no doubt as to the true nature of Satan. In the Old Testament (and once in the New Testament) he is called "Belial," which means worthless, indicating that his character is completely evil. In the New Testament he is called "Beelzebub" (the ruler of evil spirits) and "Apollyon" (the destroyer). The name "Satan" means adversary; "devil" means slanderer.

Wicked

The Lord taught His disciples to ask for deliverance from "the evil one" (Matt. 6:13, NIV). Christ also calls him "the evil one" in the parable of the sower (Matt. 13:19, NIV). Satan has been a murderer and a liar from the beginning (John 8:44). He stirred up the firstborn son of human parents to slay his brother, and he has been active ever since in multiplying every kind of evil (1 John 3:8, 12). He will do everything in his power to mar the righteousness of the believer and to intensify the wickedness of the sinner.

Powerful

The glimpses of Satan in Scripture reveal his "power and signs and lying wonders" (2 Thess. 2:9). Because of Satan's power, the unbeliever is blinded and in darkness; only faith in Christ can bring light and forgiveness of sin (Acts 26:18). By Satan's power the believer is hindered in service (1 Thess. 2:18). Only by resisting him and drawing nigh to God can the believer have victory (Jas. 4:7-8a).

Satan has power over a kingdom and rules over exalted beings called principalities, powers, world rulers, and spiritual hosts of wickedness (Eph. 2:2; 6:11-12). He is called "a great red dragon" (Rev. 12:3) to symbolize his terrible character as well as his awesome power.

Scheming

Satan is a schemer. He will take advantage of any opportunity and has a plan of attack for all conditions and all circumstances. After Jesus spent forty days in the wilderness, Satan came to tempt Him through His physical weakness (Matt. 4:2-3). At the height of Jesus' popularity, Satan again tried to tempt Him through the crowd's desire to crown Him king (John 6:15). People's weaknesses are prime targets; Satan emphasizes these weaknesses and attempts to use them for evil. Strengths and successes can also be subtly colored to meet Satan's ends. The devil is never more dangerous than when he pretends to be "an angel of light" (2 Cor. 11:14), deceiving people with what *seems* good, pure, and right. He will attack the mature believer as well as the new Christian. All Christians must be constantly aware of Satan's craftiness and be watchful so he can never have the advantage (2 Cor. 2:11).

THE WORK OF SATAN

Temptation

Satan's activities illustrate his character. The book of Job shows something of what he is doing on earth. In Job 1—2 the angels appear before God to give an account of their work. Satan is among them. On being questioned, he declares that he has been making a careful investigation of men and matters on the earth. God calls his attention to Job as "a perfect and an upright man" and asks Satan if he can find anything with which to accuse Job. Satan challenges God to let him test Job's loyalty, and God grants his request.

First Satan is permitted to destroy Job's family and property with armies, lightning, and a whirlwind. But Job remains faithful. A second conference is held in heaven, and again God calls attention to Job's loyalty despite Satan's afflictions. To this Satan replies that God did not permit him to go far enough. If God will only give him permission to afflict Job's body in addition to his other calamities, Satan is sure that

Job will curse God. Satan is permitted to tempt him further, but "in all this did not Job sin with his lips" (2:10).

However, Satan does not always tempt men by affliction. He knows people will also turn from God if they are tempted to love the world. According to 1 John 2:15-16, "all that is in the world" includes "the lust of the flesh, and the lust of the eyes, and the pride of life."

Satan appeals to the carnal nature in men, urging them to gratify their sensual desires at any cost. He would have all believe that self-gratification and pleasure are the only goals for life.

Those who have too much self-respect to waste their lives with filling every sensual desire, Satan tempts with the multitude of things around them. Possessions are often successfully used to turn people away from God.

Those who cannot be enticed with pleasure and possessions, Satan puffs up with a sense of their own importance and a desire to be important. He glorifies fallen humanity, making people believe that the power and reason to live is within themselves. As one theologian has said, "The satanic message for this age is reformation and self-development, while the message of God is regeneration by the power of the Spirit."

Deception

Satan is the prince of liars. He seems to be most effective when he deludes men into denying his existence or acts as "an angel of light" so people cannot see him working. He gets into the pulpit or the theological classroom and pretends to teach Christianity, when in reality he corrupts it! The deceiver presents his lies as truth. The gospel with which Satan deceives men (Gal. 1:6-7) praises the life of Christ but disregards His death. It magnifies Him as a teacher but gives no place to His work as Savior. As "the god of this world," Satan blinds "the minds of them which believe not, lest the light of the glorious gospel of Christ . . . should shine unto them" (2 Cor. 4:4).

In the parable of the sower, it was "while men slept" that Satan sowed the tares among the wheat (Matt. 13:24-30, 37-40). The tares resemble the wheat, and it is only with difficulty that they can be distinguished. Satan sows his children among the believers in the church, and often they cannot be distinguished by believers. They weaken and defile the church, but God promises that Satan will be judged (Rev. 12:9).

Torment

Satan "as a roaring lion, walketh about, seeking whom he may devour" (1 Pet. 5:8). No one can escape his anger against the people created to replace his lost standing in heaven (Rev. 12:12).

SATAN AUTHORS SICKNESS AND DEATH (HEB. 2:14-15)

In the final analysis, Satan is responsible for the fall of man that introduced sin and sickness to the world. The diseases that Jesus chose to heal were brought on people by the devil. It was Christ who delivered the woman whom Satan had tormented with pain for eighteen years (Luke 13:16).

SATAN PROVOKES PERSECUTION (REV. 2:10)

Satan stirred up the Jews, and later the Greeks and Romans, to persecute the early church. He prompted the tyrant Nero to destroy Christians. He invented the inquisition chamber and the cruel tortures exacted by some in the Reformation.

SATAN CAUSES BELIEVERS TO DENY CHRIST (LUKE 22:31, 61-62)

Peter wept bitterly after Satan had caused him to deny his Lord.

THE WORSHIP OF SATAN

It seems impossible that people can be found in conscious worship of Satan. Yet it is possible there are on earth today more worshipers of Satan than worshipers of God.

Idolatry is not merely the worship of wood or stone; it is in reality the worship of Satan, and the Bible warns against sacrificing "unto devils, not to God" (Deut. 32:17). Those who submit themselves to evil spirits have "changed the truth of God into a lie, and worshipped and served the creature more than the Creator" (Rom. 1:25). We need to proclaim the truth, that "they may recover themselves out of the snare of the devil, who are taken captive by him at his will" (2 Tim. 2:26).

Demonism

The worship of demons and their possession of human beings existed not only before Christ came (Lev. 17:7; Ps. 106:37) but also after His sacrificial death.

Distinction should be made between the words *devil* and *demon* or *spirit*. In revised versions of the New Testament "devil" always refers to Satan, the one "devil," the leader or head of a host of demons. A person is not possessed by the devil, but by spirits or demons. While powerful, Satan is neither omnipotent nor omnipresent; but he works through many demons. In matters of gravest importance, Satan himself probably appears. This was notably the case in the temptation of Christ.

CHRIST CAST OUT DEMONS

The Gospel writers record at least six miracles in which the Lord cast out demons.

- The unclean spirit (Mark 1:23-28; Luke 4:33-37).
- The demon in a man who was blind and dumb (Matt. 12:22).
- A legion of demons (Mark 5:1-20; Luke 8:26-39).
- The demon in a dumb man (Matt. 9:32-33; Luke 11:14).
- The demon in a girl (Matt. 15:22-28; Mark 7:24-30).
- The demon in a boy (Matt. 17:14-21; Mark 9:14-29).

That these were not cases of insanity or epilepsy is proved by the demons' superhuman strength and knowledge, recognizing Jesus as God's Son, and securing permission to dwell in animals. The demons, not the persons possessed, speak to Christ; Christ speaks to the demons, and not to the persons possessed.

THE APOSTLES CAST OUT DEMONS

Christ commissioned His disciples to cast out demons (Matt. 10:8, NASB; Mark 16:17, NASB). The early church leaders encountered demon-possession in many of the places where they taught.

- Peter, at Jerusalem (Acts 5:14-16).
- Paul, at Philippi (Acts 16:12-18).
- Paul, at Ephesus (Acts 19:11-17).

In addition to the above instances, demon-possession was encountered in Samaria and Paphos, which would suggest that it was a rather common experience. These demons manifested superhuman knowledge and power, but the apostles always possessed superior ability through the Holy Spirit (1 John 4:4).

Spiritism

Spiritism is the belief that the spirits of the dead can communicate with and present themselves to people on earth. It is generally supposed that they do this through the agency of a human being called a "medium." The truth is, the spirits of the dead do not revive; demons assume bodily forms to deceive those who wish to communicate with the dead.

The Bible speaks strongly concerning spiritism.

Expressly Forbidden (Lev. 19:31; Isa. 8:19; Micah 5:12)

The Bible condemns spiritism. Witchcraft and soothsaying are recognized as terrible realities and are given a character that is completely evil. The entire practice is condemned.

DEATH PENALTY DECREED (EXOD. 22:18; LEV. 20:27)

God fixed the death penalty for those involved with evil spirits. God's command to Joshua to destroy the Canaanites (Deut. 18:9-14) was the execution of a righteous sentence of God upon a wicked people. Israel became the executioners, that the people might "not learn to do after the abominations of those nations" (v. 9), lest they suffer a similar fate.

These abominations are listed as divination, enchantment, sorcery, consulting with familiar spirits, witchcraft, and necromancy (spiritism). Doubtless the Canaanites were also adulterers, thieves, and murderers, but it was their involvement with evil spirits that brought their final destruction.

After Samuel died and Saul had ruthlessly murdered the priests of Israel, there was no one to whom he could go for information. He ordered his servants to find him a woman possessed of a familiar spirit whom he might consult concerning the outcome of the war he was waging with the Philistines. A medium was found at Endor. Being requested to call up Samuel, she began her preparations. But God overruled the satanic powers, and the real Samuel appeared instead of the anticipated personification. The unhappy king committed suicide, not only for his bloody crimes, but "for asking counsel of one that had a familiar spirit, to inquire of it" (1 Chron. 10:13-14; cf. 1 Sam. 28:3-20).

Astrology

Astrology believes that the stars influence human lives. Astrologers need no telescope, spectroscope, micrometer, or multiplication tables to determine human destinies. A fertile imagination and a gullible public are all the equipment they need.

The accuracy of the predictions of God's prophets as compared with those of the astrologers is seen in that marvelous challenge of Isaiah to Babylon just before he revealed the name of Cyrus, its future conqueror: "Let now the astrologers, the stargazers, the monthly prognosticators, stand up, and save thee from these things that shall come upon thee" (Isa. 47:12-13).

Daniel's contest with the astrologers of Babylon is also instructive. Nebuchadnezzar revealed the shallowness of the horoscopes of his day by insisting that the "wise men" reveal the forgotten dream as well as give the interpretation of it. Listen to his estimate of these men: "If ye will not make known unto me the dream . . . ye have prepared lying and corrupt words to speak before me" (Dan. 2:9). The astrologers considered such a demand to be absurd, and though their lives were at stake, they had to admit the limitation of their art and profession that the nations had been led to hold in such high esteem. The true status of the astrologer, past and present, was revealed by the remarkable reply that Daniel made to Nebuchadnezzar: "The secret which the king hath demanded cannot the wise men, the astrologers, the magicians, the soothsayers, show unto the king; but there is a God in heaven that revealeth secrets, and maketh known to the king Nebuchadnezzar what shall be in the latter days" (Dan. 2:27-28).

Astrology today, as in former times, is linked with Satan and offers his predictions of the future as a substitute for faith in a heavenly Father. But God "frustrateth the tokens of the liars, and maketh diviners mad" (Isa. 44:25).

SUMMARY

Although Satan has been conquered, he is still the ruler of this earth. His character is completely evil. He stirs up every kind of wickedness; he blinds unbelievers and hinders the service of believers. As a ruler, he exercises awesome power. Through his scheming he is able to use all circumstances, good and bad, for his own purposes. Using people's strengths as well as their weaknesses is another deceitful tactic. He is especially dangerous when he appears as "an angel of light."

As a tempter, Satan uses affliction as well as "the lust of the flesh, and the lust of the eyes, and the pride of life" to draw people away from God. He makes people love the world and all that is in it. He is a deceiver, presenting his lies as the truth, forming a gospel that disregards Christ's work as Savior. By sowing "tares" among the "wheat," he weakens the church. He is also a tormentor causing sickness and death, persecution, and believers' denial of Christ. Many people worship Satan. Idolatry, demonism, spiritism, and astrology are all examples of involvement with evil spirits, and all are forbidden by God. Christians need to proclaim the truth against the lies of Satan.

DISCUSSION QUESTIONS

1. What do the Bible's titles for Satan reveal about his character?
2. Explain three additional characteristics of Satan.
3. How is Satan's scheming illustrated in the Scriptures?
4. What can be learned about Satan's work from the book of Job?
5. What three appeals are used in all temptations?
6. In what respect is Satan a deceiver?
7. Describe four ways in which Satan is revealed as a tormentor.

8. Explain how idolatry is Satan-worship.
9. What distinctions should be made between devil and demon (or spirit)?
10. How do we know that the demon-possessed people in the Gospels were not cases of insanity or epilepsy?
11. What is the teaching of Scripture regarding spiritism?
12. What is the Christian position on the use of astrology?
13. Discuss the relationship of Satan's activities to current world events.

RESOURCES

Beyer, Douglas. *Basic Beliefs of Christians.* Valley Forge, PA: Judson Press, 1981, Chapter 6.

Bubeck, Mark I. *The Adversary.* Chicago: Moody Press, 1975.

Dickason, C. Fred. *Angels: Elect and Evil.* Chicago: Moody Press, 1975.

Sanders, J. Oswald. *Satan Is No Myth.* Chicago: Moody Press, 1983.

Chapter Ten

RESURRECTION AND JUDGMENT

THE COMING RESURRECTION is an assured fact. Careful examination of God's Word provides overwhelming evidence. People cannot deny the resurrection without first disposing of many evidences. These evidences include all four Gospels with their concluding chapters on Christ's resurrection, the historic credibility of the book of Acts, and every other piece of writing remaining from the first century that proclaims the resurrection. To deny all these evidences would be to deny Christianity itself. The resurrection of Christ is the foundation of Christianity. To deny it is to deny history and to deny truth.

RESURRECTION OF BELIEVERS

The resurrection and eternal life are precious promises. Those whose names are written in the book of life have these promises (Dan. 12:1; Rev. 21:27).

For the Children of God

The Sadducees were the liberals of Christ's day. To their way of thinking, religion for this life was the important thing. Heaven was a vague place, and all thoughts of future existence were but idle dreams. When they asked Jesus a question concerning marriage in the resurrection, they thought they had asked Him an unanswerable question (Matt. 22:23-33). They hoped that he would either deny the resurrection or would make some statement that would contradict the law of Moses on the matter of the marriage of a relative's widow. But as usual Christ replied wisely. The amazing wisdom of His answer completely silenced them. But what is most interesting is His statement about a special resurrection of the believer: "But they which shall be accounted worthy to obtain that world, and the resurrection from the dead, neither marry, nor are given in marriage: neither can they die any more; for they are equal unto the angels; and are the children of God, being the *children of the resurrection*" (Luke 20:35-36).

For the Just

In the parable in Luke 14:12-14, Christ is addressing believers. The men and women of this world would entertain their friends with the full expectation that they would have the favor returned on another day. But God's children should give of their substance to those who are not able to repay. Why? Because "thou shalt be blessed; for they cannot recompense thee: for thou shalt be recompensed at the resurrection of the just" (Luke 14:14). If the worldly people would be included on this occasion, there would be no need to distinguish this as "the resurrection of the just." The words "of the just" are superfluous in the passage unless they refer to a distinct resurrection.

Believers' Hope

Paul relinquished everything for Jesus Christ (Phil 3:5-8). He was a great scholar, occupied a very high position, and had many friends among the exclusive and influential sect of the Pharisees to which he belonged. But all these honors meant nothing to him after he met Christ, and thereafter his one desire was that he might experience the fellowship of Christ's sufferings and the power of Christ's resurrection. As he expressed it, his one hope was that he "might attain unto the resurrection of [from among] the dead" (Phil. 3:11). The resurrection Paul desired could not have been a general resurrection of good and bad. One could experience that no matter how he lived. It was to be a resurrection of which only those who have known Christ will be participants.

Believers' Consolation

The familiar passage from 1 Thessalonians 4:13-18 is often heard at funerals. It was Paul's comfort to Christians who had lost loved ones. Among the disciples in Thessalonica were many who joyfully anticipated an early return of the Lord. As the weeks and months passed and some of their number died without seeing Christ and partaking of the glory of His return, these Thessalonians were troubled lest their loved ones who had died should not share in the joy and glory of Christ's appearing. Paul therefore comforted them with the assurance that those who are alive at the coming of the Lord will have no advantage over the Christian dead. But notice that whereas he speaks of Christian believers, living and dead, mingling together in joyous fellowship with the Lord, nothing is said about unbelievers. It is evident that those who are not Christ's will not rise with believers at His coming.

Order of Resurrections

There is much vital instruction in the resurrection chapter of 1 Corinthians 15, which is one of the longest in the New Testament. Perhaps the most interesting information found here is the order of future occurrences. The schedule of events, beginning with the resurrection of Jesus Christ, is given as follows:

- The resurrection of Christ (v. 23).
- The resurrection of the believers (v. 23).
- The reign of Christ (v. 25).
- The destruction of death (v. 26).
- The completion of Christ's reign (v. 24).

James M. Gray, former president of Moody Bible Institute, said:

The resurrection of Christ insures that of all men (vv. 20-22); for both the wicked and the good, the unbelieving and the believing, shall be raised, some to everlasting life, and some to everlasting shame and contempt (see also John 5:28, 29). But they will not be raised all at once. Christ is the first fruits, whose resurrection has already taken place. The second install- ment of the resurrection will consist of true believers, who will come forth at His second advent. The third and last will consist of the rest of the dead, who will come forth after the millennium and at the end of the world.

Revelation 20:4-6 not only confirms 1 Corinthians 15 but is much more explicit in details and time. The expression "a (or the) thousand years" is used six times in the first seven verses of Revelation 20, and it must be interpreted literally. It is important to note that the reign of Christ is preceded by the *first resurrection*, and that those who participate in it are *happy and holy*. Moreover, the rest of the dead "lived not again until the thousand years were finished" (v. 5).

RESURRECTION OF UNBELIEVERS

There are only two classes of people in relation to the resurrection. On the one hand are those who are absorbed in the pursuit of wealth, pleasure, or other material gains and know nothing higher but the things of this life.

On the other hand, there are those who believe in the coming of the Son of God and do all in their power to be ready for Him. They also must work for a living on this earth, but the things of Christ's church are more important, and their primary purpose is to complete its ministry on earth.

These two classes of people cannot be distinguished easily, but on the days of resurrection there will be no question as to their identity. Those who have "done good" because of personal faith in Jesus Christ as their Savior will come forth in the first resurrection, and those who have "done evil" at a second resurrection (John 5:29).

Revelation 20:5 states that the unbelievers—the rest of the dead— "lived not again until the thousand years were finished." There are also other characteristics that mark the second resurrection.

Judgment (Dan. 12:2; John 5:28-29; Rev. 20:13)

These passages all relate to the resurrection of the unbeliever, which is connected with the great white throne judgment. This judgment takes place at the close, and not at the beginning, of Christ's reign on earth. This resurrection might never have been mentioned in Scripture were it not that this reference is needed to explain the presence of the sinners before the judgment seat of God.

Punishment (Rev. 20:15)

The resurrection referred to in Revelation 20:15 is associated with punishment. Of necessity, therefore, the participants will be unbelievers.

JUDGMENTS OF BELIEVERS

Most people think of all judgment taking place after the resurrections. One judgment at least takes place before death. "And as it is appointed unto men once to die, but after this the judgment: So Christ was once offered to bear the sins of many; and unto them that look for him shall he appear the second time without sin unto salvation" (Heb. 9:27-28). Death is decreed on every person because of sin, and sin must be judged. The judgment of believers as sinners has already taken place through Christ's redemptive work on the cross (John 3:18; 5:24; 1 Pet. 2:24).

Judgment at the Cross (2 Cor. 5:21; Gal. 3:13; 1 Pet. 2:24)

Judgment in a criminal case is the settlement of a breach against the law of society. Judgment in a civil case is the settlement of a controversy between two individuals. But no one is tried before a judge for guilt if he has already pleaded guilty.

Christ has been appointed to judge the world, and on a day of judgment the sinner will be on trial for his sins. But if the sinner has previously pleaded guilty and accepted the pardon offered him in Jesus Christ, according to the Bible "there is therefore now no condemnation to them which are in Christ Jesus" (Romans 8:1), for by Christ "all that believe are justified from all things, from which [they] could not be justified by the law of Moses" (Acts 13:39). As soon as men plead guilty and accept

God's gracious provision for their sins, Christ will answer for them. There is no future judgment of sin for the believer. That has taken place at the cross. Peace and pardon begin right here on earth, and the future can only decree, "He which is filthy, let him be filthy still: and he that is righteous, let him be righteous still" (Rev. 22:11). Our future life is but a continuation of our present attitude toward sin and righteousness.

Judgment and Rewards (1 Cor. 3:9-15; 4:5; 2 Cor. 5:10)

These passages in Corinthians have to do solely with believers. Nothing is said about the wicked in these three chapters; so it is conclusive that Paul is speaking about Christians appearing before the judgment seat of Christ. However, this is not a judgment for sin, but for works. Judgment for sin was already accomplished for the believer by Christ. Salvation is a gift. Rewards are earned. This is a judgment of one's accomplishments. The Christian is Christ's "workmanship, created . . . unto good works" (Eph. 2:10).

All believers build on Christ as their foundation, but some put "gold, silver, precious stones" into the superstructure, and others add nothing better than "wood, hay, stubble" (1 Cor. 3:12). This judgment will test the believer's work by fire. The wise and worthy builder will receive a reward. The unwise builder, although building on Christ as a foundation the same as the other, "shall suffer loss: but he himself shall be saved; yet so as by fire" (1 Cor. 3:15).

As men are pardoned individually, so they are rewarded one by one. The result of individual acceptance of God's pardon is eternal salvation, but the result of individual service is the inheritance of the personal treasure laid up "where neither moth nor rust doth corrupt, and where thieves do not break through nor steal" (Matt. 6:20).

Paul spoke frequently about the crowns to be awarded on this day of judgment. He pictured a scene in the Olympic games where there were many runners, though only one secured the prize. But, as Paul has said, it is different with this race. Believers do not run uncertainly, for God will reward not only the winner, but all who run according to their ability. Moreover, the reward is not a fading wreath, but an incorruptible crown (1 Cor. 9:23-27).

JUDGMENTS OF UNBELIEVERS

The first two judgments concern the pardon and reward of the righteous; the last two have to do with the judgment of the wicked. It is certain that the wicked will die and rise again and appear at the great white throne judgment. As the first judgment of believers took place during their lifetime, it is interesting to note that the first judgment of unbelievers likewise takes place before death.

Judgment of the Living Nations (Matt. 25:31-46)

How often this is spoken of as the general judgment, supposed to take place in heaven at the end of the world! But Matthew 25 does not so indicate. Note that in chapter 24 Christ was talking about His return, and chapter 25 marks the events associated with His return. First, there is the marriage supper of the Lamb (vv. 1- 13); second, there is the judgment of the saints (vv. 14-30); third, we see the judgment of the living nations (vv. 31-46).

This judgment of the nations will be after the judgment of rewards and will take place at the coming of Christ to earth with His saints (Jude 14-15). During the interval between the judgment of rewards and the return of Christ to judge the earth will occur the world's greatest tribulation, as set forth in Revelation 6–19.

Joel writes that Christ will set up His judgment seat in the Valley of Jehoshaphat—that is, Palestine. Thus this judgment will take place on earth (Joel 3:11-12; Zeph. 3:8). This is most reasonable as well as significant inasmuch as Palestine is recognized as the historic, geographic, and religious center of the world, and the Jews for some time have been returning there in great numbers.

This is not a general judgment of good and bad, for there are three classes mentioned, the third being the "brethren" (Matt. 25:32, 40). "My brethren" cannot refer to the church, which has already been translated and rewarded. Neither can they be part of the nations that have been gathered for judgment. Balaam's prophecy says that Israel "shall not be reckoned among the nations" (Num. 23:9). It is evident, then, that the "brethren" are Jews who have been converted and have accepted the commission to preach the Gospel of the kingdom after the church has been removed from the earth.

The subject of this judgment in Matthew 25 is the relation of the nations to Christian Jews during the Tribulation. The wicked nations left on the earth will persecute and fight against the Jews, and Christ, at His coming with His angels and saints, will call the nations into judgment for their treatment of the Jews. Those who have treated them badly will be separated and sentenced to eternal punishment. Those who have favored the Jews—who for the most part will be God's ministers and missionaries (Isa. 66:18-19)—will join in the millennial reign of righteousness. They will form Christ's kingdom on earth, and the saints, both Jews and Gentiles, will reign with Him.

Judgment at the Great White Throne (Rev. 20:11-15)

Note the differences between the judgment of the nations, just described, and this final judgment. The former takes place at the *beginning* of Christ's thousand-year reign on earth, the latter at the close. The former deals with the *living*, the latter with the *dead*. There is no resurrection in the former; there is in the latter. The former takes place on *earth*, and the latter in *heaven*. The former deals with conduct toward the brethren, the latter with works recorded in the books.

After Christ has reigned in triumph for a thousand years on earth and has put down every enemy, His sovereignty will not be supreme until all who have rejected Him as Savior have been brought to trial. For this purpose the wicked of all the centuries will be raised from the dead and brought before Him. At some time in their lives on earth each one was confronted with the same question that troubled Pilate: "What shall I do then with Jesus which is called Christ?" (Matt. 27:22). But these unbelievers would not plead guilty of sin. They would not accept pardon in Christ. Now they will be tried by the Lord. The books will be opened, and for every idle word they shall give an account (Matt. 12:36).

"As I live, saith the Lord, every knee shall bow to me, and every tongue shall confess to God" (Rom. 14:11). Just as surely as there is a living God, the judgment must take place. There can be no stronger language in the Bible than this. He has made the earth, and He will judge it.

On that day, "there is nothing covered, that shall not be revealed; and hid, that shall not be known" (Matt. 10:26). People may have deceived their families and friends, but they cannot deceive God. They may have lied to their business associates, but they cannot lie to God.

In that day "every one of us shall give account of himself to God" (Rom. 14:12). Many forget these warning words. They try to blame someone else for their sins. The wicked will be proven guilty with overwhelming evidence against them. They have despised a crucified Savior. They laughed at God's law. But they will not laugh when the books are opened and their guilt is proven. "No sacrifice for sins is left, but only a fearful expectation of judgment and of raging fire that will consume the enemies of God" (Heb. 10:26-27, NIV).

SUMMARY

The Word of God provides assuring evidence of the resurrection. To deny the resurrection, people must first deny all the evidences and prove that they are false.

Believers are called "the children of the resurrection" (Luke 20:36).

They are referred to as participating in "the resurrection of the just" (Luke 14:14). Paul hoped for and worked toward the resurrection, for he knew there was to be a separate resurrection of believers. Those alive will have no advantage over those who have died before the Lord's return; all will join together. Christ rose first, at a later time believers will rise, Christ will reign, death will be defeated, and Christ's reign will be complete.

Unbelievers will be involved in a second resurrection. At the end of Christ's reign on earth, they will live again for judgment and punishment.

The judgment of believers already occurred at the cross, and since believers have acknowledged their guilt and accepted the pardon in Christ, there is no need for judgment. Only works will be judged and rewards given.

At the beginning of Christ's reign on earth, He will judge the living nations according to their treatment of His people, the Jews. A final judgment at the close of His earthly reign will judge all the dead according to their works. Everything will be revealed, and each person will receive God's judgment.

DISCUSSION QUESTIONS

1. What overwhelming evidence makes the resurrection an assured fact?
2. What was significant about Paul's hope of a resurrection?
3. Write a schedule of events beginning with the resurrection of Christ.
4. When does the resurrection of the unbeliever take place?
5. What is meant by the judgment of the cross?
6. Explain the judgment in relation to rewards.
7. When and where does the judgment of the living nations take place?
8. What is the difference between the judgment of the living nations and the judgment of the great white throne?

RESOURCES

Ryrie, Charles C. *Dispensationalism Today*. Chicago: Moody Press, 1973.

_____. *A Survey of Bible Doctrine*. Chicago: Moody Press, 1972, Chapter 9.

Walvoord, John F. *The Rapture Question*. Grand Rapids, MI: Zondervan, 1970.

Chapter Eleven

REWARDS OF THE RIGHTEOUS

IN THE BIBLE THE Christian learns that there are great rewards for the faithful believer. In contrast to other beliefs, only the biblical presentations of life after death evidence the high and holy qualities that distinguish a divine revelation. It apparently is not God's plan to reveal fully what He has prepared for His children, but He allows Christians just enough light to meet their needs of hope, comfort, and encouragement. Three witnesses have been permitted to give a glimpse of the glories to come.

Christ was as familiar with the unseen as with the seen. He had all His information firsthand. He "was in the beginning with God. All things were made by him; and without him was not anything made that was made" (John 1:2-3).

Paul was caught up into the highest heaven, and though the Spirit would not permit him to reveal all he saw and heard, such was his experience that he testifies that to depart and be with Christ is "far better" than to remain in this life (Phil. 1:23).

John was divinely appointed to reveal these things. On the island of Patmos John received a vision of heaven's glory, which, guided by the Spirit, he recorded in the book of Revelation (Rev. 1:9-11, 19).

GOING TO BE WITH THE LORD

At death believers immediately depart to be with the Lord. What a reward in itself! They shall not enter a dark unknown, nor a state of unconsciousness, but they will be "present with the Lord" (2 Cor. 5:8).

The eternal, glorified body is given to believers when Christ comes for His own. Then shall all the believers who are "asleep" in Jesus be joined to those who are alive and remain, and together they will meet the Lord in the air, and thus be with Him forever (1 Thess. 4:15-17). If eternal separation from God is hell's supreme torment, surely eternal union with Him is heaven's greatest joy.

ENTERING A NEW HOME

The earthly home is temporary, but all believers shall dwell forever in the house of the Lord. The new home has been specially prepared for believers by the Lord (John 14:1-3). Those who know the Lord will not be strangers or visitors in heaven.

Paul says in his first epistle to the Corinthians (2:9-10) that only the Spirit of God can know the things that God has prepared for His people.

The Holy City (Rev. 21:1-27)

The glory of man's civilization is his cities, but all these will be destroyed (2 Pet. 3:10). The city is not only the product of man's civilization but is the seat of his sin. When Abraham left the decadent civilization of Ur to dwell in tents, "he looked for a city which hath foundations, whose builder and maker is God" (Heb. 11:10). This was the Jerusalem of David's conquest, but also (according to the law of double reference) the heavenly Jerusalem that shall be revealed in the final era.

By Satan's final overthrow and the judgment of the great white throne, the world will be purged of evil inhabitants. A new heaven and a new earth will replace the old. Thus the stage will be set for the appearance of the Holy City. Note some features of this city:

MAGNITUDE

The height will be equal to its length and breadth, in that it will be built up like a pyramid (Rev. 21:16-17). The greatness of Nineveh, Babylon, Rome, Paris, and London will be totally eclipsed by the city of God. It will be the center of all creation.

The twelve gates, each with a name of a tribe of Israel, will be guarded by angels, so that only saints may enter. The twelve foundations of the wall will bear the names of the twelve apostles who laid the foundation of the kingdom of the Lamb (Rev. 21:12-21).

PURITY

The city is made of pure transparent gold and is adorned with every precious stone (Rev. 21:18-21). The whole atmosphere is that of purity, permanency, and radiance. The sun and moon will no longer be necessary. The Holy City will be more dazzling than the light of the sun or the light of the largest stars. The glory of God will light the city, and "the Lamb is the light thereof" (Rev. 21:11, 23; 22:5). Christ will always be the one by whom the Father is made known.

SANCTUARY

Because the city is a sanctuary, there will be no need of a special one. All the barriers between God and man are broken down, and the Almighty and the Lamb will dwell in the midst like a temple (Rev. 21:3, 22). This is Immanuel, "God with us," in full reality and in the highest, most intimate way.

The temple was the meeting place between God and His people and was assigned for His honor and glory. But now that the earth has been purged from sin, God will reenter it and dwell with His people. Instead of the temple there will be the throne. It is a solitary throne; it is an unshared throne; it is an eternal throne. Instead of bringing their offerings to the temple, the kings of the earth will bring their glory and honor to the throne of God.

INHABITANTS

Only those whose names are written in the Lamb's book of life will live in the Holy City (Rev. 21:7, 27). The just in Old Testament days looked for such a city. No doubt all the saints of the Lord will have their habitation there (Heb. 11:10, 13-16).

The "Paradise of God" (Rev. 22:1-5)

The apostle John describes in Revelation the paradise of God in which the Holy City lies. In it are found the river of the water of life flowing out of the throne and the tree of life. The curse is removed, and man may partake freely of both. Yet he is definitely dependent upon God.

On either side of the banks of this river will be the tree of life, the leaves of which will preserve the health of the nations. "To him that overcometh will I give to eat of the tree of life, which is in the midst of the paradise of God" (Rev. 2:7).

RECEIVING REWARDS

While it is true that every believer will dwell in this Holy City, all will not possess the same honor, wear the same crowns, or receive the commendation of "Well done." Only those faithful in life and service will receive special rewards.

Christians are adding to their accounts either works that will stand the test and be rewarded or dross that will burn and leave them empty-handed. Actions in daily life build on the foundation of Christ—either with gold, silver, and precious stones or with wood, hay, and stubble (1 Cor. 3:12-15). Several Scripture references speak of future rewards:

Verily there is a reward for the righteous. (Ps. 58:11)

He that reapeth receiveth wages, and gathereth fruit unto life eternal. (John 4:36)

Knowing that whatsoever good thing any man doeth, the same shall he receive of the Lord. (Eph. 6:8)

Knowing that of the Lord ye shall receive the reward of the inheritance: for ye serve the Lord Christ. (Col. 3:24)

Basis of Rewards

One cannot work for salvation. "For by grace are ye saved through faith; and that not of yourselves: it is the gift of God: not of works, lest any man should boast" (Eph. 2:8-9). But after salvation, God promises to reward every good work. There is a difference between the Bible references that deal with *salvation*, the "free gift" (Rom. 5:15-16, 18), and those that speak of *rewards*, which are earned by works. The apostle Paul did not doubt his salvation when he feared he might be a "castaway" (or disapproved), but he did feel that, though he preached to others, he might be preaching in the energy of the flesh rather than for the glory of God, and so suffer loss of reward (1 Cor. 9:26-27).

Christians will be rewarded according to their *walk*. Notice the words of the Lord: "I know thy works, and charity, and service, and faith, and thy patience, and thy works" (Rev. 2:19). Christians will be rewarded for the way they live as well as for what they do. By walking "worthy of the Lord unto all pleasing, being fruitful in every good work" (Col. 1:10) and adding Christian living to faith in Christ, they shall have an *abundant* entrance into the everlasting kingdom of the Lord and Savior (2 Pet. 1:5-11).

Christians will also receive rewards according to their *works* (1 Cor. 3:8, 13-15; Rev. 14:13). "Behold, I come quickly; and my reward is with me, to give every man according as his work shall be" (Rev. 22:12) is the promise of the Son of God. When believers stand before the judgment seat of Christ, they will be rewarded not according to good intentions, holy ambitions, or large promises, but strictly in proportion to their faithfulness in multiplying the talents they had received (Matt. 25:21). "He which soweth sparingly shall reap also sparingly; and he which soweth bountifully shall reap also bountifully" (2 Cor. 9:6). One cannot judge what is of true worth in God's eyes, for human eyes are blinded by spectacular service, and the perspective can be faulty.

It is possible to do much in the name of Christ or the church that is not done for Christ at all. It is also possible to perform many humble duties and hidden services of love for Christ that the world never sees. A great sermon preached in man's wisdom and oratory, to please a large congregation, may not stand at all in that day before the fire of God, whereas a simple, sincere testimony of Christ's saving power may shine forth as a gem.

Crowns as Rewards

THE INCORRUPTIBLE OR VICTOR'S CROWN (1 COR. 9:25-27)

After the Grecian games were all over, the runners, wrestlers, and successful contestants assembled before the judges' stand, an elevated seat on which the judges sat, and each winner was given a crown of laurel leaves. Although this was a corruptible crown that would soon fade, Paul probably had it in mind when he spoke of the incorruptible victor's crown. A man who would compete in those games would deny his body many indulgences in order to win the race. Similarly, Paul tells us, this incorruptible crown is for one who will "keep under [his] body"—that is, who does not yield to fleshly desires. Such victors do not permit themselves to be weakened for service by selfish desires or to be diverted from the Master's work by worldly pleasures.

THE CROWN OF LIFE (JAS. 1:12; REV. 2:10; CF. MATT. 5:12; ROM. 8:17-18)

This is sometimes called the martyr's crown. However, coupled with the two primary passages listed above are numerous others referring to the special reward awaiting those who suffer much for Christ. God has a crown of life for all believers who endure persecution. The martyrs of every age, and of the Tribulation period especially, will receive this crown.

THE CROWN OF GLORY (1 PET. 5:2-4)

This is the elder's or pastor's crown, to be given by the Chief Shepherd when He shall appear. It is for faithful ministry. Much is said in God's Word about true and false shepherds of the flock. The faithful minister points in but one direction—toward the cross. Many ministers today cater to the perishing praise of their audience or the wealth of their members or the acknowledgment of the learned rather than seeking God's crown of glory. Others who are faithful in preaching the infallible Word of God and the message of the shed blood of the Son of God are being bitterly persecuted. For these faithful shepherds the crown of glory awaits.

THE CROWN OF REJOICING (1 THESS. 2:19; CF. DAN. 12:3; PHIL. 4:1)

All cannot win the crown of glory, but every Christian may attain the crown of rejoicing, for this is the soul-winner's crown. Every believer is not called to preach, but everyone is called to sow the precious seed of God's Word and to be constantly seeking to win others to Christ. Great will be our rejoicing in heaven when we see those who have been led to salvation through our testimony and the patient teaching of God's Word.

THE CROWN OF RIGHTEOUSNESS (2 TIM. 4:7-8)

This is the crown for those who love Christ's future appearing. Why a crown of righteousness for loving and looking for the second coming of the Lord? John answers this in 1 John 3:2-3: "Beloved, now are we the sons of God, and it doth not yet appear what we shall be: but we know that, when he shall appear, we shall be like him; for we shall see him as he is. And every man that hath this hope in him purifieth himself, even as he is pure."

SUMMARY

There are many promises in the Bible concerning future rewards for the righteous. Christ, Paul, and John were able to speak of these glories. Christ knew them; Paul and John were given glimpses.

At death, believers go to be with the Lord and will remain with Him eternally. The new home with God is indescribable in beauty and is specially prepared for believers. It will be a holy city, unlike the cities on earth. Only those whose names are found in the book of life will be its inhabitants. No sanctuary will be needed because God's presence fills the city. The light will be from God and the Lamb, brighter than the sun or any star. The wall and gates are made of jewels. The foundations bear the names of the twelve apostles, each gate the name of a tribe of Israel. Huge in magnitude, its length, breadth, and height will be equal. Purity permeates the city. This city lies in the Paradise of God where the water of life flows, and the tree of life gives leaves for the preserving of the health of the nations.

Believers have accepted salvation, and all of them will live in the Holy City; but individual rewards will be given according to each Christian's walk and work. Each day's actions will be burned and purified at this judgment of rewards. Some will burn up, and some will remain.

Crowns will be believers' rewards. These will be incorruptible, eternal crowns for those who did not allow selfish desires to hinder service to God. The crown of life is a special reward for martyrs and those who suffered persecution. To faithful pastors and leaders goes the crown of glory. Soul-winners are presented with a crown of rejoicing. The crown of righteousness is especially for those who love and look for Christ's return.

DISCUSSION QUESTIONS

1. What happens to the believer at death?
2. Describe the believer's new home.
3. Characterize the Holy City.
4. Why is there no temple in the Holy City?
5. What assurances does the believer have of rewards in heaven?
6. Upon what basis will these rewards be given?
7. What is meant by the victor's crown?
8. Compare the crown of life with the crown of glory.
9. Why is the crown of glory called the pastor's crown?
10. What is the soul-winner's crown?
11. Who will receive the crown of righteousness? Why?

RESOURCES

Smith, Wilbur M. *The Biblical Doctrine of Heaven.* Chicago: Moody Press, 1980.

Chapter Twelve

PUNISHMENT OF THE WICKED

SOME PEOPLE BELIEVE that hell does not exist. Their idea of the mercy of God would be inconsistent with such a place. They say it is too awful a concept to be true. In the Garden of Eden Satan proposed only a slight change in God's word by inserting "not" into God's command to make it state, "Ye shall not surely die" (Gen. 3:4; cf. 2:17). Satan's addition of one small word was accepted, and the world was lost.

Others do not believe that hell is eternal. They explain that a compassionate God would not punish men forever. This is a great help to the Devil's cause.

Then there are those who believe there is a hell but cannot agree that anyone is going there. With them, all people are good as soon as they die. All were sincere, all meant well, and all, *they hope*, go to heaven. This is a common delusion. It is easy to understand the feelings of the little girl who asked her mother where all the wicked people were buried, for she found no mention on the gravestones of any but the good.

This is not a pleasant doctrine. It was not pleasant for Moses to stand before Pharaoh and proclaim the overthrow of Egypt, for Elijah to stand before Ahab and proclaim punishment for Israel's sins, for Jeremiah to predict the downfall of Jerusalem, for Stephen, Peter, and Paul to preach to their persecutors.

No teacher was more loving than the Savior, and yet no one ever spoke more severely about the punishment of the wicked. Hell and destruction were ever before Him. To Him the punishment of the wicked was clear and essential, and to those who look upon Him as their Savior from hell, the divine record He left is full of truth and meaning.

Terrible as it is to think of eternal anguish, it must be true or our tender Lord would not have said it. The same lips that voiced the Beatitudes and told of the many mansions in heaven referred to "everlasting fire" and "weeping and wailing and gnashing of teeth." There can be no doubt. Jesus Christ settled the fact of the future punishment of the wicked.

PARTICIPANTS OF PUNISHMENT

All those whose names are not found written in the book of life will be punished (Rev. 20:15). These will be raised up at the second resurrection and judged guilty according to their sins. In this vast multitude there will be those whom the Bible calls children of Satan, hypocrites, unbelievers.

Christ was very particular to point out that Satan has his children in this world. Their chief characteristic is that they do not love righteousness but are rather the enemies of righteousness. And because Christ's righteousness is not in their hearts, envy, malice, murder, and falsehood rule their lives (Matt. 13:38-42; John 8:44).

No one had more to say about hypocrites than did Christ. He constantly exposed their falseness. Satan is the great deceiver (Rev. 12:9), and those who, like him, pretend to be one thing and are something else must eventually be punished with him (Matt. 23:13-15; 24:51).

People need not be murderers or hypocrites to find their way to hell. Everyone guilty of sin is under condemnation. Only those whose names are written in the book of life because they believed in the atonement of Jesus Christ will be saved. All unbelievers are damned (Luke 12:46; John 3:18; 8:24).

PURPOSE OF PUNISHMENT

The wicked are said to "die in [their] sins" (John 8:21). They hang onto their sins to the very last. "Wrath" indicates the settled mind of God toward the persistently wicked (John 3:36); "indignation" is the outburst of that wrath at the day of judgment (Rev. 14:10).

But God is also "longsuffering" and desires to lead sinners to repentance (Rom. 2:4-9). He is "not willing that any should perish, but that all should come to repentance" (2 Pet. 3:9). He has no pleasure in the punishment of the wicked (Ezek. 18:23, 32; 33:11). He not only gave man an opportunity in the beginning to live forever, but He provided for man's redemption after he had fallen. What more could He have done as a righteous ruler? A righteous God must punish sin.

PLACE OF PUNISHMENT

"Where is hell?" asked the skeptic. "Anywhere outside of heaven," was the answer. While it is true that to miss heaven is hell, and that eternal torment may well be realizing the truth too late, hell is not "just anywhere."

Hell (Sheol, Hades) (Job 2:2; 1 Pet. 5:8; Rev. 20:2-3, 10)

Satan is not now in hell—yet. Satan is the god of this world, and he and his angels are now very busy on this earth; but their day of judgment, and confinement, will come, as will that of all who reject Christ. The word "hell" is *hades* in Greek and *sheol* in Hebrew. It means the place of departed unbelieving spirits.

Lake of Fire (Gehenna) (Matt. 10:28; Rev. 19:20; 20:14)

In very plain and definite words the Lord declared that in the future life people will have bodies, and that the bodies of the lost will remain in a literal, physical place of torment. The word *Gehenna*, which Christ used, represents the same place and punishment as the "lake of fire" mentioned in the book of Revelation. Gehenna is a place of punishment after death. As it receives both soul and body, it comes into existence, therefore, after the resurrection.

Gehenna was the name of a valley near Jerusalem where the garbage and refuse of the city were constantly burning. Jesus used it to typify what is elsewhere expressed in Scripture as "everlasting burnings" (Isa. 33:14), "everlasting fire" (Matt. 25:41), "unquenchable fire" (Mark 9:43; Isa. 66:24), and "the lake of fire" (Rev. 20:14).

PERIOD OF PUNISHMENT

The words "everlasting" and "forever" are used repeatedly in Scripture to indicate that the punishment is endless. In fact, the same words that are used to speak of the reward of the righteous are likewise employed to designate the duration of the penalty of the wicked (Dan. 12:2; Matt. 25:46; Jude 13; Rev. 14:11; 19:3; 20:10). The one lasts as long as the other; and only if there is an end to the joy of heaven will there be a termination to the misery of hell.

Some change Scripture and seek to comfort themselves in the belief that the use of the word *destruction* means annihilation. But this is destruction of opportunity rather than of existence. How can those who are annihilated be said to be tormented, to weep and wail? How can they be said to plead for admission into heaven and to reason on the subject (Luke 16:23-24)?

NATURE OF PUNISHMENT

Spurgeon said, "Can you bear to see a fellow-creature in pain? His agony draws forth our sympathies. But you cannot compare the pains of this life with what is to come."

Banishment (Matt. 13:49-50; 25:41; Luke 16:26; 2 Thess. 1:9)

God now confers many blessings upon the wicked. God "sendeth rain on the just and on the unjust" (Matt. 5:45). But when He once says, "Depart from me, all ye workers of iniquity" (Luke 13:27), that will be the last they will see of everything that is good and upright and lovely. There will be no voice of prayer, no hymn of praise in hell. There will be no pursuit of knowledge, no acquisition, no occupation, no relief, no hope. Hell is everything evil and abandoned.

Darkness (Matt. 8:12; 22:13; 25:30; Jude 13)

The picture is that of an evening banquet. The wicked are thrust out from the merriment of the dinner party into the darkness and gloom outside. Those who have been in the arctic regions say that an even greater hardship than the severe cold are the months of lingering darkness with accompanying depression. The darkness of hell will be impenetrable and eternal.

Fire (Mal. 4:1; Matt. 3:12; 13:40, 50; Luke 16:23-24)

It is an accepted law of language that a figure of speech is less intense than the reality. There is no pain like that of burning. Fire is the most destructive and devouring of all elements. Fire is of all elements most opposed to life. Creatures can live in air, earth, and water, but nothing can live in fire.

But the most terrible characteristic of this fire is that it does not consume those who must dwell in its flames. They are tormented in the flame, and the rich man is pictured by the Lord as piteously pleading for one drop of water to cool his parched tongue.

Remorse (Isa. 66:24; Matt. 8:12; 13:42, 50; 22:13)

What is meant by the phrase, "where their worm dieth not" (Mark 9:44, 46, 48)? This "worm" is probably memory. When God says, "Remember," men will never be able to forget. They will remember their sins. They will everlastingly remember God's mercies. They will never be able to forget that they heard the Gospel and neglected the privilege of being saved. It is this that will bring bitter pangs of remorse. There will be perpetual weeping over lost opportunities.

Christ speaks of hell, and it seems that people would desire to do everything in their power to escape. But such is not the case. Despite the fact that

God has done all He can do to save people from this awful fate, they willfully neglect His salvation. Most vividly did Christ sketch the picture of the rich man in hell pathetically begging that someone be raised from the dead to warn his doomed relatives. But would men listen to someone raised from the dead? Lazarus was raised from the dead, and did the Jews listen to him? No; they sought to kill him. Christ was raised from the dead, and still people did not listen to Him or the good news of salvation.

SUMMARY

Many people attempt to deny the existence of hell, to deny that it is eternal or that anyone will go there. But Christ Himself spoke often of hell and of punishment for the wicked.

Those whose names are not written in the book of life will be punished. These will include the children of Satan who do not love righteousness, hypocrites, and all who do not believe in Christ as Savior. These people must be punished, for God is holy, and therefore He must punish sin.

Satan is now allowed to roam the earth, but one day he will be cast into hell and the lake of fire; and the wicked will be punished with Satan forever. This punishment does not mean complete annihilation but conscious torment. This torment includes banishment from all that is good, impenetrable darkness, fire that does not consume, and remorse over lost opportunities to receive Christ.

DISCUSSION QUESTIONS

1. In what way does Satan attempt to conceal the existence of a place of punishment?
2. Describe the participants of punishment.
3. What is the chief characteristic of the children of Satan?
4. What is the real purpose of punishment?
5. Discuss the place of punishment for the wicked.
6. In what respect was Gehenna a symbol of the lake of fire?
7. Describe the four penalties involved in the punishment of the wicked.
8. How does Scripture describe the fire of hell?
9. Explain the punishment of remorse.
10. What has this study meant to you personally?

RESOURCES

Demaray, Donald E. *Basic Beliefs*. Grand Rapids, MI: Baker Book House, 1958, Chapter 14.

Book Three:
Evidence
and
Truth

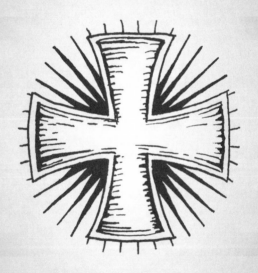

ROBERT J. MORGAN

CONTENTS

INTRODUCTION: CAN CHRISTIANITY BE PROVEN?

YEARS AGO WHEN I began pastoring, I faced an unexpected problem. Each Sunday after preaching to my small congregation, I would go home wondering if my sermons were true. What if Christianity was just a grand hoax? What if it was all a myth?

These doubts drove me to study apologetics, from the Greek *apologia*, meaning "defense." Paul used this word in 2 Timothy 4:16 and Philippians 1:7, 16. Peter wrote, "Always be prepared to give an *answer* to everyone who asks you to give the reason for the hope that you have" (1 Pet. 3:15, emphasis mine). I found that apologetics—the defense of the truth of Christianity—demonstrates that our faith is not a blind leap into the dark but a sensible step into the light.

Faith is not foolishness, exemplified by the man who started across thin ice on a pond, saying, "I just believe! I have faith this ice will hold me up." His faith was all wet—or it will be shortly.

Unrealistic faith collapses in college classrooms when challenged. It cringes when hearing about newly discovered "proof" of evolution. It harbors nagging doubts when facing a crisis. But genuine faith is believing on the basis of powerful evidence, not in spite of inadequate evidence. To be valid, Christianity must be logical and real with a "provable" quality to it. And as any courtroom observer knows, proof requires evidence. *That evidence exists!*

The body of evidence for the truth of Christianity is staggering, and I believe the truth of Christianity can be established to a 99 percent level of certainty. The remaining 1 percent is the step of faith you take when you "confess with your mouth, 'Jesus is Lord,' and believe in your heart that God raised him from the dead" (Rom. 10:9).

I am glad I grappled with doubts during earlier days, for it drove me to burrow out the facts and uncover the evidence. I found an intellectual basis for my faith that satisfies both my heart and my mind. This book was written to provide Christians with reassurance about the validity of their faith while giving them a thumbnail sketch of how to answer those who are examining Christianity. Here, then, is a summary of the evidence that demonstrates the truthfulness of Christianity—beyond reasonable doubt.

Chapter One

EXHIBIT A: THE RESURRECTION OF CHRIST

The Empty Tomb

LUKE, THE FIRST-CENTURY physician/scientist/chronicler, was a historian of first rank whose meticulous research and verifiable accuracy put him head and shoulders above his secular peers. His two surviving works, the Gospel of Luke and the Acts of the Apostles, both advance the view that Jesus of Nazareth rose physically from the tomb on the first day of the week.

In telling us this, Luke does not expect us just to swallow it by blind faith. He presents it as an event in history, verifiable and backed by evidence. He opens his Gospel by telling us that, prior to composing his biography of Christ, he "carefully investigated everything from the beginning" so that we would "know the certainty of the things" we have been taught (Luke 1:3-4). He opens his Acts of the Apostles with these words: "After his suffering, he showed himself to these men [the apostles] and gave *many convincing proofs* that he was alive. He appeared to them over a period of forty days" (Acts 1:3, emphasis mine).

The "many convincing proofs" substantiate the resurrection of Christ for good reason. All of Christianity hinges on the Resurrection. As the apostle Paul says, without the resurrection of Christ "our preaching is useless and so is your faith. . . . If Christ has not been raised, your faith is futile; you are still in your sins. Then those also who have fallen asleep in Christ are lost. If only for this life we have hope in Christ, we are to be pitied more than all men" (1 Cor. 15:14, 17-19).

Scientist Henry Morris put it this way: "The bodily resurrection of Jesus Christ from the dead is the crowning proof of Christianity. If the resurrection did not take place, then Christianity is a false religion. If it did take place, then Christ is God and the Christian faith is absolute truth."[1]

What were these "convincing proofs" that Luke carefully investigated from the beginning? What evidence exists for the literal, physical, bodily resurrection of Jesus of Nazareth from a Jerusalem cemetery on the world's first Easter?

Look at it negatively. Suppose we believe that the body of Jesus Christ is now nothing more than a decomposed corpse, perhaps a bare skeleton or mere dust, still buried somewhere in Israel. To cling to that belief, we would have a formidable task. We would have to discount a mountain of evidence and explain away "many convincing proofs."

THE RELIABILITY OF THE HISTORIANS

A later chapter will deal more fully with the reliability and accuracy of the biblical documents, but a prior word is necessary now. The story of the ancient world is recorded by several historians of old, such as Homer, Josephus, Tacitus, Xenophon, Herodotus—called "the father of history," and Thucydides, who is credited as being one of the most trustworthy of ancient sources. All of them suffer in comparison to the historical pinpoint accuracy of Luke.

Several years ago the Scottish scholar Sir William Mitchell Ramsay determined that Luke had made one error after another in the details of his books. Ramsay set out to prove it, traveling throughout Turkey and the Middle East, studying the history, geography, and topography described in the Acts of the Apostles. In every point of dispute, Ramsay found himself on the losing side. Luke was correct, even in minute details. Ramsay later wrote that "no period in ancient history is so assured and well attested" as the times described by Luke. "There are few events which cannot be dated to the year, and sometimes to the month, and even to the day."[2]

Ramsay wrote, "You may press the words of Luke in a degree beyond any other historian's, and they stand the keenest scrutiny and the hardest treatment."[3] Ramsay's conclusions are summarized this way: "The author of Acts [and thereby of the Gospel of Luke] is not to be regarded as the author of historical romance, legend, or third- or second-rate history. Rather he is the writer of an historical work of the highest order."[4]

With that in mind, remember that Luke painstakingly and confidently described the death, burial, and resurrection of Jesus Christ in his Gospel, chapters 23 and 24; and he repeatedly made reference to the Resurrection in the book of Acts.

The brilliant Wilbur Smith said:

> Of all the writers in the New Testament, Luke was the one who knew better than any of them, from his own medical experience, that it was utterly impossible for a dead body to come to life again by its own power. He was also a man who would have no faith in such a great doctrine as the resurrection of Christ, were it based upon a vision, a hallucination, mental excitement, or the blowing of the wind, or the rattling of a window. It was the conviction of this scientist and scholar, true Grecian and true Christian, that the Lord manifested himself to his disciples in many proofs.[5]

To reject the Resurrection, you have to disregard the demonstrated reliability of one of the foremost historians of the first century, a man who has been proven accurate even in the minutia of his narrative.

THE DIVERSITY OF THE ACCOUNTS

Closely connected is a related evidence, one that may seem strange at first—the diversity of the resurrection accounts. Luke, as we have seen, was the consummate historian, but he was only one of four Gospel writers. There were three others: Matthew, Mark, and John. Matthew was a tax collector by trade, Mark a preacher, and John a fisherman. When you compare the resurrection narratives of these four men, you immediately find differences in the details. I remember a friend in high school telling me that he could not believe in the Resurrection because Matthew, Mark, Luke, and John gave accounts that differed from one another.

I submit that the divergences among the four accounts are, in fact, a powerful evidence *for*, rather than *against*, the truthfulness of the records.

How can that be?

Although the four accounts differ from one another, they do not contradict each other. For example, Matthew begins his account of Easter Sunday by saying, "After the Sabbath, at dawn on the first day of the week, Mary Magdalene and the other Mary went to look at the tomb" (Matt. 28:1). Mark begins his account by saying, "When the Sabbath was over, Mary Magdalene, Mary the mother of James, and Salome brought spices so that they might go to anoint Jesus' body" (Mark 16:1).

Matthew has two women visiting the tomb at daybreak. Mark has three. Is that a contradiction? No, it is just a difference, and differences are not necessarily contradictions. For example, suppose you arrived at church one Sunday to find a visiting minister filling the pulpit. You asked the person on your left, "Where's Pastor Jones?" She replied, "He's on vacation." Then you asked the person on your right, "Where's Pastor Jones?" He said, "He and his wife are on vacation." Would you exclaim, "There's a contradiction here! Someone's telling a lie! Someone's fabricating a myth"? Of course not. You would easily realize that the ones on your right and left were not making up false stories independent of one another. Neither, obviously, were they in collusion. They were just relating the same fact from two different but noncontradictory perspectives.

Diversities in the stories are not necessarily contradictions in the history. On the contrary, these minor divergences provide powerful evidence that the accounts are true. In a court of law, when you have two or three witnesses whose stories are all presented exactly alike, you begin to suspect that they have gotten together ahead of time to rehearse their accounts. You strongly suspect collusion. But if each person tells the story from his or her own perspective, each adding different details and yet not contradicting the testimony of the others, you can more easily assume you are getting a genuine story.

Henry Morris observes:

> The mere fact that there does appear on the surface to be numerous superficial discrepancies and omissions in the account is clear proof that the writers were not engaged in some kind of collusion. It is a well-known rule of evidence that the testimonies of several different witnesses, each reporting from his own particular vantage point, provide the strongest possible evidence on matters of fact when the testimonies contain superficial contradictions which resolve themselves upon close and careful examination. This is exactly the situation with the various witnesses to the resurrection.[6]

THE EMPTY TOMB ITSELF

The third piece of evidence for the Resurrection is the empty tomb itself. Consider the significance of the fact that nobody in first-century Judea disputed that the tomb was empty. Three different groups verified the absence of Christ's body from the grave. First, His friends admitted the tomb was empty. Second and more surprising, His enemies freely admitted that the tomb was empty, and they scrambled to fabricate an explanation for it. Never forget that both the Jews and the Romans—the enemies of Christ, the ones responsible for His death—never tried for one moment to dispute the empty tomb. They could not. They could have shut down the Christian movement in short order had they only produced Christ's body. But they could not, and they did not even try.

The third group comprised the general population of Jerusalem. As Paul later observed, "this thing was not done in a corner" (Acts 26:26 KJV). Do not forget that the Resurrection occurred during a major Jewish holiday, and the Holy City was overflowing with multitudes of Jewish pilgrims and Roman soldiers.

When I was in Jerusalem, in the Old City near the Temple Mount, I wanted to visit the two traditional sites of the crucifixion and resurrection of Christ—the Church of the Holy Sepulcher and Gordon's Garden Tomb. Christ was most likely buried at one or the other of these spots. It took me less than five minutes to walk to the former and less than ten to walk to the latter. These spots were easily accessible to the crowds, and we know from Luke 24 that the whole countryside was captivated by the news of Jesus' death and reported resurrection. The two disciples traveling to Emmaus, recorded in chapter 24, expressed surprise that the stranger who joined them had not heard the news. They said in effect, "You must be the only person in Jerusalem who doesn't know about this."

Multitudes had undoubtedly crowded into that cemetery garden and around that tomb, and no one—not one witness!—saw a body there. No one—not His friends, not His enemies whether Jewish or Roman, and not His fellow countrymen—questioned the historical fact of the empty tomb.

So those who deny the resurrection of Jesus Christ have some explaining to do. They have to work around the reliability of historians, diversity of the accounts, and disappearance of the body.

THE PRESENCE OF THE GUARD

But there is more evidence. They must also explain how the body of Christ disappeared underneath the noses of the crack team of Roman soldiers guarding the tomb. According to Matthew 27:62-66, the enemies of Christ appealed to the Roman Governor Pontius Pilate to dispatch troops, probably numbering from ten to thirty, to guard the tomb. Why? The chief priests and Pharisees recalled that Jesus had predicted His own resurrection in advance. "We remember that while he was still alive that deceiver said, 'After three days I will rise again'" (Matt. 27:63).

So Pilate sent his troops to guard the tomb for three days to prevent His disciples from stealing the body and claiming that He had risen from the dead. This guard, as you can imagine, was highly-disciplined, well-armed, and subject to brutal punishments in the event of failure. Now do you really think it possible for such a military contingent stationed around the tomb to miss a ragged, frightened band of fishermen sneaking into the burial garden, breaking the Roman seal, rolling away the cumbersome stone, creeping inside the tomb, hoisting the body of Jesus onto their shoulders, stumbling out of the tomb, and racing from the garden?

It seems far more likely that in officially sealing the tomb and dispatching a contingent of elite Roman soldiers, the enemies of Christ unwittingly provided us with another piece of powerful evidence for the only logical explanation for the empty tomb—the resurrection of Christ.

Albert L. Roper was a prominent Virginia attorney, a graduate of the University of Virginia and its law school, who eventually became mayor of the city of Norfolk. He once began a thorough legal investigation into the evidence for the resurrection of Christ, asking himself the question: Can any intelligent person accept the resurrection story? After examining the evidence at length, he came away asking a different question: Can any intelligent person deny the weight of this evidence?[7]

One of the most interesting books in my library was written by a man who set out to disprove the resurrection of Jesus Christ. He was an English journalist named Frank Morison. He viewed Christianity with scorn, deciding that if he could prove that Christ's resurrection was a mere myth, he could debunk the Christian religion.

He poured over the evidence, absorbing all the information he could and marshaling all his arguments. Not only was he unable to disprove the Resurrection, but he was compelled on the weight of the evidence to become a Christian himself.

And his book? It is a powerful argument in favor of the Resurrection, called *Who Moved the Stone?* It is "essentially a confession," Morison says, "the inner story of a man who originally set out to write one kind of book and found himself compelled by the sheer force of circumstances to write quite another."[8]

SUMMARY

The apostle Paul once asked King Agrippa, "Why should any of you consider it incredible that God raises the dead?" (Acts 26:8). Far from being foolish and mythical, the Resurrection is logical, sensible, and evidenced by "many convincing proofs."

The only incredible thing about it is that so many people reject the evidence and spurn the Savior whose body no longer resides in the tomb of Joseph of Arimathea in Jerusalem.

This is the risen Savior. This is He who said in John 11:25: "I am the resurrection and the life. He who believes in me will live, even though he dies; and whoever lives and believes in me will never die."

FOR FURTHER DISCUSSION

1. Jerry, a Christian friend of yours, tells you, "I don't need any evidence for my faith. Jesus said it, and that's enough for me." How would you respond?
2. Thomas, an unchurched friend, says, "I wish I could believe in Christianity, but it's just too fantastic. You have to believe in supernatural things, in miracles, in resurrections. Everyone knows those things don't really happen." How would you respond?

FOR APPLICATION

1. Study a map of Jerusalem, locating the traditional sites of Jesus' death, burial, and resurrection.
2. Prepare a chart comparing the four resurrection accounts in the Gospels, putting them in parallel columns and seeking to harmonize the divergent perspectives among the four.
3. Brainstorm and compile a list of ways in which the world would be different today had Jesus not physically risen from the dead.

Chapter Two

EXHIBIT A: THE RESURRECTION OF CHRIST

The Eyewitnesses

ANYONE WHO STUDIES the subject of Christian evidences soon bumps into Josh McDowell's *Evidence That Demands a Verdict*, a book that has provided countless Christians with well-organized, tightly-researched materials on apologetics.

McDowell entered the university as a young man looking for a good time and searching for happiness and meaning in life. He tried going to church but found religion unsatisfying. He ran for student leadership positions but was disappointed by how quickly the glamour wore off. He tried the party circuit, but he woke up Monday mornings feeling worse than ever.

He finally noticed a group of students engaged in Bible study, and he became intrigued by the radiance of one of the young ladies. He asked her a reason for it. She looked him straight in the eye, smiled, and said, "Jesus Christ."

"Oh, for heaven's sake," he retorted, "don't give me that garbage about religion."

She replied, "I didn't say religion; I said Jesus Christ."

The students invited him to examine intellectually the claims of Christ and the evidence supporting Christianity. He accepted their challenge and, after much study and research, finally admitted that he could not refute the body of proof supporting Christianity. McDowell received Christ as his Savior, and his research became the background for his book *Evidence That Demands a Verdict*.

One of the major factors in his conversion to Christianity was his inability to ignore the historical resurrection of Jesus Christ, a point he made later to a student at the University of Uruguay who asked him, "Professor McDowell, why can't you intellectually refute Christianity?"

"For a very simple reason," replied McDowell. "I am not able to explain away an event in history—the resurrection of Jesus Christ."[1]

The first-century historian Luke asserted that Jesus "gave many convincing proofs that he was alive" (Acts 1:3), and the apostle Paul added his own confirmation by writing in 1 Corinthians 15:4-8 "that he was raised on the third day according to the Scriptures, and that he appeared to Peter, and then to the Twelve. After that, he appeared to more than five hundred of the brothers at the same time, most of whom are still living, though some have fallen asleep. Then he appeared to James, then to all the apostles, and last of all he appeared to me also."

In the previous chapter, we considered four evidences for the Resurrection. In the passage above, Paul suggests several other proofs.

THE PREDICTIONS OF HIS RESURRECTION

Notice the four little words Paul uses to describe Christ's resurrection in both verses 3 and 4: "Christ died for our sins *according to the Scriptures*, that he was buried, that he was raised on the third day *according to the Scriptures*" (emphasis mine).

In using that phrase "according to the Scriptures," Paul is telling us that one of the confirmations of the resurrection of Christ is that it occurred exactly as the Scriptures had predicted. Both Jesus Christ Himself and the Old Testament before Him had described in advance what would happen. The prophet Isaiah, for example, in a passage that has been confirmed by the Dead Sea Scrolls, predicted, "He was assigned a grave with the wicked, and with the rich in his death, though he had done no violence, nor was any deceit in his mouth. Yet it was the LORD's will to crush him and cause him to suffer, and though the LORD makes his life a guilt offering, he will see his offspring and prolong his days, and the will of the LORD will prosper in his hand. After the suffering of his soul, he will see the light of life and be satisfied" (Isa. 53:9-11).

You may want to study other passages such as Genesis 3:15; Psalm 2:7-9; Psalm 16:9-11; Psalm 22:14-25; Psalm 30:2-9; Psalm 40:1-3; Psalm 110:1; Psalm 118:21-24; Hosea 5:15—6:3; Zechariah 12:10, and the example of Jonah whose exit from his waterlogged "grave" after three days foreshadowed the Lord's emergence from the tomb.

Regarding Christ's own words, it is interesting that His enemies did us the favor of pulling out His resurrection predictions and reinforcing them for all of history. How? By using them in His trial to condemn Him. One of the accusations made against Him was that He had claimed, "I am able to destroy the temple of God and rebuild it in three days" (Matt. 26:61). And following His death, the chief priests and Pharisees went to Pilate requesting the stationing of a Roman guard at the tomb, for they remembered that "while he was still alive that deceiver said, 'After three days I will rise again'" (Matt. 27:63).[2]

Jesus' predictions of His resurrection spanned His ministry, appearing like signposts at the beginning, in the middle, and at the end of His earthly career. During His early ministry, He declared, "Destroy this temple, and I will raise it again in three days" (John 2:19), referring to the temple of His body. At mid-ministry, He said, "For as Jonah was three days and three nights in the belly of a huge fish, so the Son of Man will be three days and three nights in the heart of the earth" (Matt. 12:40). And during His final trek toward Calvary, He repeatedly predicted His resurrection in words like these: "The Son of Man is going to be betrayed into the hands of men. They will kill him, and on the third day he will be raised to life" (Matt. 17:22-23).

It came to pass just as the Old Testament and its promised Messiah had predicted.

THE EYEWITNESS ACCOUNTS OF CHRIST'S APPEARANCES

The apostle Paul proceeds to give us more collaborating proof: "He appeared to Peter, and then to the Twelve. After that, he appeared to more than five hundred of the brothers at the same time, most of whom are still living, though some have fallen asleep. Then he appeared to James, then to all the apostles, and last of all he appeared to me also" (1 Cor. 15:5-8).

Ever experience an "Elvis sighting"? Some rock-and-roll fans are so distraught over the "king's" death that they deny it altogether, claiming he shows up here and there at fast-food businesses and music concerts. Do the "Jesus sightings" of the first century belong to this sort of tabloid chicanery?

Absolutely not. Following His resurrection, Jesus remained on earth for forty days, appearing at least ten times to various individuals and groups, showing Himself alive by "many convincing proofs." The genuineness of these eyewitness reports and the historical reliability of the accounts are virtually beyond question.

Wilbur Smith added an insightful point about these appearances when he wrote:

> About a year ago, after studying over a long period of time, this entire problem of our Lord's resurrection, and having written some hundreds of pages upon it at different times, I was suddenly arrested by the thought that the very kind of evidence which modern science, and even psychologists, are so insistent upon for determining the reality

of any object under consideration is the kind of evidence that we have presented to us in the Gospels regarding the Resurrection of the Lord Jesus, namely, the things that are seen with the human eye, touched with the human hand, and heard by the human ear. This is what we call empirical evidence. It would almost seem as if parts of the Gospel records of the Resurrection were actually written for such a day as ours when empiricism so dominates our thinking.[3]

Some people assume that Christ only appeared to the believers and that we must therefore impugn these eyewitnesses as having biased accounts. That is not true for two reasons. First, despite Jesus' predictions, none of His disciples expected Him to rise from the dead. They were all skeptics who were so astounded by the Resurrection that they only gradually grew convinced. Thomas was particularly adamant in his refusal to believe that Christ had arisen. "Unless I see the nail marks in his hands," he said, "and put my finger where the nails were, and put my hand into his side, I will not believe it" (John 20:25).

And there were skeptics among the five hundred who met Him on the mountainside in Galilee. "Some doubted," Matthew 28:17 says. Yet they could not refute their own eyewitness accounts.

But Jesus not only appeared to skeptics. He showed up before the eyes of some who were openly hostile. We know of two enemies in particular, both mentioned here in 1 Corinthians 15, who became convinced of Christ's resurrection. The first was Jesus' own half-brother James, who had openly ridiculed and rejected Christ throughout the Gospels. Yet in the book of Acts, we see him assuming courageous leadership in the early church, withstanding threats of torture, danger, and death. What suddenly happened to transform James from an agnostic brother to a courageous martyr? First Corinthians 15:7 says, "Then he appeared to James."

Paul mentions another enemy who was transformed by the Resurrection. "Last of all he appeared to me also," the apostle says (1 Cor. 15:8). The appearance of the risen Savior to Saul of Tarsus on the Damascus Road is the final post-resurrection appearance in the New Testament apart from the apocalyptic visions of Christ in the book of Revelation. And it is one of the most eventful, for it instantly transformed the fiercest enemy of Jesus Christ into the greatest missionary the church has ever known.

THE TRANSFORMATION OF THE APOSTLES

How do you explain this fact? On Friday you have a group of men huddled in misery, depressed and dejected, denying their own Savior like spineless cowards. On Monday those same men are ready to face the lash, the prison, the sword, the stocks, the snarling beasts in the arena, and death itself—all the while proclaiming the Gospel to the very ones who only days before had murdered their leader. Never for a moment during the entire remainder of their days did any of these men lose their nerve or deny their Savior. They willingly poured out the rest of their lives, suffering shame and pain, leaving hearth and home, spilling their own sweat and blood to turn the world upside down.

What happened between Friday night and Monday morning?

They saw the risen Savior. John Stott suggests, "Perhaps the transformation of the disciples of Jesus is the greatest evidence of all for the resurrection. It was the resurrection which transformed Peter's fear into courage, and James' doubt into faith. It was the resurrection which changed the Sabbath into Sunday and the Jewish remnant into the Christian Church. It was the resurrection which changed Saul the Pharisee into Paul the apostle, and turned his persecuting into preaching."[4]

THE CHANGE IN THE DAY OF WORSHIP

As Stott suggests, another evidence for the reality of the Resurrection involves the shift from Saturday to Sunday as the Christian day of worship. The Jews viewed the seventh day of the week as the Sabbath, their day of rest and praise. But from the beginning—from Resurrection morning—Christians have celebrated the first day of the week as the "Lord's Day," commemorating each week the rising of Christ from the dead.

The first Christians, remember, were staunch Jews who fiercely defended their day of worship as specified in the fourth commandment, a Sabbath to be strictly observed. In fact, many rules and rituals had arisen around the Sabbath Day, and the consequences of shifting worship from the seventh to the first day were profound religiously, emotionally, and legally. The Sabbath had been observed every week for 1,500 years. Yet during one week, in one day, on Resurrection morning itself, all of that changed for these Jewish believers. It changed suddenly, naturally, and permanently. What could have produced such a change? Nothing but the Resurrection.

REFERENCES IN SECULAR HISTORIES

We can also draw historical evidence for the Resurrection from the secular histories of antiquity. You would not expect non-Christian sources to emphasize the Resurrection the way biblical historians do. But no one can ignore the existence of the man Jesus Christ or the presence of a strong band of men and women in the first century who were absolutely convinced Jesus had risen from the dead.

The earliest references we have to Christ come from archaeology— inscriptions found on burial caskets dated between A.D. 40 and 50 outside of Jerusalem. One casket contains the words, "Jesus, help!" and the other one bears the words, "Jesus, let him who rests here arise."

Archaeologists have also found an inscription in Nazareth, the hometown of Jesus, repeating an edict from a first-century Roman emperor warning in sharp and urgent language against the removing of bodies from sealed tombs.

The Jewish historian Josephus described many details that corroborate the gospel accounts, according to Dr. Mireille Hadas-Lebel, ancient history scholar and professor at the National Institute of Oriental Languages and Civilizations in Paris. Dr. Hadas-Lebel observes that Josephus mentions the census ordered by Quirinius, the cruelty of King Herod, the preaching of John the Baptist, and the condemnation of "a man named James, the brother of Jesus who was called Christ." Another passage in Josephus's writings describes Jesus as a wise man who was crucified and "on the third day he appeared to them restored to life . . . and the sect of Christians, so called after him, has still to this day not disappeared."

Dr. Hadas-Lebel addresses the speculation that portions of the Josephus passages were added later by Christian copyists and editors. Her conclusions represent those most widely accepted in the academic world today. The passages are basically authentic. Some descriptive phrases may have been scribbled in the margins by ancient Christian copyists and later added into the text. For the most part, the passages in Josephus referring to Christ can be well trusted, for we find Eusebius of Caesarea quoting them in the fourth century.[5]

The historian Tacitus described the strength and resilience of the Christians in Rome during the persecution of Nero in A.D. 64. We also have references to Christ and to the church in the writings of Pliny to the Emperor Trajan about the year A.D. 110. The Roman historian Seutonius speaks of Christ in his *Life of Claudius* and *Lives of the Caesars*.

In addition to the secular historians, we have the writings of the Apostolic Fathers—Clement of Rome, Ignatius, Hermas, Barnabas of Alexandria, Papias, and Polycarp—all of them living in the first century and attesting to the historicity of the risen Christ.

All this combined with the clear accounts in the Gospels leaves us with more information about the life of Jesus Christ than of any other figure in the ancient world. No competent, objective historian today denies the existence of Jesus of Nazareth. And no one can deny that something of an extraordinary nature happened in the garden tomb of Joseph of Arimathea that profoundly changed the history of the world.

THE THEOLOGICAL FIT

Among the remaining pieces of evidence is one that packs more punch than appears at first glance. I believe we find powerful testimony in support of the Resurrection by observing how perfectly this event fits into the entire structure of biblical theology. Returning to Paul's statements in 1 Corinthians 15, we find him viewing the resurrection of Christ as the essential spinning core of the Christian faith: "I want to remind you of the gospel . . . that Christ died for our sins according to the Scriptures, that he was buried, that he was raised on the third day according to the Scriptures. . . . And if Christ has not been raised, our preaching is useless and so is your faith" (vv. 1, 3-4, 14).

The resurrection of Christ is so woven into the warp and woof of the biblical plan of salvation that the entire Bible, from Genesis to Revelation, is held together by it. The whole plan of salvation depends on it. The Bible says, "He was delivered over to death for our sins and was raised to life for our justification" (Rom. 4:25).

The Bible was written over a period of 1,600 years in sixty-six installments. But when you step back and see it as a whole, its entire message spins around the axis of the empty tomb. As soon as sin entered into the human story, God predicted a Savior and reassured humanity of a way of redemption, a plan of salvation. The entire Old Testament points toward the coming Savior who would defeat sin, death, and the grave. And the entire New Testament describes His death and resurrection— and the eternal life He thus imparts. Without the resurrection of Christ, nothing in the Bible makes sense.

But not only does the resurrection of Christ fit the theology of Scripture; it also fits perfectly into the life of Christ. It is the kind of event we would expect, given the identity of the Nazarene. "It is fitting that a supernatural person should enter and leave the earth in a supernatural way," wrote John Stott. "This is in fact what the New Testament teaches and the Church believes. His birth was natural, but His conception was supernatural. His death was natural, but His resurrection was supernatural."[6]

SUMMARY

So if you reject the resurrection of Christ, you have to explain away a massive body of evidence that includes, but is not limited to:

- the reliability of the most accurate historian of the first century.
- the diversity of the resurrection accounts.
- the empty tomb itself.
- the presence of the Roman guards.
- the Resurrection's remarkable fulfillment of Scripture.
- the eyewitness accounts of the Lord's appearances.
- the transformation of the apostles, including Paul.
- the change from the Sabbath to the Lord's Day.
- the way the Resurrection fits perfectly into all of biblical teaching.

Years ago in England two men set out to disprove Christianity. One was a well-known English jurist and literary scholar named Lord Littleton. The other was Gilbert West. They agreed that if Christianity was to be discredited, it was necessary to do two things—disprove the Resurrection and explain the conversion of Saul of Tarsus in a way that satisfied the skeptics. The two men divided these tasks between themselves, Littleton taking the problem of Saul and West agreeing to research the Resurrection. They invested over a year for their studies and then met together to compare notes. Each one was astonished to discover that the other had become a Christian. The evidence was too strong, the truth too undeniable. It still is.

FOR FURTHER DISCUSSION

1. How would you answer someone who claimed that Jesus' disciples stole the body and fabricated the story of the Resurrection as a hoax? How would you respond to those who claim that Jesus was not fully dead when He was buried and that the cool dampness of the tomb awakened Him, making it appear that He rose from the dead?
2. Describe the risen body of Christ. In what ways will the resurrected bodies of believers "be like his glorious body" (Phil. 3:21)?

FOR APPLICATION

1. Read through one of the epistles of Paul, listing all the references to the resurrection of Christ and jotting down every item mentioned by the apostle as an implication of the Resurrection.
2. In a group setting, try role playing in which someone presents evidences for the historical reality of the resurrection of Christ to a "skeptic."
3. Prepare your testimony, emphasizing what the resurrection of Christ means to you.

Chapter Three

EXHIBIT B:
THE CREATION

The Existence of Creation

PAUL GENTUSO WAS a budding evolutionist until he studied the human hand in medical school. "In anatomy class," he said, "we dissected a human hand. In investigating the hand, I first removed the skin, then isolated the individual tendons and muscles as I worked my way to the bones. The tendons of the hand are aligned in tendon sheaths, like self-lubricating pulleys, allowing the hand to work in a tireless, noiseless, almost effortless fashion. It was perfectly designed to carry out all the work it was called to do, everything from lifting a small object to lugging a tree trunk."

The experience deeply affected Paul. Until then he had entertained serious doubts about God's existence. "In seeing how each tendon was perfectly aligned along the axis of each finger and how each finger moved in a coordinated fashion when tugged by individual tendons," he said, "it became obvious to me that there was a creator who had intelligently designed and created the human hand. This was the first time in my adult life that I could say with assurance that a creator existed. It was really a spiritual experience for me. I went from doubt to certainty based on seeing God's creation."

Paul later became a Christian and now serves as a missionary physician in Cote d'Ivoire. He is not the only one to abandon his faith in evolution in the light of the evident design of creation. A controversial biology textbook being used in some of America's public schools, *Of Pandas and People*, was coauthored by Dean Kenyon, a tenured molecular biology professor at San Francisco State University. Dr. Kenyon, whose research interest is specifically the origin of life, was an ardent evolutionist who earlier had coauthored *Biochemical Predestination*, a biology textbook based on evolutionary presuppositions that became a standard text in the field of biology and origins. But the more he studied the marvel of life with all its complexity and apparent design, the more Dr. Kenyon questioned the hypothesis that it all just evolved from primordial nothingness.

I was astonished several years ago to read these words from his pen: "I no longer believe that the arguments in *Biochemical Predestination* and in similar books by other authors add up to an adequate defense of the view that life arose spontaneously on this planet from nonliving matter."[1]

Now Dr. Kenyon has authored this newer textbook that does not refer to God or to the Creation as such, but proposes what it calls "Intelligent Design." Here is what the *Wall Street Journal* said:

> [*Of Pandas and People* deploys] accepted scientific laws to argue that the world is too complex to be explained by Charles Darwin's mindless natural forces. Therefore, [the authors reason] an "intelligent agent" must have sat at the drafting table. But the book stops short of identifying this agent. The book has won allies with impeccable academic credentials. Phillip E. Johnson, a University of California, Berkeley, law professor and staunch defender of intelligent-design theory, calls the book a pioneering effort to challenge evolutionary doctrine. "What we need," he says, "is honest non-dogmatic science education that is as honest about what evolutionary biologists don't know as what they do know."[2]

For most of this century, science has tried to discount the existence of God and deny the reality of a creator. But the more it explores the mysteries and marvels of the universe, the more difficult it becomes to ignore the evidence of the Creation.

The truthfulness of Christianity, however, rests on an even deeper assumption, the reality of God Himself. In other words, Christianity is based on theism, the belief in the existence of God (the Greek word for God being *theos*).

If there is no God, then Christianity is gibberish. But there is a God, and He has not left Himself without a witness. Just as Christianity has a central, documenting proof—the Resurrection—so theism has a central, documenting proof—the Creation. The psalmist wrote, "The heavens declare the glory of God; the skies proclaim the work of his hands. Day after day they pour forth speech; night after night they display knowledge. There is no speech or language where their voice is not heard" (Ps. 19:1-3). The apostle Paul concurred, saying, "For since the creation of the world God's invisible qualities—his eternal power and divine nature—have been clearly seen, being understood from what has been made" (Rom. 1:20).

THE VERY EXISTENCE OF THE UNIVERSE

Anyone who wants to deny the existence of Almighty God has to provide an answer to one supreme question: Where did the universe come from? I remember hearing a science professor reduce to shreds the arguments of an agnostic student by simply asking him a series of repetitive questions. Where did life come from? "It evolved from chemicals in some sort of primeval pond," said the student. Where did the primeval pond come from? "From elements existing as residue of the Big Bang." Where did the Big Bang come from? "From a speck of matter that exploded." Where did the speck of matter come from? That is where the discussion ended, for the student's only answer was, "I don't know."

Since that is not a very satisfying answer, scientists try to couch it in sophisticated language. They talk about the universe "exploding into existence" and the "spontaneous generation" of matter.

But increasingly, honest scientists are admitting the deficiency of such language. R. C. Sproul, a scholar with degrees from the Free University of Amsterdam, Geneva College, and Grove City College, who lectures widely on apologetics, wrote:

> For something to come from nothing it must, in effect, create itself. Self-creation is a logical and rational impossibility. For something to create itself, it must be able to transcend Hamlet's dilemma, "To be or not to be." Hamlet's question assumed sound science. He understood that something (himself) could not both be and not be at the same time and in the same relationship. For something to create itself, it must have the ability to be and not be at the same time and in the same relationship. For something to create itself, it must be before it is. This is impossible. It is impossible for solids, liquids, and gasses. It is impossible for atoms and subatomic particles. It is impossible for light and heat. It is impossible for God. Nothing anywhere, anytime, can create itself.[3]

What would you think, for example, if an apple suddenly materialized from thin air on top of this book? What if it just "poofed" into existence? Can you imagine it appearing by "spontaneous generation"? If such a thing happened, you might call it magic or perhaps a miracle, but you would not call it science.

Scientists have been unable to dispute the simple truth that nothing comes from nothing. For example, the evolutionist and agnostic Robert Jastrow, America's Science Laureate, wrote several textbooks on evolution and served as Professor of Geophysics at Columbia University and Professor of Space Studies-Earth Sciences at Dartmouth College, as a regular columnist for *Science Digest* magazine, and as Founder/Director of NASA's Goddard Institute of Space Studies in New York. Several years ago he shocked the scientific community by admitting that he was unable to explain the existence of the universe without God. He wrote in his book *God and the Astronomers*: "For the scientist who has lived by his faith in the power of reason, the story ends like a bad dream. He has scaled the mountains of ignorance; he is about to conquer the highest peak; as he pulls himself over the final rock, he is greeted by a band of theologians who have been sitting there for centuries."[4]

About a decade after Jastrow's quote, scientists were further shaken by the announcement by NASA that it had discovered the possible origin of the universe in cloudlike structures detected by the Cosmic Background Explorer satellite, which seem to prove that the universe was created during a moment in the past rather than having always existed. Following that announcement, Dr. Frederick B. Burnham, science historian and director of the Trinity Institute in New York City, confessed that many scientists would consider the idea that God created the universe "a more respectable hypothesis at this point in time than at any time in the last 100 years."[5]

There is, in other words, an undeniable law of cause and effect in the universe. Everything that exists is the result of a chain of events that has its root in some omnipotent First Cause. Furthermore, by studying the effects, we can draw some implications about the First Cause. Henry Morris states: "Every observed phenomenon is an effect, and its cause must be adequate to produce it. No effect can be quantitatively greater or qualitatively extrinsic to its cause. Every effect must be assimilated in principle to its cause."[6]

Simply put, since the universe appears almost limitless in extent, the First Cause must be virtually infinite. Since the universe appears almost endless in duration, the First Cause must be virtually eternal. Since the universe pulsates with energy, the First Cause must be virtually omnipotent. Since the universe is phenomenally complex and contains intelligent life, the First Cause must be virtually omniscient. Since the universe contains feeling and emotions and love and human relations, the First Cause must be personal. Since the universe contains goodness and righteousness and love and justice, the First Cause must be moral.

"Thus," says Morris, "reasoning from cause-and-effect leads us to conclude that the great First Cause of all things is an infinite, eternal, omnipotent, omnipresent, personal, emotional, moral, spiritual, living Being. And this, of course, is nothing less than a description of the God of the Bible."[7]

THE COMPLEXITY OF THE UNIVERSE

The second layer of evidence from creation has to do with the complexity of the existing universe. One of the most famous proponents of this truth was the British theologian and naturalist William Paley, who formulated the famous "Watchmaker Argument." Suppose, Paley said, we were walking along and came to a stone. We might ask where the stone came from, and our companions might say that the stone had been there forever. But suppose, continuing down the path, we came to a watch, with its hands and face and dials and gears and its intricate, precise workmanship. If we asked where the watch came from, the obvious answer would be that someone had made it. Someone had owned it. Someone had lost it. Such a precise and finely crafted instrument would not have come into existence just by pieces of dust and debris blowing together.

The universe is billions and billions of times more complex than a wristwatch; hence, the complexity of the universe is itself powerful and indisputable evidence for the existence of a creator. *Time* Magazine ended a recent year by devoting its cover story to the subject "What Does Science Tell Us About God?" The lead article was written by an unbeliever, Robert Wright, who called himself a fairly hard-core scientific materialist. But in the course of the article, Dr. Wright admitted:

> There is more to this universe than meets the eye, something authentically divine about how it all fits together. One intriguing observation that has bubbled up from physics is that the universe seems calibrated for life's existence. If the force of gravity were pushed upward a bit, stars would burn out faster, leaving little time for life to evolve on the planets circling them. If the relative masses of protons and neutrons were changed by a hair, stars might never be born, since the hydrogen they eat wouldn't exist. If, at the Big Bang, some basic numbers—the "initial conditions"—had been jiggled, matter and energy would never have coagulated into galax-

ies, stars, planets or any other platforms stable enough for life as we know it. And so on.[8]

Similarly, Dr. Hugh Ross, a scientist with his Ph.D. in astronomy from the University of Toronto, wrote in his book *Creation and Time*:

> Until recently the universe was measureless. Now we can see and measure many of its limits and characteristics. In making these measurements, astronomers discovered the anthropic principle, the maxim that the universe has been built for humankind. As of October 1993, twenty-five different characteristics of the universe were recognized as precisely fixed. If they were different by only slight amounts, the differences would spell the end of the existence of any conceivable life. To this list of twenty-five can be added thirty-eight characteristics of our galaxy and solar system that likewise must fall within narrowly defined ranges for life of any kind to exist.
>
> The degree of fine-tuning necessary for the support of life supersedes by many orders of magnitude the best human beings have ever achieved in the design and construction of instruments, machines, or anything else. Three of the characteristics of the universe must be fine-tuned to a precision of one part in 10^{37} or better. That's supernatural![9]

I recently read a monograph by Dr. Owen Gingerich, Research Professor of Astronomy and History of Science at Harvard University and a senior astronomer at the Smithsonian Astrophysical Observatory. Gingerich referred to his friend, Fred Hoyle, a highly respected scientist of the first caliber, who was an atheist. Hoyle discovered the remarkable nuclear arrangement of the carbon atom, which is so uniquely and perfectly designed that if its composition and resonance level had been altered in the slightest way, life would be absolutely impossible.

Dr. Gingerich heard a rumor that Fred Hoyle claimed nothing had shaken his atheism as much as his discoveries regarding the carbon atom. But in their discussions together, Dr. Gingerich never mustered the courage to ask Dr. Hoyle if he had made the statement.

Then Dr. Gingerich ran across an article by Fred Hoyle in a Cal Tech publication. The article stated:

> Would you not say to yourself, "Some supercalculating intellect must have designed the properties of the carbon atom, otherwise

the chance of my finding such an atom through the blind forces of nature would be utterly minuscule." Of course you would. . . . A common sense interpretation of the facts suggests that a super-intellect has monkeyed with physics, as well as with chemistry and biology, and that there are no blind forces worth speaking about in nature. The numbers one calculates from the facts seem to me so overwhelming as to put this conclusion almost beyond question.

Dr. Owen Gingerich observed, "Fred Hoyle and I differ on lots of questions, but on this we agree: A commonsense and satisfying inter-pretation of our world suggests the designing hand of a superintelli-gence."

Then Gingerich added: "For me, it makes sense to suppose that the superintelligence, the transcendence . . . has revealed itself through the prophets in all ages, and supremely in the life of Jesus Christ. . . . [And] just as I believe that the Book of Scripture illumines the path-way to God, so I believe that the Book of Nature, with its astonishing details like the resonance levels of the carbon atom, also suggests a God of purpose and a God of design. And I think my belief makes me no less a scientist."[10]

SUMMARY

I do not want to leave the impression that most scientists today are evangelical Christians, although many are. Increasing numbers of sci-entists are clearly being driven by their research and discoveries to recon-sider the reality of God.

I draw encouragement from knowing that in this age of skepticism and doubt, many of the world's most eminent scientists know and trust in God—and in Jesus Christ. And their faith in Christ makes them no less scientists, for as the psalmist said three thousand years ago: "The heavens declare the glory of God; the skies proclaim the work of his hands" (Ps. 19:1).

FOR FURTHER DISCUSSION

1. Western science stemmed from medieval Christian philosophies and institutions, believers seeking to learn more about God's creation. Why do you think the scientific community at large has since aban-doned faith in God and become purely materialistic and agnostic or atheistic? Why are numbers of them now returning to a consideration of theism?

2. How would you answer a high school or college student who, deeply influenced by the teaching of evolution, asked you how anyone could still believe in the biblical account of the Creation?

FOR APPLICATION

1. Share your nature-centered hobbies one evening in a group setting. Those who collect rocks or grow flowers or peer through telescopes or collect insects can each share from their observations, perhaps bringing samples, as to the design of creation.
2. In a group setting, try role playing. Present to a "skeptic" evidences from creation for the existence of God.
3. There is probably a Christian in your community involved in a scientific career, perhaps teaching science or working as a researcher or practitioner. Make an appointment for him or her to talk to you or your group.

Chapter Four

EXHIBIT B:
THE CREATION

The Complexity of Creation

JOEY NEVER DOUBTED for a moment the truthfulness of the Bible until he entered a small, private university where he took Introduction to Biology. His persuasive agnostic professor presented evolution as established fact, deliberately drawing Christians into debates in which he humiliated them. By the end of the semester, Joey's faith was badly shaken, and for a while he wondered if Christianity could be intellectually defended. It was not until later, after a period of agonizing doubt and extensive research, that he discovered a cadre of evangelical scientists and professors whose tough-minded, no-nonsense answers reassured him and, in fact, left him stronger in his faith than before.

Joey's experience is not uncommon. The state of California, for example, has formulated guidelines for teachers to use when responding to questioning students. "I understand that you may have personal reservations about accepting this scientific evidence," the teacher is to say, "but it is scientific knowledge about which there is no reasonable doubt among scientists in this field."

Some professors go further. Oxford scientist and author Richard Dawkins said, "It is absolutely safe to say that if you meet somebody who claims not to believe in evolution, that person is ignorant, stupid, or insane (or wicked, but I'd rather not consider that)."[1]

Well, if so, increasing numbers of eminent scientists and authorities are "ignorant, stupid, or insane," for an entire generation of young scholars is joining forces with many established leaders in the scientific world to call evolution what it really is—a dogmatic philosophy unsubstantiated by the legitimate scientific findings of the past hundred years.

Colin Patterson is a senior paleontologist at the British Natural

History Museum and the author of the museum's general text on evolution. He gave a lecture at the American Museum of Natural History some time ago comparing creation with evolution, and this is part of what he said:

> Can you tell me anything we know about evolution, any one thing . . . that is true? I tried that question on the geology staff at the Field Museum of Natural History and the only answer I got was silence. I tried it on the members of the Evolutionary Morphology seminar in the University of Chicago, a very prestigious body of evolutionists, and all I got there was silence for a long time, and eventually one person said, "I do know one thing—it ought not to be taught in high school."[2]

I found Patterson's quote in Phillip Johnson's book *Darwin on Trial*. Johnson, a graduate of Harvard and the University of Chicago, is a lawyer and a professor of law who served as a law clerk for Chief Justice Earl Warren of the United States Supreme Court and has taught law for over twenty years at the University of California at Berkeley. He decided to evaluate the evidence for evolution from the perspective of an attorney. After exhaustive studies and research, he wrote *Darwin on Trial*, a book that rocked the scientific world. Johnson's conclusion in a nutshell is that the confirmatory evidence for evolution is miserably lacking on every front. Yet scientists continue to cling to this pseudoscience, as he calls it, because to abandon it would leave them with no explanation for the origin of life apart from a creating God, which they refuse to consider.

The Bible's classic statement on origins offers a better explanation, one that increasing numbers of authorities are embracing: "In the beginning God created the heavens and the earth" (Gen. 1:1). Just as the Resurrection is Exhibit A for the veracity of Christianity, so the Creation is Exhibit A for the veracity of theism. That is why Paul, addressing the pagan philosophers of Athens, started at this point: "The God who made the world and everything in it is the Lord of heaven and earth" (Acts 17:24).

THE COMPLEXITY OF THE UNIVERSE

In chapter 3, we examined the first two aspects of the evidence from creation—the very existence of the universe and the complexity of the universe. Here is additional evidence that the complexity of the universe points to the Creator God.

The universe is a cosmos, not a chaos. It has order and design, and I would like to explore this theme further. Perhaps you are reading this book in the glow of an electric light. That electricity is produced in enormous generators, harnessed at a power plant, and transmitted through a complex system of public utility wires that flash it into your room. Would anyone suggest that the utility systems of your city happened by blind accident or by random chance?

Yet in the muddy waters of the Amazon lives an olive-brown eel that grows eight feet long and has six built-in electric generators composed of thousands of modified muscle cells called electroplaques. It can produce enough electricity to stun and even kill those it touches, its electrical circuitry being far more complex and intricate than the wiring of my house or yours. Is it chance or design?

Whenever you board a jetliner, perhaps you lean back in your seat, sip a soft drink, and chat with your seatmate. But in the control tower, air traffic controllers are watching radar screens that show every moving aircraft. Radar systems, first invented by scientists for the U.S. Navy during World War II, are now very sophisticated, operated by highly trained professionals. In its simplest form, radar consists of sending out radio signals that bounce off targets and echo back to satellite receivers, which then transmit data through computers onto the radar screens in the tower. Did this system assemble itself by accident?

Yet virtually all over the world live small mammals with odd wings covering their skeleton-like arms and fingers. These animals—bats—fly in the dark at high speeds and with great precision. For centuries scientists wondered how. It was assumed that bats possessed enhanced eyesight enabling them to see in the dark; but in the 1780s an Italian zoologist blinded some bats and released them into a room crisscrossed with silk threads. The bats flew through the room without touching so much as the tiniest thread. In the 1940s two American scientists placed some bats in front of a new electronic instrument that could detect ultrasonic sounds. The men heard no sound, but the patterns on the screen showed that the bats were uttering high-pitched cries. We now know that bats have a remarkable built-in radar technology more advanced than that of the military.

We could cite countless examples—the "bridges" created by spiders, the "aerodynamics" of a wren or a robin, the "navigation" of a sparrow, the "management principles" of honeybees.

"The scientific foundation for the proposed evolutionary origin of life is very weak at best," says Garret Vanderkooi, Professor of Chemistry and

Biological Sciences at Northern Illinois University and author of numerous research articles in journals of chemistry and biochemistry. It "contains holes which even speculation proves inadequate to fill. Anyone who observes nature must admit that it has the appearance of being the product of design rather than chance. This is the case regardless of whether one's observations are made at the level of field biology or of molecular biology."

Why then, Vanderkooi asks, do scientific writers so doggedly cling to evolution? He answers his own question: "These writers arbitrarily rule out even the possibility of a supernatural origin for life and hence are forced to the conclusion that evolution happened, although they do not know how, and in spite of the evidence which says it is impossible."[3]

THE BEAUTY OF THE UNIVERSE

Have you ever snorkeled off the coast of a tropical island? Have you peered into the saltwater aquarium of your local pet store? Have you ever visited a botanical garden and soaked in the beauty of a thousand varieties of flowering shrubs and plants? Ever stood on the edge of a vast chasm, gazing at rugged rocks and hills and valleys and canyons? Ever visited the zoo and noticed the colors of the animals, the richness of their fur, the patterns adorning their hides, the shape of their bodies, the tenderness of parents toward their young? Ever peered through a microscope at the hidden world contained in water drops from a pond or through a telescope at the mind-boggling array of endless galaxies?

Is this all-encompassing splendor the blind product of random accidents? Well, ask this: If we visited an art museum to view a painting of a beautiful landscape with trees and a river, fluffy white clouds, and a pasture dotted by flowers, would we assume the artwork was an accident? Did a delivery truck wreck, spilling cans of paint onto a canvas? Or would we assume that an artist of fabulous skill had created the beauty and signed his name at the bottom?

The beauty of the universe is God's signature. "The heavens declare the glory of God; the skies proclaim the work of his hands" (Ps. 19:1).

THE BIBLE'S ACCURACY REGARDING
THE UNIVERSE

Another evidence for the existence of God is found in the accuracy of the Bible's descriptions regarding scientific matters. While the Bible is not a science textbook, and while much of its language is figurative and poetic, yet when it does speak on scientific issues, it assumes a knowledge that has only recently become known to scientists. Apologists call this body of evidence *prescience*—the "occurrence, in Scripture, of accurate statements reflecting an in-depth knowledge of scientific concepts far before mankind had laid the technological base for such things to be known. Prescience is not just occasional, but is present in abundance, especially in the Old Testament."[4] Good examples are the sanitation and dietary laws of the Pentateuch.

Over a hundred years ago, Ignaz Semmelweis worked as a doctor in a hospital in Vienna, a clinic infamous for its high mortality rate among expectant women. Childbirth fever, as it was called, resulted in the death of one in six new mothers. Semmelweis studied the problem carefully and developed a theory that made him the laughingstock of Vienna. He suggested that the disease was being transported on the hands of doctors and that all doctors should scrub their hands before treating patients, especially following autopsies. The physicians started scrubbing their hands, and the mortality rate immediately plunged. But the doctors quickly tired of having to "waste" so much time scrubbing, and Semmelweis was fired. Nobody believed that such a thing as germs or bacteria or disease could be carried on a doctor's fingers or hands.

Yet three thousand years ago in the book of Numbers, God gave the children of Israel specific written procedures about washing their hands in running water whenever they had touched the carcasses of dead animals or humans. The sanitation procedures were quite strict, and the reason given in Exodus 15:26 was the avoidance of disease.

In the last few years, thousands of news reports have warned us about the dangers of blood cholesterol and the tendency of cholesterol to clog the blood vessels and create the danger of heart attack. One of the greatest sources of cholesterol is animal fat. Yet thousands of years before doctors knew about blood cholesterol, Moses told the Hebrews to trim all excess fat from their meats. They were allowed to use the fat for soap and waterproofing their tents, but it was not to be eaten.

In attempting to read through the Bible, we sometimes grow weary with all the rules and regulations we encounter in Exodus, Numbers, and Leviticus. But a more careful study of these books would amaze us. They are filled with health-inducing practices and procedures thousands of years ahead of their time, based on scientific truths that are only now being uncovered by modern medicine, science, and technology—all of which is exactly what you would expect if the universe was created by the God who also gave us His own inspired Scripture. His world and His Word are two sides of the same cosmic coin.[5]

THE PSYCHOLOGICAL AND SOCIOLOGICAL IMPLICATIONS OF CREATION

There is another—a pragmatic—reason for accepting divine creation of the universe. It results in human dignity and happiness, whereas the results of the evolutionary hypothesis are dark, sinister, and deeply troubling. Scientists, after all, gather evidence for their theories by conducting experiments and finding out what works and what does not.

So does evolution "work"? Does it result in psychological and sociological health and happiness? It is a well-known, if seldom-mentioned, fact of history that Darwin's survival-of-the-fittest and materialist evolutionary conjectures, seized upon by Karl Marx, provided the foundation for both Hitler's Holocaust and Stalin's genocide.[6]

In America Darwin's influence has been more subtle, but think of it in this way: What would you expect of a generation that had been taught evolution from earliest schooldays? If Darwin is right, we are nothing but accidental byproducts of evolutionary dust on an insignificant world lost somewhere in the vastness of a hostile universe and doomed to perish in a short period of time. We are nothing more than a match that blazes for a moment and then is extinguished forever. We are without any divine guidance, without any moral absolutes. We have no spirit and no soul; therefore, we become obsessed with our bodies, obsessed with pleasure. All we are, as the song says, is "dust in the wind."

What does such a belief do to optimism and hope? To moral values? To the sanctity of life? To human dignity? To the sacredness of home and family? To law and order?

Dostoyevsky once remarked that if God is dead, then everything is justifiable. Philosopher Ravi Zacharias put it like this: "There is nothing in history to match the dire ends to which humanity can be led by following a political and social philosophy that consciously and absolutely excludes God."[7]

If, on the other hand, creation is true, then we are formed by a loving God in His own image, the crown of His creation, and heirs of eternal life through His Son, Jesus Christ. We are people of dignity and worth, surrounded by a fantastic universe that He made for our enjoyment. We are guided by sound moral principles leading to human health and happiness, and we are comforted by all the promises in the Book He has given. We have hope even during life's darkest hours, and we have value beyond that of any other living creature.

Which option seems most sensible to you?

SUMMARY

Hugh Ross was born in Montreal shortly after World War II. He became intrigued with the stars and the sky very early in life, and by age eight he was peering through his own telescope and spending hours in the library, reading books on physics and astronomy. By the time he was sixteen, he was presenting lectures on astronomy, and at seventeen he won the British Columbia Science Fair with his project on variable stars. Shortly after, he became the director of observations for the Vancouver branch of the Royal Astronomical Society of Canada. He earned his doctorate in astronomy from the University of Toronto and went on to do research on quasars and galaxies as a postgraduate fellow at the California Institute of Technology.

As Ross studied the heavens, he increasingly realized that the existence, complexity, and beauty of the universe pointed undeniably to a master designer and creator. He began to study the great religions of the world, reading the holy books of various faiths; but again and again he found himself disappointed. These books were full of scientific foolishness, of myth, conjecture, and ignorance. It was not until he read a Gideon Bible that it all began to make sense to him. As he read the Scripture, he said:

> I was amazed with the quantity of historical and scientific references and with the detail in them. I committed myself to spend at least an hour a day going through the Bible to test the accuracy of all its statements on science, geography, and history. At the end of eighteen months, I had to admit to myself that I had been unsuccessful in finding a single provable error or contradiction. I was now convinced that the Bible was supernaturally accurate and thus supernaturally inspired.[8]

He discovered something else, too. As he combed through the Bible looking for statements relating to science, he found the ones relating to salvation. He came to recognize that the God of the universe had become a man, Jesus Christ, who had died to provide forgiveness for those who trust Him for eternal life. "At 1:06 in the morning," he said, "I signed my name on the back page of my Gideon Bible, stating that I had received Christ as my Lord and Savior."

He found that the pathway through the stars and the trail through the Bible both led him to the same Almighty God. That is a discovery worth making.

FOR FURTHER DISCUSSION

1. What do Psalm 8 and Psalm 139 tell us about the role of creationism in developing spiritual and psychological health? What are some psychological implications for rejecting the Creator (see Isa. 45:9; Ps. 14:1; 53:1)?

2. How is the evolutionary hypothesis filtered into our culture by the entertainment industry? How can we best counter the influence such exposure might have on our children and resist the teaching of evolution in our community and local public schools?

FOR APPLICATION

1. Analyze Psalm 19. Make two columns and list the characteristics of God's two "books"—creation (vv. 1-7) and the Word (vv. 8-11). What conclusion did the psalmist reach at the end of the passage?

2. Conduct a group visit to a zoo, aquarium, botanical garden, planetarium, or art museum. Compile a list of the beauty you observe, and discuss the significance of beauty in the universe.

3. Undertake a project to supply your church library, public library, school library, and science teachers with materials about origins written by evangelical scholars.

Chapter Five

EXHIBIT C: THE FULFILLMENT OF PROPHECY

Historical Prophecy

A TATTERED GROUP OF Christians disembarked from the *Mayflower* and established a colony at Plymouth Harbor in 1620. They had sailed from England in search of religious freedom, and while anchored near Cape Cod, they made a covenant with one another, the Mayflower Compact. We now recognize the document as the first agreement for self-government ever put into force in America. The Pilgrims had undertaken their voyage, they said, to plant a new colony on these shores "for ye glorie of God, and advancemente of ye Christian faith." They thought of themselves as the new Israelites, as God's people who had left the land of oppression to possess a new and promised land.

William Bradford, who wrote the Mayflower Compact, later became the governor and the historian of Plymouth Colony. Imagine Bradford standing on the *Mayflower*'s deck in the cold of that December morning, addressing his shivering followers just before they left the ship. Suppose he said something like this:

> My fellow Pilgrims, today, December 26, 1620, we are setting foot on an untamed land and possessing an uncharted world. We will settle here in Plymouth Colony, encountering many hardships. But from these ragged beginnings a mighty nation will emerge— one that will become the home of the brave and the land of the free. As subjects of the British monarchy, the colonial government in this new land will endure for over one hundred years; but eventually our descendants will throw off England's yoke, fighting a war of independence and drafting a constitution dedicated to the proposition that all men are created equal. Our citizens will elect a leader, a president, and an assembly, a congress. America's boundaries

will push westward, driving out those noble tribes of Native Americans who now spread their teepees in the land of the setting sun. More and more states will join the union, but eventually a conflict will arise between them over the issue of human slavery. The states to the south will secede from the others, causing a great civil war that will rage long and bloody and desperate; but the union will be preserved through the courage and tenacity of a simple lawyer named Lincoln. An ensuing reconstruction period will usher in a great era of industrial growth, and America will become a global power, only to be thrust into a terrible and far-flung war that will engulf all the world. Our descendants will win that war, but will quickly stumble into an economic depression that will leave this land on the brink of ruin. Then another war will rage, a conflagration in which fifty million will die, and our posterity will prevail only by using a terrifying weapon of apocalyptic dimensions against the land of the rising sun. But following their costly victory, this land will lose its moral bearing; references to God will be expunged from public domains; sexual perversion and violence will swallow up the nation; entertainment will become the supreme pastime, and the Christianity we have come here to preserve will again be threatened.

Well, of course, Bradford never said any such words or made any such predictions, for no one can forecast specific events before they occur. We do not know what will happen two minutes from now, much less two years or two decades or two centuries ahead. No one can foretell the future with accuracy and detail and certainty.

Yet 3,500 years ago, standing on the banks of the Jordan River, Moses leaned on his staff and foretold his nation's history in advance. Other prophets added more and more details. The history of the Jews, prophesied in the Bible, was recorded in as much detail as my hypothetical example above.

Numerous specific predictions and prophecies are given in Scripture hundreds and sometimes thousands of years in advance. We can easily document that these predictions have come to pass exactly as predicted. According to Scripture, God provided these prophecies for the purpose of proving that His Word is trustworthy and authoritative. In other words, prophecy in the Bible is given to confirm the truth of Christianity.

The Lord said in the closing verses of Deuteronomy 18: "You may say to yourselves, 'How can we know when a message has not been spoken by the LORD?' If what a prophet proclaims in the name of the LORD does not take place or come true, that is a message the LORD has not spoken. That prophet has spoken presumptuously" (vv. 21-22).

In other words, how can we know if the Bible is true? We can ask: Does it make specific predictions about the future that come true? "I am God, and there is no other; I am God, and there is none like me. I make known the end from the beginning, from ancient times, what is still to come" (Isa. 46:9-10).

"Prophecy," says an old book on Christian evidences, "is a species of miracle. Prophecy which is fulfilled under circumstances that forbid the supposition of mere coincidence or accident, and the supposition that it causes its own fulfillment through some influence exerted by it, necessarily involves supernatural agency."[1] This kind of prophecy is unique to the Bible. No other religion on earth contains such an abundance of predictions and prophecies about the future, much of it minute in its specifications; and no other religion can document detailed fulfillments of its predictions in human history.

For our purposes, we can divide biblical prophecy into three categories—prophecies concerning Israel, prophecies concerning other nations, and prophecies concerning the Messiah. The next chapter will deal with Messianic prophecy, but in this chapter we will look briefly at the first two categories.

PROPHECIES CONCERNING ISRAEL

In the Old Testament, many passages giving the entire history of the nation of Israel in advance occur and recur. In Deuteronomy 29 and 30, just before the Israelites entered the Promised Land, Moses predicted a day when this very people, the Jewish nation, would be driven out of Palestine and dispersed among the nations of the world. But he also predicted a later day when the Jews would be regathered to Palestine and would again possess the land given to their forefathers. To put this prophecy in focus, look at the Bradford illustration again. What if Bradford had made a similar prediction?

> We are going to leave this boat and establish a colony that will eventually be an independent nation. But by and by our descendants, because of their sin, will be driven from America's shores, back to the corners of Europe, to the far quadrants of Asia, to the most remote spots of the world. They will be dispersed among distant nations while powerful forces of evil will occupy this land. But after years

of dispersion, they will be regathered from the four winds of the heavens and will again repossess and repopulate this land.

It never entered Bradford's mind to make such a prediction, of course, and for good reason. It is not logical for a group of exiles establishing a new home to predict such a scenario. But that is exactly what Moses predicted as he prepared the children of Israel for their occupation of Palestine. In Deuteronomy 29, he told these eager, ambitious, nationalistic Israelites that though they were taking over the Promised Land, another day would come when by their own foolishness they would be driven from the territory they were about to possess. He then predicted the land would become "a burning waste of salt and sulfur—nothing planted, nothing sprouting, no vegetation growing on it" (v. 23). However, he predicted that afterward "the LORD your God will restore your fortunes and have compassion on you and gather you again from all the nations where he scattered you. Even if you have been banished to the most distant land under the heavens, from there the LORD your God will gather you and bring you back. He will bring you to the land that belonged to your fathers, and you will take possession of it" (Deut. 30:3-5).

Jeremiah predicted that this banishment from the land would last seventy years, and after that (Isaiah added) the Jews would be allowed to return to Jerusalem through the edict of a world ruler named Cyrus.

There is more. The Bible further predicted a Messiah would come to Israel, but the Jews would reject and kill Him; He would be cut off; He would be pierced for the transgressions of His people (Isa. 53:5; Dan. 9:26). The Old Testament then predicted another banishment; and in Deuteronomy, Moses described the kind of life the Israelites would experience during their dispersion:

> You will be uprooted from the land you are entering to possess. Then the LORD will scatter you among all nations, from one end of the earth to the other. There you will worship other gods—gods of wood and stone, which neither you nor your fathers have known. Among those nations you will find no repose, no resting place for the sole of your foot. There the LORD will give you an anxious mind, eyes weary with longing, and a despairing heart. You will live in constant suspense, filled with dread both night and day, never sure of your life (Deut. 28:63-66).

That account, which sounds like the written record of a Holocaust survivor, is a perfect description of the entire history of the Jewish dispersion.

But the Bible becomes even more specific. The prophet Hosea said: "For the Israelites will live many days without king or prince, without sacrifice or sacred stones, without ephod or idol" (Hos. 3:4). In other words, the Jews would spend many days without a political system and without a temple or sacrifices. The Bible also predicted (for example, in Psalm 83) that the Jews would live in perpetual antagonism with their neighbors and half-brothers, the Arabs.

Incredibly, the Bible says that this second dispersion and banishment would also end by the Jews returning to the land of Israel. In other words, the Old Testament predicted that a Jewish Diaspora will happen not once, but twice! Isaiah 11:11-12 contains one of the most incredible predictions in Scripture:

> In that day the LORD will reach out his hand *a second time* to reclaim the remnant that is left of his people from Assyria, from Lower Egypt, from Upper Egypt, from Cush, from Elam, from Babylonia, from Hamath and from the islands of the sea. He will raise a banner for the nations and gather the exiles of Israel; he will assemble the scattered people of Judah from the four quarters of the earth (emphasis mine).

It happened exactly as Isaiah predicted. The Babylonians came in 587 B.C. and drove the Jews from Palestine; but seventy years later the Jews returned. The Messiah came and was cut off, literally pierced for the transgressions of His people. The Romans drove them from the land in A.D. 70; and in our own era, in 1948, the Lord reached out His hand a second time to reclaim the remnant of the Jews and return them to the land of Israel.

These are only a few of the predictions made about the nation of Israel, but from these passages let us summarize. The predictions involving Israel include these:

1. The Jews would possess Palestine and consider it their Promised Land.

2. They would disobey the law.

3. As a result, they would be driven from the land.

4. They would return to the land seventy years later.

5. A Messiah would come to them, but He would be cut off, pierced for the transgressions of His people.

6. They would again be driven from the land.

7. They would be dispersed to the four corners of the world.

8. During their dispersion, the land of Israel would become barren and dry, a burning waste of salt and sulfur.

9. Also during this dispersion, the Jews would be the object of unbelievable cruelty and persecution and constant suspense.

10. They would have no political leader, no king, no temple.

11. They would encounter perpetual antagonism from the Arab world.

12. Amazingly, after many years, they would return a second time to possess the Promised Land.

13. Jews would come from the far corners of the globe to repopulate Israel.

If William Bradford had stood on the deck of the *Mayflower* and made such a precise list of predictions, outlining an incredible course for the future history of the Pilgrims and their descendants, we would have called him deranged. Yet we can see how perfectly every detail of biblical prophecy is being fulfilled—every time we watch the evening news.

The return of Israel is unique in world history. Never before has an ancient people after two thousand years of exile, of nonexistence, of being dispersed and intermingled among all the nations of the earth, returned to their ancient homeland and reestablished their nation with their ancient language and currency. Where are the Edomites? Where are the Hittites? Where are the Jebusites?

Dr. William F. Albright, who was for many years professor of Semitic languages at Johns Hopkins University and one of the foremost archaeologists of modern times, said, "No other phenomenon in history is quite so extraordinary as the unique event represented by the restoration of Israel. . . . At no other time in world history has a people been destroyed, and then come back after a lapse of time and reestablished itself. It is utterly out of the question to seek a parallel for the recurrence of Israel's restoration after 2,500 years of further history."[2]

Even more to the point, it was all predicted in advance and in detail. No wonder when Frederick the Great of Prussia asked his court chaplain to prove to him the existence of God, the chaplain pointed to a Jew. What a privilege to live in our era, our moment in history, in which biblical prophecy is being fulfilled before our very eyes. What a moment to trust in God, preach the Gospel, and await the return of the King of Kings.

PROPHECIES CONCERNING OTHER NATIONS

God's prophecies are not limited to Israel; and although there are many other examples, the following items are suggested for further study.[3] The prophet Daniel, for example, gives us an overview of human history in its totality, specifically predicting the sequence of empires that would dominate the ancient world. In Daniel 2 King Nebuchadnezzar has a dream that Daniel interprets as being from God. In this vision, the Lord outlines the Babylonian, Persian, Greek, and Roman Empires in advance. Other chapters of Daniel expand and detail these prophecies.

The prophet Nahum provides predictions about the city of Nineveh, and their amazing fulfillment is among the most unusual in Scripture.

The destruction of the city of Tyre is described in Ezekiel 26 in specific detail, prophecies remarkably fulfilled by subsequent history.

The destruction of Jerusalem is accurately predicted thirty years in advance by Jesus in Matthew 24. Other verses in that chapter, along with predictive portions in the writings of John, Paul, and Peter, describe with power the tone and tenor of the "last days" of human history.

SUMMARY

All of this adds to the body of evidence, for "above all, you must understand that no prophecy of Scripture came about by the prophet's own interpretation. For prophecy never had its origin in the will of man, but men spoke from God as they were carried along by the Holy Spirit" (2 Pet. 1:20-21).

FOR FURTHER DISCUSSION

1. What events in current international affairs reinforce the view that Christ's return is at hand? How does previously fulfilled prophecy assure us about as-yet-unfulfilled prophecy?
2. What benefits come from studying prophecy? How would you respond to someone who said, "I'm not very interested in biblical prophecy. I like the parts of the Bible that tell me how to live today, but prophecy is for those who live in yesterday or tomorrow"?

FOR APPLICATION

1. Comb the magazines and newspapers for current news about the Middle East. Without being overly specific, discuss your view of how current world events may be paving the way for Christ to return.

2. Plan a personal or group study of the prophet Daniel. Read through the book of Daniel alongside a conservative commentary such as *Daniel: The Key To Prophetic Revelation* by John Walvoord.

3. Study 2 Peter 3, making a list of the qualities that: (1) will characterize the unbeliever during the last days, and (2) should characterize the believer during the last days.

Chapter Six

EXHIBIT C: THE FULFILLMENT OF PROPHECY

Messianic Prophecy

AT FIRST GLANCE, Jesus Christ and Alfred Hitchcock may appear to have little in common, but in at least one way they remind me of one another. Both men step from nowhere into pre-drawn silhouettes that fit them perfectly. While growing up, I watched Hitchcock do this week after week at the beginning of his television show. The program would open with an opaque configuration of a portly man; and a moment later Hitchcock would glide into this profile and pronounce a sinister "good evening."

In the same way, when Jesus Christ appeared in human history, He stepped into a pre-planned profile that molded itself around Him with astonishing accuracy, like a perfect silhouette. Every phase of His back-ground, birth, life, ministry, death, burial, and resurrection had been pre-drawn by the Old Testament prophets, and the fit was so exact that the New Testament writers used it as a centerpiece of evidence proving His divine identity. As A. T. Pierson put it, the Old Testament writers added "feature after feature and touch after touch and tint after tint, until what was at first a drawing without color, a mere outline or profile, comes at last to a perfect portrait with the very hues of living flesh."[1]

Consider, for example, the incident on the Emmaus Road in Luke 24. It was late afternoon on the day of Christ's resurrection, and two disci-ples were returning home from Jerusalem. While hiking along, they discussed the tragedy they had just experienced, the death of Christ by Roman crucifixion; and they discussed the rumors of the disappearance of His body from the tomb. Jesus Himself drew alongside them, but they were prevented from recognizing Him.

This is an oddity in Scripture. Nowhere else in the New Testament did Jesus disguise Himself, as it were. Nowhere else were His disciples prevented from identifying Him. Why did Jesus not want these two men to know who He was? "[Jesus] said to them, 'How foolish you are, and how slow of heart to believe all that the prophets have spoken! Did not the Christ have to suffer these things and then enter his glory?' And beginning with Moses and all the Prophets, he explained to them what was said in all the Scriptures concerning himself" (Luke 24:25-27).

When they arrived in Emmaus, Jesus joined the disciples for supper, and, as He ate with them, their eyes were opened to recognize Him. Then He suddenly vanished. The men immediately left for Jerusalem saying, "Were not our hearts burning within us while he talked with us on the road and opened the Scriptures to us?" (Luke 24:32). Finding the others in Jerusalem, they were exchanging stories when Jesus suddenly appeared among them saying, "This is what I told you while I was still with you: Everything must be fulfilled that is written about me in the Law of Moses, the Prophets and the Psalms" (Luke 24:44).

To return now to our primary question: Why did Jesus disguise Himself at first? Why were the Emmaus disciples kept from recognizing Him? Since nothing like this appears anywhere else in the Bible, there must have been a specific reason. There was. Jesus wanted His disciples to know beyond any shadow of doubt that He was the Messiah, King of Kings, and Prince of Peace risen from the dead. He had two ways of proving this. The first was to appear physically before them and by His concrete, resurrected body provide empirical proof of His resurrection.

But the second way was more important, more convincing, and more durable. He could prove His resurrection by showing them how He alone fulfilled—and with utmost perfection—the predictions and prophecies about His life, death, and resurrection made hundreds of years before by Old Testament prophets. So the roadside stranger led these two disciples on a tour of biblical prophecy, and by the time He had finished, they were so convinced that Christ was the risen Messiah that their hearts burned like a fire within them. Only after they had been convinced through fulfilled prophecy did He allow them to be convinced by visual evidence.

By hiding His real identity and directing us into the Old Testament, Christ pointed us to the overwhelming body of evidence for the veracity of Christianity found in the fulfillment of Old Testament Messianic prophecy.

THE MESSIAH'S FAMILY TREE

First, the Old Testament predicted the Messiah's family tree. The Jews, more than anyone else in antiquity, valued their ancestry and kept meticulous records of their genealogies. Priests, for example, who could not trace their family backgrounds were removed from office; and national genealogical tables for all the families of Israel were carefully preserved in Jerusalem until they were all destroyed in the destruction of that city by Roman forces in A.D. 70. Interestingly, the only genealogical records surviving the destruction of Jerusalem were those of Jesus Christ, which had been preserved by being included in the Gospels. This means that A.D. 70 ends the window of possibility into which any other Jew could establish his claim to be in the Messianic lineage.

What is that lineage? In Genesis, it states that of the three sons of Noah, the Messiah would come through Shem (Gen. 9:26-27; Luke 3:35). Of the descendants of Shem, the Messiah would come through Abraham (Gen. 12:2-3; 22:18). Of the two sons of Abraham, the Messiah would come through Isaac (Gen. 21:12). Of the two sons of Isaac, He would come through Jacob (Gen. 35:10-12; Num. 24:17). Of the twelve sons of Jacob, the Messiah would come, not from the noble Joseph, but from the scoundrel Judah (Gen. 49:10; Ps. 78:67-68). Of the descendants of Judah, all were rejected except the family of Jesse (Isa. 11:1-2). Of the sons of Jesse, all were rejected but the youngest, David (Jer. 23:5).

The Lord narrowed down the Messiah's family tree until it could only be a descendant of Abraham through Isaac, Jacob, Judah, Jesse, and David. The first words of the New Testament are: "A record of the genealogy of Jesus Christ the son of David, the son of Abraham" (Matt. 1:1).

THE MESSIAH'S BIRTH AND MINISTRY

According to the Old Testament, not only would Jesus be born from David's family, but in David's city—Bethlehem. Micah 5:2 says, "But you, Bethlehem Ephrathah, though you are small among the clans of Judah, out of you will come for me one who will be ruler over Israel, whose origins are from of old, from ancient times."

Isaiah 7:14 predicts, "Therefore the Lord himself will give you a sign: The virgin will be with child and will give birth to a son, and will call him Immanuel."

Malachi 3:1 and 4:5 say that the Messiah would be preceded by an Elijah-like figure who would live in the wilderness and cry out a message warning people to prepare the way for the Lord.

It was foretold that the coming Messiah will fill three different offices, which had only been fulfilled in one other person in human or Jewish history, the Genesis figure named Melchizedek—namely, prophet, priest, and king (Deut. 18:18; Ps. 110:4; Zech. 9:9).

It was foretold that the Messiah would exhibit superlative character traits, that He would be holy, righteous, good, faithful, innocent, zealous, meek, forgiving, patient, loving, and full of justice (Isa. 9:6-7; 11:1-5; 52:13—53:12).

It was foretold that His ministry would begin not in Judah or Jerusalem as one might expect, but in a predominantly Gentile area in the northern reaches of Israel called Galilee (Isa. 9:1).

It was foretold that His ministry would climax in Jerusalem, which the Messiah would enter humbly, riding on a young donkey before suddenly appearing boldly in the temple (Zech. 9:9; Hag. 2:7; Mal. 3:1).

It was also foretold that the Messiah's ministry would contain the element of the miraculous. He would heal the blind and deaf and lame (Isa. 35:5-6), and He would teach the people, uttering parables (Ps. 78:2). We are told, as incredible as it seems, that this long-awaited prophet, priest, and king would be publicly rejected by His own people, the Jews (Ps. 118:22). We are told that He would be betrayed by a friend for thirty pieces of silver, and the silver would be thrown on the temple floor and be used to buy a potter's field (Ps. 41:9; 55:12-14; Zech. 11:12-13).

THE MESSIAH'S DEATH

It was foretold that the Messiah would be smitten, and His followers would disperse like sheep who have suddenly and violently lost their shepherd (Zech. 13:7). It was foretold that the Messiah would be attacked and rejected, accused by false witnesses, and He would remain silent, refusing to come to His own defense (Ps. 35:11; 38:13; Isa. 53:7). It was foretold that He would be beaten and whipped and slain for the transgressions of those He came to save, and His death would be painful. Isaiah 53 and Psalm 22, as woven together below, present a powerful and remarkable portrait of the details of the execution of the Messiah, including these elements:

• *He was plunged into sorrow and rejected by both God and man*— "He had no beauty or majesty to attract us to him, nothing in his appearance that we should desire him. He was despised and rejected by men, a man of sorrows, and familiar with suffering. Like one from whom men hide their faces he was despised, and we esteemed him not. Surely he took up our infirmities and carried our sorrows, yet we considered him stricken by God, smitten by him, and afflicted" (Isa. 53:2-4).

• *He was publicly disrobed, and His clothing was gambled away by His executioners*—"I can count all my bones; people stare and gloat over me. They divide my garments among them and cast lots for my clothing" (Ps. 22:17-18).

• *He was executed with criminals*—"[He] was numbered with the transgressors" (Isa. 53:12).

• *His hands and feet were pierced*—"But he was pierced for our transgressions" (Isa. 53:5); "They have pierced my hands and my feet" (Ps. 22:16).

• *He would question why God had forsaken Him*—"My God, my God, why have you forsaken me?" (Ps. 22:1).

• *Nearby mockers would deride Him*—"All who see me mock me; they hurl insults, shaking their heads: 'He trusts in the LORD; let the LORD rescue him. Let him deliver him, since he delights in him'" (Ps. 22:7-8).

• *He would suffer acute thirst after massive losses of bodily fluids. His bones would be twisted from their joints, and His heart would melt and break from grief*—"I am poured out like water, and all my bones are out of joint. My heart has turned to wax; it has melted away within me. My strength is dried up like a potsherd, and my tongue sticks to the roof of my mouth; you lay me in the dust of death" (Ps. 22:14-15).

• *Despite severe pain and sorrow, He would utter no complaints*—"He was oppressed and afflicted, yet he did not open his mouth; he was led like a lamb to the slaughter, and as a sheep before her shearers is silent, so he did not open his mouth" (Isa. 53:7).

• *This amazing rejection, humiliation, and death of the Messiah would prove redemptive, being God's plan for saving His people*—"Surely he took up our infirmities and carried our sorrows. . . . But he was pierced for our transgressions, he was crushed for our iniquities. . . . the Lord has laid on him the iniquity of us all . . . for the transgression of my people he was stricken. . . . Yet it was the LORD's will to crush him and cause him to suffer. . . . For he bore the sin of many, and made intercession for the transgressors" (Isa. 53:4-12).

• *His corpse would be laid to rest in the borrowed tomb of a rich man*— "He was assigned a grave with the wicked, and with the rich in his death" (Isa. 53:9).

• *After His suffering and death, He would again see the light of life*— "Though the Lord makes his life a guilt offering, he will see his offspring and prolong his days, and the will of the LORD will prosper in his hand. After the suffering of his soul, he will see the light of life and be satisfied" (Isa. 53:10-11).

• *His death would justify many*—"By his knowledge my righteous servant will justify many, and he will bear their iniquities" (Isa. 53:11).

• *Following His return to life, He would be considered great*— "Therefore I will give him a portion among the great" (Isa. 53:12).

THE MATHEMATICAL POSSIBILITY

These are some of the prophecies made about Christ hundreds of years before His birth. Overall, about three hundred predictions stretch through all the books of the Old Testament. Peter Stoner, former Chairman of the Departments of Mathematics and Astronomy of Pasadena City College, Chairman of the Science Division of Westmont College, and Professor Emeritus of Science at Westmont, wrote a book called *Science Speaks*, in which he applied the mathematical principles of probability to various Old Testament predictions. In the chapter relating to Messianic prophecy, Stoner selected eight of the many predictions in Scripture relating to Christ's life and ministry and formulated the mathematical probability of their coming true in one man. He and his students wanted to know what the chances were that any one man, in accordance to predictive prophecy, would be born in Bethlehem, preceded by a forerunner, enter Jerusalem as a king riding a donkey, be betrayed by his friend for thirty pieces of silver, be placed on trial and though innocent make no defense for himself, and be crucified.

What is the chance that any man might have lived from the day of these prophecies down to the present time and fulfilled all eight of these predictions? His answer? The chance calculates to 1 in 10^{17}. What kind of chance is that? Cover the state of Texas with silver dollars to a depth of two feet, then mark one of those silver dollars and drop it somewhere into the pile, stirring thoroughly. The chance of a blindfolded man choosing the marked silver dollar is equal to the chances of all eight of those prophecies' being fulfilled in one man in history.

Yet there are not eight but three hundred predictions.[2]

THE BIG PICTURE

But there is something else. We should not only consider the three hundred predictions scattered here and there throughout the Old Testament but the whole tenor and tone of these thirty-nine books. If all we see are the specific predictions, we have not grasped the whole picture. It is impossible to read the Old Testament without noticing that the entire warp and woof of its content is held together by the threads of redemptive anticipation.

A. T. Pierson observed, "No miracle which He wrought so unmistakably set on Him the seal of God as the convergence of the thousand lines of prophecy in Him, as in one burning focal point of dazzling glory. Every sacrifice lit, from Abel's altar until the last Passover of the Passion week, pointed as with flaming fingers to Calvary's Cross."[3]

For example, in Genesis we read of Adam and Eve disobeying the Lord, resulting in death and a curse falling over all the earth. While meeting the fallen couple immediately afterward, God promised to provide a way of escape, of salvation. He promised to send One who would crush the serpent's head though being hurt Himself in the process (Gen. 3:15). As a token, an innocent animal was slaughtered to provide covering for the two sinners.

In Exodus we read of the Passover lamb, the blood of which would atone for sin; yet this sacrifice seemed to be pointing to something more. It appears that a scarlet cord was being stitched into the story. Moses promised the people that one day the Lord would raise up "a prophet like me," whose words would save the people (Acts 3:22). Even the heathen prophet Balaam, touched momentarily by the Holy Spirit, said, "I see him, but not now; I behold him, but not near. A star will come out of Jacob; a scepter will rise out of Israel" (Num. 24:17). We want to ask, "Whom were Moses and Balaam talking about?"

Job came along and cried, "I know that my Redeemer lives, and that in the end he will stand upon the earth" (Job 19:25). We want to ask, "Who is this Redeemer? Whom is Job talking about?" Then the prophets came along, all of them talking about a future coming Savior. Isaiah said, "For to us a child is born, to us a son is given, and the government will be on his shoulders. And he will be called Wonderful Counselor, Mighty God, Everlasting Father, Prince of Peace" (Isa. 9:6). We would like to ask Isaiah, "Whom are you talking about? Who is this strange child?"

We continue reading, soon coming to the end of the Old Testament, to the final book, Malachi. In Malachi 3 God promised to send His messenger to pave the way for the coming king. But in the next chapter, Malachi finished his writing, and the Old Testament abruptly ends with the cryptic words: "or else I will come and strike the land with a curse" (Mal. 4:6).

Is that any way to end a book? For a thousand years through thirty-nine installments stretching from Genesis to Malachi, the story has been building, issues have been raised, promises have been made, the anticipation has grown. Everything has pointed to a Savior who would be of the lineage of Abraham and David and who would deliver humanity from sin and despair. But the story abruptly concludes with the depressing words: "or else I will come and strike the land with a curse."

It seems like an incomplete story. It seems as if we have come to an intermission with only the first half of the story told. *Surely*, we think, *there must be more, another part, a completion.*

THE REST OF THE STORY

Then we turn the page, passing over four hundred years of history, and we find the Gospels, with the words: "A record of the genealogy of Jesus Christ the son of David, the son of Abraham" (Matt. 1:1).

As we continue reading, we meet someone who has descended from Shem, through Abraham, through Isaac, through Jacob, through Judah, through Jesse, and through David. We see One who was born of a virgin and named Immanuel. We see one who was born in the city of Bethlehem, though it was small among the clans of Judah. We see someone who was preceded by a forerunner after the tradition of Elijah. We see someone who was superlative in character traits, being holy, righteous, good, faithful, innocent, zealous, meek, forgiving, patient, loving, and full of justice—who, in the tradition of Melchizedek, was prophet, priest, and king. We see someone who began His ministry in Galilee and climaxed it in Jerusalem, and He healed the sick and taught the masses. We see One who was rejected by His own people, betrayed by a friend for thirty pieces of silver, deserted by His followers, accused by false witnesses, beaten and whipped and publicly stripped, His clothing being gambled away by soldiers. We see One who was executed between two criminals, whose hands and feet were pierced. We see One who suffered acute thirst, dying a death in which His bodily fluids were poured out, His bones were twisted out of their joints, and His heart melted like wax within Him. We see One who was buried in the borrowed grave of a rich man, and who, following His suffering, again saw the light of life. We see One who was wounded for our transgressions and bruised for our iniquities. We see the One whom all the world has awaited.

SUMMARY

Finally, we see One who said, "How foolish you are, and how slow of heart to believe all that the prophets have spoken! . . . Everything must be fulfilled that is written about me in the Law of Moses, the Prophets and the Psalms" (Luke 24:25, 44).

And when we see Him, it is not hard to believe, given the evidence. It is hard not to believe. For this is the One of whom it was written, "Blessed is he who comes in the name of the LORD" (Ps. 118:26).

FOR FURTHER DISCUSSION

1. Suppose you had a skeptic join your group. What objections might he make to the material contained in this chapter? How would you answer those objections?
2. The apostles pointed to the empty tomb and fulfilled prophecy as the major evidences confirming Christ's claims. Why does our humanistic civilization ignore or reject such strong confirmations?

FOR APPLICATION

1. Paraphrase Isaiah 53, pondering each word and sentence. Notice that the chapter not only describes the events of Christ's passion but also the theological implications behind them.
2. Prepare an evangelistic presentation based on the way Christ fulfilled Messianic prophecy. Be prepared to share, either formally or casually, this material with a questioning unbeliever.
3. Compare the prophecies about Christ's first coming with some of the major predictions about His second coming. How are they similar? How are they different? Make a study chart, listing the one on the left side and the other on the right side.

Chapter Seven

EXHIBIT D: TWIN WITNESSES—THE SAVIOR AND THE SCRIPTURES

The Unequaled Christ

THE FRENCH MATHEMATICIAN and philosopher Auguste Comte was talking about religion one day with the Scottish essayist Thomas Carlyle. Comte suggested they start a new religion to replace Christianity, based on positive thinking and mathematical principles. Carlyle thought a moment and replied, "Very good, Mr. Comte, very good. All you will need to do will be to speak as never a man spake, and live as never a man lived, and be crucified, and rise again the third day, and get the world to believe that you are still alive. Then your religion will have a chance to get on."

In surveying the evidence for the reliability of Christianity, we have looked at the empty tomb, the complexity of creation, and the fulfillment of prophecy. Now we come to the person of Christ Himself, about whom A. T. Pierson said, "He stands absolutely alone in history; in teaching, in example, in character, an exception, a marvel, and He is Himself the evidence of Christianity. He authenticates Himself."[1]

Christ alone, in His history and in His character, serves as a material witness in His own behalf. Anyone who wants to discredit Christianity must somehow explain away the uniqueness of Jesus of Nazareth.

DID CHRIST REALLY EXIST?

Early in the nineteenth century, it became fashionable in some circles to discount the uniqueness of Christ by questioning His very existence in history. In Germany some of the higher critics openly doubted the historicity of Christ, suggesting that the stories about Him were myths like those of the Greek and Roman gods, or perhaps shadowy legends like those of King Arthur and Camelot.

Today virtually no reputable historian tries to disavow the existence of Christ, because the evidence is irrefutable. The Epistles can be dated back to the first century; the Gospels can be dated very early; the existence of the church can be traced to the years immediately following the Resurrection. We also have many references to Christ in the writings of the first- and second-century church fathers such as Polycarp, Eusebius, Irenaeus, Ignatius, and others. Beyond that, there are inscriptions about Jesus of Nazareth on burial caskets in Jerusalem dating to the fourth decade of the first century and references to Christ and Christianity by ancient secular historians, including Tacitus, Seutonius, Josephus, and Thallus. In addition, we see references to Christ among the writings of officials of the ancient Roman government such as Pliny the Younger and the Emperors Trajan and Hadrian.

In fact, we know more about the life of Jesus Christ than about any other single figure in antiquity. The historian Will Durant, author of the massive *Story of Civilization*, devoted an entire volume of 751 pages to the years surrounding the life of Christ, and he entitled it *Caesar and Christ*. In it he noted the stylistic differences between the Gospels, but he concluded:

> The contradictions are of minutiae, not substance; in essentials the synoptic gospels agree remarkably well, and form a consistent portrait of Christ. No one reading these scenes can doubt the reality of the figure behind them. That a few simple men should in one generation have invented so powerful and appealing a personality, so lofty an ethic and so inspiring a vision of human brotherhood, would be a miracle far more incredible than any recorded in the Gospels. After two centuries of Higher Criticism the outlines of the life, character, and teachings of Christ remain reasonably clear, and constitute the most fascinating feature in the history of Western man.[2]

Simply put, Jesus is absolutely unequaled in history. Consider the following five areas in which Christ towers alone, unmatched, superlative, and far beyond any other man or woman since the beginning of the human race.

UNEQUALED IN HIS MAGNETISM

First, He is unequaled in His magnetism. In John 12:32, Jesus said, "But I, when I am lifted up from the earth, will draw all men to myself."

The media today is always on the prowl for people brimming with personal magnetism. It glamorizes those who carry themselves with a charismatic grace and charm, a power of personality. Franklin Roosevelt had it, and so did John F. Kennedy and Ronald Reagan.

I recently heard a reporter describe her impression of Reagan as he arrived in Washington, having just been elected president of the United States. She admitted she disliked Reagan's policies and philosophy, but she said that when she saw him emerge from the airplane, tall and handsome and self-assured, dressed in a dark overcoat with a white scarf around his neck, when she saw his thick, dark hair catching the snowflakes, and when she watched him bounce confidently down the steps, she was mesmerized. "There was an irresistible power to his presence," she said. "It drew you in. It was like an electric force."

It helps, if you are an actor, an actress, or a politician, to dispense this kind of charisma. A few in each generation have it, but only one person has ever radiated a magnetic field so powerful that it transcends centuries and millennia. Only one has impacted the world to such an extent that we recognize His centrality in history every time we date a letter or mark a calendar. Only one person has exercised supreme influence over every ensuing generation, touching both peasants and potentates, rich and poor, young and old, men and women. Only one person has given such comfort to the living and hope to the dying. Only one person has, like a bipolar magnet, attracted so many while at the same time, and with equal force, repelled so many.

Philip Schaff put it very well when he wrote:

> This Jesus of Nazareth, without money and arms, conquered more millions than Alexander, Caesar, Mohammed, and Napoleon; without science and learning, He shed more light on matters human and divine than all the philosophers and scholars combined; without the eloquence of schools, He spoke such words of life as were never spoken before or since and produced effects which lie beyond the reach of orator or poet; without writing a single line, he set more pens in motion, and furnished themes for more sermons, orations, discussion, learned volumes, works of art, and songs of praise than the whole army of great men of ancient and modern times.[3]

UNEQUALED IN HIS TEACHING

Christ is also unequaled in His teaching. When He stepped from the carpentry shop at age thirty and began addressing the Galilean multitudes with His Sermon on the Mount, they were "amazed at his teaching, because he taught as one who had authority, and not as their teachers of the law" (Matt. 7:28-29). A. T. Pierson observed that Christ taught the Scriptures as if He were its author rather than its commentator. How incredible, Pierson said, that He "comes forth from the carpenter's shop, where like all other well-trained Hebrew youth, he had learned his father's trade, and his first public utterance is the most original and revolutionary address on practical morals which the world has ever heard."[4]

His hometown of Nazareth marveled at His teaching, asking, "Where did this man get this wisdom and these miraculous powers? Isn't this the carpenter's son? Isn't his mother's name Mary, and aren't his brothers James, Joseph, Simon and Judas? Aren't all his sisters with us? Where then did this man get all these things?" (Matt. 13:54-56). Mark 11:18 tells us that when the chief priests and teachers of the law heard Him, they began "looking for a way to kill him, for they feared him, because the whole crowd was amazed at his teaching."

Even the military was challenged. When the chief priests sent the temple soldiers to arrest Christ, they came back empty-handed. The Pharisees, furious, asked, "Why didn't you bring him in?" The guards had a simple reply: "No one ever spoke the way this man does" (John 7:46).

And the remarkable thing about Jesus' teaching was the cohesive way He pulled together all spiritual truth into the reality of the Gospel. He taught that He Himself was the centerpiece of Scripture, the centerpiece of history, and the centerpiece in the plan of God for redeeming the human race. "For God so loved the world," he told Nicodemus, "that he gave his one and only Son, that whoever believes in him shall not perish but have eternal life" (John 3:16).

UNEQUALED IN HIS CLAIMS

Closely related is a third area of Christ's uniqueness. He is unequaled in the claims He made for Himself, for He claimed to be both God and man, with both natures being assimilated perfectly in one personality. It is interesting to remember that the only charge of which the Jewish leaders could convict Jesus, the only thing that stuck and led to His condemnation and execution, was His claim to be God.

Yet at the same time His favorite title for Himself was Son of Man. John Chrysostom said in the fourth century:

I do not think of Christ as God alone, or man alone, but both together. For I know He was hungry, and I know that with five loaves He fed 5,000. I know He was thirsty, and I know that He turned the water into wine. I know He was carried in a ship, and I know that He walked on the sea. I know that He died, and I know that He raised the dead. I know that He was set before Pilate, and I know that He sits with the Father on His throne. I know that He was worshipped by angels, and I know that He was stoned by the Jews. And truly some of these I ascribe to the human, and others to the divine nature. For by reason of this He is said to have been both God and man.

This is vital to us theologically, for according to the Scriptures, Christ had to be God in order to save us. In Isaiah 43:11 the Lord said, "I, even I, am the LORD, and apart from me there is no savior." Yet He had to also be human. Our salvation could only have been purchased by the death of an absolutely sinless and spotless sacrifice, for the Bible also says, "without the shedding of blood there is no forgiveness" (Heb. 9:22). A baby was thus conceived in a virgin's womb by the Holy Spirit, and He was named Jesus, for He came to save His people from sin.

UNEQUALED IN HIS RESURRECTION

No other leader of any other religion ever authenticated his message by rising from the dead. And no other leader of any other religion ever proved himself alive by "many convincing proofs." Consider the fact that Jesus staked His entire reputation and ministry on the proposition that He would rise again. As pointed out in chapter 2, Christ predicted at the beginning, in the middle, and at the end of His ministry that He would rise from the dead. "Destroy this temple," He said, referring to His body, "and I will raise it again in three days" (John 2:19).

"For as Jonah was three days and three nights in the belly of a huge fish," He asserted, "so the Son of Man will be three days and three nights in the heart of the earth" (Matt. 12:40). "The Son of Man is going to be betrayed into the hands of men," He said. "They will kill him, and on the third day he will be raised to life" (Matt. 17:22-23). In making these predictions, He was staking the future of the Gospel on His ability to return to life following His execution. And in fulfilling the predictions, He was authenticating His message and proving Himself with power to be the Son of God.

No other figure in history has ever made such claims, and no one else has ever risen from the dead by his own power. None but Christ.

UNEQUALED IN HIS IMPACT ON HISTORY

Last of all, He is unequaled in human history. An unknown author once summed it up with these well-worn words:

> He was born in an obscure village, the child of a peasant woman. He worked in a carpenter shop until he was thirty. Then for three years he was an itinerant preacher. He never wrote a book. He never held an office. He never had a family or owned a house. He never went to college. He never traveled 200 miles from the place where he was born. He never did one of the things that usually accompany greatness. He had no credentials but himself. He was only thirty-three when the tide of public opinion turned against him. His friends ran away. He was nailed to a cross between two thieves. When he was dead, he was laid in a borrowed grave through the pity of a friend. Nineteen centuries have come and gone, and today he is the central figure of the human race, and the leader of the column of progress. I am far within the mark when I say that all the armies that ever marched, all the navies that ever sailed, all the parliaments that ever sat, all the kings that ever reigned, put together, have not affected the life of man on earth as has that One Solitary Life.

Lew Wallace was a famous general and literary genius of the nineteenth century who, along with his friend Robert Ingersoll, decided to write a book that would forever destroy "the myth of Christianity." For two years, Wallace studied in the libraries of Europe and America. Then he started his book. But while writing the second chapter, he found himself on his knees crying out to Jesus Christ in the words of Thomas, "My Lord and my God." The book he was writing became the great novel about the times of Christ, *Ben Hur.*

Bill Murray was a businessman who grew up in a home that had rejected God so completely that his mother once told him, "I don't care if you become a drug addict or a bank robber or if you bring home a boyfriend instead of a girlfriend. There's just one thing I don't want you to do in life—become a Christian."

So Bill grew up sexually promiscuous, moving from one marriage to another, from one sexual partner to another. He began drinking and drugging; wanting more and more possessions, he worked himself to exhaustion. He collapsed inwardly and found himself praying to the God he had rejected, "Please, get me out of this mess!" Going to an all-night bookstore, he found a Bible buried under a stack of pornographic magazines, and he began reading about Jesus Christ. He was especially drawn to Luke's Gospel, and, as he read it, he grew convinced that Jesus was unique in history, unequaled in His magnetism, His teachings, His claims, His resurrection, and His impact on history.

Bill received Christ as his Savior, and it changed his life. He gave up his drinking, drugging, promiscuous sex, and rampant materialism. He found the inner peace and joy he had always been looking for. Bill Murray, ironically, is the son of atheist Madalyn Murray O'Hare, who used him as the plaintiff in the Supreme Court case that outlawed prayer in the public classrooms of America.

C. S. Lewis likewise came to Christ almost against his will, convinced by the evidence that Christianity was true. He used the power of deduction, later explaining:

> A man who was merely a man and said the sort of things Jesus said would not be a great moral teacher. He would either be a lunatic, or else he would be the Devil of Hell. You must make your choice. Either this man was, and is, the Son of God; or else a madman or something worse. You can shut Him up for a fool, you can spit at Him and kill Him as a demon; or you can fall at His feet and call Him Lord and God. But let us not come with any patronizing nonsense about His being a great human teacher. He has not left that open to us. He did not intend to.[5]

SUMMARY

There are only three logical options when it comes to Jesus. Either He was a liar, a hoax, a deceiver, an impostor—in which case you have to explain how He could also have been the greatest spiritual leader and the most selfless atoning sacrifice the world has ever known; or He was a lunatic—in which case you have to explain how He could have been the wisest teacher the world has ever seen; or He is the God-man—which is just who He claimed to be.

Liar, lunatic, or Lord.

The answer, it seems, is obvious.

FOR FURTHER DISCUSSION

1. How would you respond to someone who questioned the existence of Christ in human history? What would you say if the person questioned the accuracy of the Gospels in describing Him?
2. In what ways was Jesus Christ unlike all other men and women in history? In what ways was He like us?

FOR APPLICATION

1. Find a passage in the Gospels in which Christ amazed the crowds. Spend some time visualizing the scene. In group study, brainstorm the details of the scene. Think of the human dimensions—might it have been an overcast day? Cold and rainy? Might it have been hot? Were people sweating? Was a baby nearby crying? Try to place yourself in the setting and begin to feel the wonder and surprise of the multitudes at the remarkable presence of Christ.

2. Make a list of the wonders of Christ's personality, attributes, and actions. Find hymns or Scripture songs that praise Him for those things and plan a simple service of worship and adoration.

3. In one sentence, have various group members answer the question of Mark 4:41: "What manner of man is this?" (KJV).

Chapter Eight

EXHIBIT D: TWIN WITNESSES—THE SAVIOR AND THE SCRIPTURES

The Solidarity of Scripture

"TO MY OWN MIND," wrote J. Sidlow Baxter, "the most satisfying proofs that the Bible is divinely inspired are not those which one 'reads up' in volumes of religious evidences or Christian apologetics, but those which we discover for ourselves in our own study of the Book. To the prayerful explorer the Bible has its own way of revealing its internal credentials."[1]

The nineteenth-century scholar A. T. Pierson agreed: "Every study of the Bible is a study of the evidences of Christianity. The Bible is itself the greatest miracle of all."[2]

That discovery once reassured a young man named Morgan—G. Campbell Morgan. He had grown up in a Christian home, never questioning that the Bible was the Word of God. But in college his faith was severely challenged, and he began to entertain doubts. "The whole intellectual world was under the mastery of the physical scientists," he later said, "and of a materialistic and rationalistic philosophy. Darwin, Huxley, Tyndall, Spencer, Bain. There came a moment when I was sure of nothing."

In those days opponents of the Bible appeared every Sunday in great lecture and concert halls across England, attacking Christianity and the Bible; and these brilliant atheists and agnostics troubled the young student. He read every book he could find, both for and against the Bible, both for and against Christianity, until he was so confused, so riddled with doubt that he felt he could not go on.

In desperation he closed his books, put them in his cupboard, and turned the lock. Going down to a bookshop, he bought a new Bible, returned to his room, sat down at his desk, and opened it. He said, "I am no longer sure that this is what my father claims it to be—the Word of God. But of this I am sure. If it be the Word of God, and if I come to it with an unprejudiced and open mind, it will bring assurance to my soul of itself." As he looked into the book before him, studying its form, structure, unity, and message, he was amazed. He later said, "That *Bible* found *me*. I began to read and study it then, in 1883, and I have been a student ever since."[3]

In this chapter we will study the unity, wonder, and cohesiveness of the Scriptures. If there is a God, if He has revealed Himself through Jesus Christ, and if that message is recorded in a book that He Himself has inspired, then we should find evidence for that in that book. The Bible should authenticate itself. It should be different from every other book and give evidence of supernatural origin, design, and insight.

It should be a book like no other.

Well, consider this. The first portions of the Bible were written during the days of Moses, perhaps in the fifteenth century B.C. The final section was probably written by John near the end of the first century A.D. So the time span covered by the biblical writers is 1,500 or 1,600 years.

Can you imagine beginning a book now, having your son add to it thirty or forty years from now, then his son after him, and other descendants continuing into the twenty-second century, then to the twenty-third, on to the year 3000, then to 3300 and so forth? Can you imagine this book being finished in the year A.D. 3600—about sixteen centuries from now? Even if we could imagine it, what would such a book be like? A disjointed jumble of oddly matched observations and speculations?

We cannot even imagine it.

Not only that, but the Bible was written in sixty-six installments by over forty authors, and these authors were from every strata of society. Some were rich and some were poor. Some were renowned and others were unknown. Some were kings; others were peasants. Among the authors of Scripture were fishermen, scholars, politicians, philosophers, theologians, shepherds, farmers, and rabbis.

These sixty-six installments were written in many places—deserts and mountains, prisons and palaces, islands and tents. They were written in various emotional states; some of the writings reflect great joy and others dismal despair. The Bible was written in three languages—Hebrew, Aramaic, and Greek—on three different continents—Europe, Asia, and Africa.

And these sixty-six installments written over 1,600 years by forty men in three languages on three continents cover hundreds of controversial subjects.

Yet these writings fit marvelously together into one cohesive, neverending story, with an appropriate beginning, a logical ending, a consistent theme, and a central character around which every part revolves. There is an organizing theme and an obvious scheme. No one has described this phenomenon better than A. T. Pierson:

> In such a book there would not be likely to be unity; for all the human conditions were unfavorable. No other book was ever composed or compiled in circumstances so disadvantageous to a harmonious moral testimony and teaching. Here are some sixty or more separate documents, written by some forty different persons, scattered over wide intervals of space and time, strangers to each other; in three different languages, in different lands with marked diversities of literary style, and by men of all grades of culture and mental capacity, from Moses to Malachi; and yet in not one respect are their doctrinal and ethical teachings in conflict; from beginning to end, we find in them a positive oneness of doctrine, which amazes us. Even where, at first glance, there appears to be conflict, as between Paul and James, we find on closer examination that instead of standing face to face, beating each other, they stand back to back, beating off common foes. And, most wonderful of all, this moral unity could not be fully understood till the book was completed. The process of preparation, like a scaffolding about a building, obscured its beauty—even the workmen upon it could not appreciate its harmony—but when John added the capstone and declared that nothing further should be added, the scaffolding fell, and a great cathedral was revealed.[4]

Pierson goes on to suggest that we try an experiment that I will word according to my own frame of reference. I have a set of books called the Harvard Classics that includes some of the greatest books ever written. There are works by Augustine, Emerson, Milton, Homer, Plutarch, Pascal, and others. Suppose I take ten of those books written by ten different authors, all in English, who lived and wrote over a period of one hundred years. Suppose I extract references from those ten books about, not hundreds of controversial subjects, but only one. And suppose I splice these extracts together. Would I have a unified volume with plot and plan, scheme and theme, unity and design—all in full agreement?

No. I would have a conglomeration.

But with the Bible you do not have a conglomeration. You have a circle and a thread.

THE CIRCLE

By circle, I mean that when you read the first three chapters of Genesis and the last three chapters of Revelation, you find the story of the Bible coming full circle. The issues and dilemmas raised in Genesis 1—3 are addressed and perfectly resolved in Revelation 20—22. Compare these verses from the first and last chapters of the Bible:

"In the beginning God created the heavens and the earth." (Gen. 1:1)
   "Then I saw a new heaven and a new earth, for the first heaven and the first earth had passed away." (Rev. 21:1)

"Now the LORD God had planted a garden in the east, in Eden; and there he put the man he had formed." (Gen. 2:8)
   "I saw the Holy City, the new Jerusalem, coming down out of heaven from God, prepared as a bride beautifully dressed for her husband. And I heard a loud voice from the throne saying, 'Now the dwelling of God is with men.'" (Rev. 21:2-3)

"Then the man and his wife heard the sound of the LORD God as he was walking in the garden in the cool of the day." (Gen. 3:8)
   "He will live with them. They will be his people, and God himself will be with them and be their God." (Rev. 21:3)

"And the LORD God made all kinds of trees grow out of the ground— trees that were pleasing to the eye and good for food. In the middle of the garden [was] the tree of life." (Gen. 2:9)
   "On each side of the river stood the tree of life, bearing twelve crops of fruit, yielding its fruit every month. And the leaves of the tree are for the healing of the nations." (Rev. 22:2)

"A river watering the garden flowed from Eden." (Gen 2:10)
   "Then the angel showed me the river of the water of life, as clear as crystal, flowing from the throne of God and of the Lamb down the middle of the great street of the city." (Rev. 22:1-2)

"The gold of that land is good." (Gen. 2:12)

"The wall was made of jasper, and the city of pure gold, as pure as glass. . . . The great street of the city was of pure gold, like transparent glass." (Rev. 21:18, 21)

"The LORD God took the man and put him in the Garden of Eden to work it and take care of it." (Gen. 2:15)
   "And his servants will serve him." (Rev. 22:3)

"The LORD God commanded the man, '. . . you must not eat from the tree of the knowledge of good and evil, for when you eat of it you will surely die.'" (Gen. 2:16-17)
   "He will wipe every tear from their eyes. There will be no more death or mourning or crying or pain, for the old order of things has passed away." (Rev. 21:4)

"Now the serpent was more crafty than any of the wild animals the LORD God had made. . . . So the LORD God said to the serpent, '. . . I will put enmity between you and the woman, and between your off-spring and hers; he will crush your head, and you will strike his heel.'" (Gen. 3:1, 14-15)
   "And I saw an angel coming down out of heaven, having the key to the Abyss and holding in his hand a great chain. He seized the dragon, that ancient serpent, who is the devil, or Satan, and bound him. . . . And the devil . . . was thrown into the lake of burning sulfur." (Rev. 20:1-2, 10)

"Cursed is the ground because of you." (Gen. 3:17)
   "No longer will there be any curse." (Rev. 22:3)

"So the LORD God banished [man] from the Garden of Eden. . . . After he drove the man out, he placed on the east side of the Garden of Eden cherubim and a flaming sword flashing back and forth." (Gen. 3:23-24)
   "On no day will its gates ever be shut." (Rev. 21:25).

In the Bible's first three chapters, God created the heavens and the earth, but it was spoiled. In the last three chapters, He recreates them.

In the first three, His prepared paradise was lost; in the last three, it is regained.

In the first three, fellowship with God was severed. In the last three, it is reestablished. In the first three, the tree of life was removed; in the last three, it is recovered.

In the first three, the river and gold of Eden were lost; in the last three, we discover a city of gold with a river running through it.

In the first three, death entered the human story. In the last three, death is abolished. In the first three, the serpent showed up in the Garden; in the last three, he is thrown into the lake of burning sulfur.

In the first three chapters, a curse fell on the earth; in the last three, the curse is lifted. In the first three, humanity was banished from paradise; in the last three, we discover our eternal home.

Any good book opens with a dilemma, a question, a hook quickly leading into a scintillating plot with theme, structure, ups and downs, and ins and outs before finally resolving itself with a conclusion that unravels the tangles, pulls all the strands together, and (hopefully) ends happily.

Such books do not just happen. They are created by authors of great skill and ability. When you open the Bible, you see God creating the heavens and the earth and placing human beings in paradise to enjoy fellowship with one another and with Himself. You see the serpent and sin, with death occurring, and mankind being driven from paradise into a sin-cursed world.

Sixty-six books later, you end the story with God re-creating the heavens and the earth, again placing human beings in paradise to enjoy fellowship with one another and with Himself. You see the serpent, sin, and death judged, the curse lifted, and men and women, washed in the blood of the Lamb, living abundantly and eternally.

The story comes full circle.

THE THREAD

But there is also a thread stretching from the Garden of Eden to the New Jerusalem, from Genesis to Revelation. This crimson thread tells us how God reclaimed paradise for fallen sinners, how He saved us from death and restored us to glory. We will trace it, beginning in Genesis 3.

Genesis 3 says that following the disobedience of the first couple, "The LORD God made garments of skin for Adam and his wife and clothed them" (Gen. 3:21). When Adam and Eve disobeyed God, they became aware of their nakedness. They felt ashamed of themselves and had an instinctive desire to "cover up," to hide. The Lord killed an animal, shedding its blood, to provide a covering for man's sin. The next chapter gives us an indication of the kind of animal needed for such a sacrifice: "Now Abel kept flocks, and Cain worked the soil. In the course of time Cain brought some of the fruits of the soil as an offering to the LORD. But Abel brought fat portions from some of the firstborn of his flock. The LORD looked with favor on Abel and his offering" (Gen. 4:2-4). It was a lamb. From the earliest chapters of Genesis, written by Moses long before Isaiah or John or Paul, a theme emerges—the doctrine of the Lamb.

This doctrine emerges more fully in Genesis 22: "'The fire and wood are here,' Isaac said, 'but where is the lamb for the burnt offering?' Abraham answered, 'God himself will provide the lamb for the burnt offering, my son'" (vv. 7-8).

In Exodus the theme becomes clearer. In chapter 12 the Lord said: "Tell the whole community of Israel that on the tenth day of this month each man is to take a lamb for his family, one for each household. . . . Take care of them until the fourteenth day of the month, when all the people of the community of Israel must slaughter them at twilight. Then they are to take some of the blood and put it on the sides and tops of the doorframes of the houses where they eat the lambs. . . . On that same night I will pass through Egypt and strike down every firstborn . . . and I will bring judgment on all the gods of Egypt. . . . The blood will be a sign for you on the houses where you are; and when I see the blood, I will pass over you" (vv. 3, 6-7, 12-13).

Leviticus states what kind of lamb is acceptable. Some twenty times, the Lord told the priests that the lamb must be spotless and without blemish: "When anyone brings from the herd or flock a fellowship offering to the LORD . . . it must be without defect or blemish to be acceptable" (Lev. 22:21).

It fell within the ministry of Isaiah to begin applying these principles to a great coming Redeemer. Returning to Isaiah 53, we read: "He was led like a lamb to the slaughter, and as a sheep before her shearers is silent, so he did not open his mouth" (Isa. 53:7). Up to this point, the sacrificial lamb has always been an animal, but now Isaiah shows us that the Lamb of God is a person, one who will be "pierced for our transgressions . . . crushed for our iniquities," for "we all, like sheep, have gone astray . . . and the LORD has laid on him the iniquity of us all" (Isa. 53:5, 6).

Then we turn to John's Gospel and notice the dramatic and surprising way John the Baptist introduces the Messiah. He does not say, "Behold the King of Kings and Lord of Lords." He does not say, "Here now at last after all these centuries is the Messiah." He does not say, "Here is the God-man, the divine made human." He says something totally unexpected: "Look, the Lamb of God, who takes away the sin of the world!" (John 1:29).

In Acts 8 the connections are made even clearer as Philip witnesses to the Ethiopian: "The eunuch was reading this passage of Scripture: 'He was led like a sheep to the slaughter, and as a lamb before the shearer is silent, so he did not open his mouth.' . . . The eunuch asked Philip, 'Tell me, please, who is the prophet talking about . . . ?' Then Philip began with that very passage of Scripture and told him the good news about Jesus" (Acts 8:32, 34-35).

Peter punches the point home in his epistle: "For you know that it was not with perishable things such as silver or gold that you were redeemed from the empty way of life handed down to you from your forefathers, but with the precious blood of Christ, a lamb without blemish or defect. He was chosen before the creation of the world, but was revealed in these last times for your sake. Through him you believe in God, who raised him from the dead and glorified him, and so your faith and hope are in God" (1 Pet. 1:18-21).

And finally we see this theme reach a crescendo in the book of Revelation: "Then I saw a Lamb, looking as if it had been slain, standing in the center of the throne, encircled by the four living creatures and the elders. . . . Then I looked and heard the voice of many angels, numbering thousands upon thousands, and ten thousand times ten thousand. They encircled the throne and the living creatures and the elders. In a loud voice they sang: 'Worthy is the Lamb, who was slain, to receive power and wealth and wisdom and strength and honor and glory and praise!'" (Rev. 5:6, 11-12).

The Bible ends with these words: "I did not see a temple in the city, because the Lord God Almighty and the Lamb are its temple. The city does not need the sun or the moon to shine on it, for the glory of God gives it light, and the Lamb is its lamp. . . . Nothing impure will ever enter it, nor will anyone who does what is shameful or deceitful, but only those whose names are written in the Lamb's book of life" (Rev. 21:22-23, 27).

There is a thread that progressively unrolls throughout Scripture, from Genesis to Revelation, pulling all the books together around one master theme: God loves us, we disobeyed Him, and He redeemed us through the blood of the Lamb.

Abel showed us the necessity of the Lamb. Abraham showed us the provision of the Lamb. Exodus showed us the slaying of the Lamb. Leviticus showed us the character of the Lamb. Isaiah showed us the personality of the Lamb. John the Baptist identified the Lamb. Peter described the enthronement of the Lamb, and Revelation tells us about the Lamb's endless reign and the eternal life of those whose names are written in the Lamb's book of life.[5]

SUMMARY

So if you want to debunk Christianity, you have a formidable task. You have to deny the empty tomb of Jesus Christ. You have to explain away the creation and complexity of the universe. You have to ignore fulfilled prophecy, both historical and Messianic. You have to disregard the uniqueness of Jesus Christ. You have to explain how a book written over 1,600 years by forty authors in three languages on three continents, covering hundreds of controversial subjects, can fit together as though written by a master author, having an opening and closing that come full circle and a unified theme that runs like a crimson thread from beginning to ending.

No wonder it convinced a skeptic named Morgan.

FOR FURTHER DISCUSSION

1. The Bible frequently refers to itself as food for the soul. How is the Bible like food, and how is Bible study like eating?
2. How is the Bible different from all other books? How is it similar to other books?

FOR APPLICATION

1. In a concordance, trace the word *blood* through the New Testament. Compile a list of truths about the blood of Christ.
2. On a chalkboard or wall chart, list the parallels between the first three chapters and the last three chapters of the Bible.
3. Compose a response to someone who believes that the Bible is a good and valuable book, but who is not convinced it is the infallible and inerrant Word of God.

Chapter Nine

EXHIBIT E: THE HISTORICAL RELIABILITY OF THE BIBLE

The Reliability of the Biblical Documents

VISITING THE ROTUNDA of the National Archives in Washington is an almost sacred experience. The hallowed room, round and regal and as solemn as a cathedral, is designed to preserve one of the greatest documents in human history—the American Declaration of Independence. This venerable document rests under green-filtered glass in a bronze case filled with inert helium gas and is lowered every night into a climate-controlled vault some twenty-two feet below the floor.

Christians also have a founding document on which our spiritual faith and freedom are based, one more fabulous than even the Declaration of Independence. It is the Bible, composed over 1,600 years in sixty-six installments, written in three languages on three continents. It has a central theme and a unifying scheme; and Christians, believing it inspired by God, consider it infallible, inerrant, and sufficient for all human need.

When we say the Bible is without error, we are talking about the original books and parchments—the actual original documents produced by the inspired authors themselves. The original autographs, as they are called. We do not claim that the copies of those documents are inerrant. If I wanted, for example, I could transcribe Psalm 23 right now and deliberately add or subtract words. I could say, "The Lord is my Friendly Alpine Shepherd . . ." That unfortunate rendition would involve adding words to Scripture and thereby be an errant copy. So while the originals were inerrant, it is possible that mistakes and distortions have crept into our text during the transmission process through the centuries. The copies are not necessarily infallible, only the originals—which we no longer have.

That raises a question. Can we really trust the Bible? Is Scripture sufficiently trustworthy to stake our lives upon it? The first question in the mind of a skeptic is not whether the Bible is theologically inspired, but whether the Bible is historically reliable. That question demands a twofold answer.

ACCURATE IN ITS COMPOSITION

First, is the Bible accurate in its composition? Were the biblical documents written by biographers and historians who told the truth and who actually lived during the times they describe? Some people claim that the Gospels, for example, were pieced together by unknown authors or editors from oral traditions and from various fables that may or may not have factual basis in history. "We don't really know who wrote the Gospels," they might claim, "and we certainly can't believe all the miracles and the material about the Jesus-figure. It's part legend, part fable with maybe a shred of history somewhere in the shadowy past."

But it takes time for fables and legends to develop, and we have copies and fragments of the Gospels dating to within a generation of the apostles. Increasingly, liberal thinkers who had dated the composition of New Testament books in the second and third centuries have been forced by recent scholarship and archaeological discoveries to push their dates back to the first century. A few years ago, Young-Kyu Kim demonstrated that an early collection of Paul's letters (P^{46}) should no longer be dated at A.D. 200 but a full hundred years earlier, to the late first century. Two scholars, German papyrologist Carsten Thiede and journalist Matthew D'Ancona, in their book *Eyewitness to Jesus*, claim that the date of three scraps of parchment housed at Magdalen College, Oxford, and containing fragments from Matthew's Gospel can be dated to the first century. Their conclusions have created a stir.

We do not have space to study each New Testament book, but one is particularly illustrative, the Gospel of Luke. Few scholars question the traditional authorship of Luke. It is generally agreed that the third Gospel and the book of Acts were written by the physician Luke, and it is widely admitted that Luke wrote his Gospel prior to writing Acts. Acts can be dated sometime in the early sixties of the first century, so the Gospel of Luke must be dated somewhat earlier. Notice the way he begins his Gospel: "Many have undertaken to draw up an account of the things that have been fulfilled among us, just as they were handed down to us by those who from the first were eyewitnesses and servants of the word" (Luke 1:1-2).

Luke was explaining that many accounts of the life of Christ were in circulation in the mid-first century. Many biographers and writers had published works about Jesus, some of them actually based on eye-witness accounts. Others, however, were less reliable: "Therefore, since I myself have carefully investigated everything from the beginning, it seemed good also to me to write an orderly account" (Luke 1:3).

Luke was undeniably brilliant, possessing remarkable literary abilities and a deep knowledge of the Greek language. He was the only non-Jewish author of the Bible. Yet he wrote more of the New Testament than any-one else—28 percent. He was a physician and a scientist. He was a writer and a medical missionary. He has proved himself a historian of first rank. Here he tells us that before writing his Gospel, he did the work of an investigative journalist, recording his findings in an orderly manner based on careful investigation: "It seemed good also to me to write an orderly account for you, most excellent Theophilus, so that you may know the certainty of the things you have been taught" (Luke 1:3-4).

Did Luke deliver? Absolutely. He tied everything into history and gave us historical anchors all along the way, both in his Gospel and Acts. His historical pegs have proven accurate even in minute points. For example, notice the way he began chapter 2: "In those days Caesar Augustus issued a decree that a census should be taken of the entire Roman world. (This was the first census that took place while Quirinius was governor of Syria.) And everyone went to his own town to register" (Luke 2:1-3).

Luke did not just say that Joseph and Mary traveled to Bethlehem. He said they traveled there because of a census instituted by Caesar Augustus and that this particular census occurred while a man named Quirinius was governor of Syria. A hundred years ago, critics had a field day with that statement, finding no evidence in history to suggest that Caesar ever issued such a decree. Furthermore (critics charged) there was nothing to suggest that Quirinius was ever governor of Syria at the time prescribed by Luke.

Then a series of discoveries were made. Sir William Ramsay, the Scottish archaeologist, dug up first-century documents showing that the Roman Empire conducted a regular taxpaying census every four-teen years and that this system originated in the days of Caesar Augustus. Another document was found in Egypt, an edict of G. Vibius Maximus written on papyrus, describing the procedure used in such a census, directing taxpayers to return to their ancestral towns to register. Another inscription discovered by Ramsay in Antioch showed that with brief interruptions, a man named Quirinius functioned as military governor in Syria from 12 B.C. to A.D. 16.

Notice in the next chapter, Luke 3, how meticulously Luke nails down his historical references: "In the fifteenth year of the reign of Tiberius Caesar—when Pontius Pilate was governor of Judea, Herod tetrarch of Galilee, his brother Philip tetrarch of Iturea and Traconitis, and Lysanias tetrarch of Abilene—during the high priesthood of Annas and Caiaphas, the word of God came to John son of Zechariah in the desert" (Luke 3:1-2).

Sound like misty legend and fabricated fable? Anything but! Luke tacks John's ministry to the wall of history using six different pins. John the Baptist appeared when (1) Tiberius Caesar was in his fifteenth year of rule; (2) Pontius Pilate was governor of Judea; (3) Herod was tetrarch of Galilee; (4) Herod's brother Philip was tetrarch of Iturea and Traconitis; (5) Lysanias was tetrarch of Abilene; and (6) Annas and Caiaphas were sharing the office of high priest. Most of these facts are easy to verify, but a couple of them caused problems. A hundred years ago, critics were attacking Luke's reference to Lysanias, saying, "The only Lysanias mentioned in history was killed in 36 B.C., sixty years before John the Baptist." But the critics were stilled when archaeologists excavated an inscription near Damascus, stating that a man named Lysanias was indeed tetrarch of Abilene at the time mentioned by Luke.

The skeptics also made hay with Pontius Pilate. For most of modern history his name has been absent on every historical document we have from the ancient world. Critics charged that Pilate was a fabrication. But a stone excavated in Caesarea has the name Pontius Pilate plainly engraved for all the world to see. He was governor of Judea during the very time given by Luke, and he was headquartered at Caesarea.

I mentioned in an earlier chapter how William Ramsay traveled to the Middle East to disprove Luke's historical references and how, to his great surprise, he found the writings of Luke accurate in their tiniest details. This is even more remarkable when we consider that every other historian in the ancient world—men like Polybius, Quintilian, Xenophon, Josephus, and even Thucydides—did not hesitate to misrecord the facts to suit their own purposes. But in Luke we find the singular historian from antiquity who has been proven right at every point.

In summary, we have documents reaching to within a generation of the original writers, and the details that emerge from the New Testament's pages show these documents to be historically reliable and well-researched. They were accurate in their composition. That leads to our second question: Is the Bible trustworthy in its transmission?

TRUSTWORTHY IN ITS TRANSMISSION

By transmission, we mean the process by which the biblical documents were copied and recopied through the ages from the original autographs down to the age of the printing press. Were the handwritten copies and the copies of copies kept reasonably pure, so that we have a Bible that, practically speaking, reflects accurately the words of the original autographs?

What about the Old Testament? Until recently we had the problem of few known ancient Hebrew manuscripts, for the Jews destroyed tattered and worn copies out of reverence for the Word of God. We also know that prior to A.D. 900, Jewish history was in turmoil, and national life was disrupted by war, banishment, and dispersion.

But we also know that scribes and copyists were meticulous beyond belief. They even devised elaborate systems for numbering every letter and word; if a scribe was off by even one letter, they would destroy the whole manuscript. We had good reason to believe that the Old Testament had been faithfully transmitted; but nonetheless our oldest extant (existing) copy of a Hebrew manuscript dated from about A.D. 1000, and there was no way to compare it to more ancient copies to see if errors had intruded.

Until 1947. A boy in the Dead Sea village of Qumran threw a rock at one of his goats. When the stone flew through the opening of a small cave, the boy heard a shattering sound. He climbed up the cliff and into the cave to make one of the greatest archaeological discoveries of all time—the Dead Sea Scrolls—ancient scrolls hidden in clay jars in caves to preserve them from the invading Romans.

For the first time, we had Hebrew manuscripts from pre-Christian times. Fragments of almost every book in the Bible have been found, and the book of Isaiah is preserved in one complete copy and in another tattered copy. The result? Gleason Archer says, "Even though the two copies of Isaiah discovered in Qumran Cave 1 near the Dead Sea in 1947 were a thousand years earlier than the oldest dated manuscript known (A.D. 980), they proved to be word for word identical with our standard Hebrew Bible in more than 95 percent of the text. The 5 percent of variation consisted chiefly of obvious slips of the pen and variations in spelling."[1]

Dr. R. Laird Harris compared our oldest Hebrew manuscript of Isaiah 53 with the tattered Isaiah found at Qumran. He found seventeen letters that were different. "Ten of these are mere differences of spelling, like 'honor' or 'honour,' and make no change at all in the meaning. Four more are very minor differences, such as the presence of the conjunction which is often a matter of style. The other three letters are the Hebrew word for 'light,' which is added in verse 11. Out of 166 words in this chapter only this one word is really in question [after 1,000 years of transmission], and it does not at all change the sense of the passage. This is typical of the whole manuscript."[2]

We have other ways to affirm the quality of the textual transmission of the Old Testament. About two hundred years before Christ, for example, a group of Jewish scholars in Alexandria translated the Scriptures from Hebrew into Greek. We can compare the ancient Greek versions with the Hebrew text of the Old Testament.

We also have an ancient Samaritan Pentateuch and the Targums (oral paraphrases of Old Testament passages). All of these sources provide enormous evidence that the Hebrew text of the Old Testament has been preserved in trustworthy fashion; and though there are variations here and there, no major doctrine is impacted. The variations, for the most part, involve matters of spelling, style, and grammar.

What about the New Testament? Here we are on even firmer ground, for we have an abundance of ancient manuscripts on which painstaking research has been performed. The original autographs and the earliest copies were written on papyrus, and they were read and reread until they wore out. In the fourth century, copiers began using a more durable material, parchment made from the skins of animals. Parchment became the primary writing material for a thousand years, before paper began to be widely used in the thirteenth century.

It would be fascinating to know what happened to the original autographs. Tertullian wrote in about A.D. 208 that the apostles' "own authentic writings" (*authentica*) were read in the churches. We do not know whether he meant that Paul's actual originals were still being read or that the church was using faithful copies. At any rate, our oldest fragment of the New Testament reaches almost back to the days of the apostles themselves.[3] The Ryland Fragment, dating from the early second century, contains five verses from the Gospel of John. Scholars date it at approximately A.D. 125. Since the Gospel of John was probably written about

A.D. 100, this particular fragment was in circulation within a quarter of a century or so of the original.

It is interesting that the German higher critics and the European textual critics of the nineteenth century shook the faith of many by claiming that John's Gospel was written by an unknown author one or two hundred years after John's death. They claimed that the theological symbolism and depth of John's Gospel would have taken that long to evolve, and thus it was not really written by John and does not really date from the first century. Then the Lord allowed this little fragment to be discovered in Egypt, and it happened to contain verses from the Gospel according to John. With one small discovery, thousands of skeptical lectures, books, articles, and dissertations were blown down like a scarecrow in a storm.

We also have the Chester Beatty Papyri, dating from about A.D. 200, containing large portions of the New Testament. We have two complete New Testaments, the Sinaiticus and the Vaticanus, both dating back to the 300s.

In addition to this and the other five thousand Greek manuscripts, we have many ancient translations or versions, including Jerome's Vulgate—the New Testament translated into Latin in the late 300s. We have old Syriac and Latin translations dating to about A.D. 150 and an early Egyptian translation made in about 200. We have countless quotations from the New Testament preserved in the writings of church fathers of the first, second, and third centuries and in the Lectionaries (readings used in public worship).

In short, the number of manuscripts in support of the reliability of the New Testament text (and their chronological proximity to the original writings) is far beyond anything else known in human literature. There are only nine or ten good manuscripts of Caesar's *Gallic War*, for example, and the oldest extant manuscript is a thousand years later than the original. There are only seven copies of Plato, and the time span between the original and the copy is 1,200 years. Thucydides lived about the time of Malachi, and he wrote his history near the end of the Old Testament era. The earliest extant copy we have of Thucydides dates from A.D. 900, 1,300 years later than the original. How many ancient copies of Thucydides come from A.D. 900 or later? Only eight. Yet no one questions the accuracy of Thucydides. He is viewed as a first-rate historian.[4]

However, we have not ten or eleven manuscripts, but five thousand Greek manuscripts of the New Testament, dating to within twenty-five years or so of the actual writings. We have translations, quotations, and readings going back to the earliest times of the Christian church. "From the standpoint of literary evidence," writes Professor Berkeley Mickelsen, "the only logical conclusion is that the case for the reliability of the New Testament is infinitely stronger than that for any other record of antiquity."[5]

When we compare all these manuscripts, we do find occasional variations in the style and spelling and sometimes in wording. That is why many translations have footnotes, showing that a certain word or passage here and there can be rendered in an alternate way. There are actually two different families of Greek manuscripts, and New Testament scholars spend much of their time discussing the differences between them. Yet the vast majority of verses are identical, and the manuscripts provide a unified witness. No key doctrine of the Christian faith is in any way invalidated or threatened by textual uncertainty.

Does this prove the Bible is the inspired Word of God? No. But it shows us that the Bible provides a reliable foundation for our faith. It is trustworthy, both in its accurate composition and in its reliable transmission. "Many people say the Bible is a myth," Vance Havner once quipped. "But they're myth-taken, myth-guided, and myth-erable."

SUMMARY

When you hold the Gospels in your hand, you are holding documents that give us reliable accounts, well researched by biographers and writers including the most eminent historian of the ancient world, of a man from Nazareth who lived for thirty years as a village carpenter. He preached for the next three years, making claims for Himself that no other had ever made, and driving home His claims with so much evidence that He overturned the Jewish theology of His audience and convinced them that He was, in fact, the Messiah of Israel and the Master of the world. He healed the blind, raised the dead, and filled the hopeless with joy. He allowed Himself to be executed in a most excruciating manner, and then His grave was found vacated. He showed Himself alive by many convincing proofs and so changed the world that today, after two thousand years of human history, His message is more widely believed than ever before. These things were investigated thoroughly from the beginning and written in an orderly account that we might have a solid basis for faith, that we may know the certainty of the things we have been taught.

FOR FURTHER DISCUSSION

1. Why is it vital to insist upon and defend the infallibility and inerrancy of the Scriptures? Why is such an insistence and defense valid and reasonable?

2. What if other writings were discovered from the hands of the apostles? For example, the apostle Paul must have written many letters that never became part of Scripture and have been lost to history. If such a letter were found, should it be considered inspired and infallible? Should it be added to our canon of Scripture?

FOR APPLICATION

1. Using sources from the bibliography, compile a listing of the major ancient manuscripts now in our possession.

2. Appoint a group member to locate a video or to tape a television show about the mysteries of the Bible, especially dealing with the Dead Sea Scrolls. After watching, discuss its significance to apologetics.

3. Discuss the question of circular reasoning as it relates to bibliology. We believe in Christ because the Bible tells us about Him. We believe in the Bible, because Christ affirmed it as inspired. Logically speaking, how do we frame our arguments for the trustworthiness of Scripture without falling into the circular reasoning trap?

Chapter Ten

EXHIBIT E: THE HISTORICAL RELIABILITY OF THE BIBLE

The Evidence of Archaeology

IN ADDITION TO the archaeological discoveries mentioned in the last chapter, there are thousands of other artifacts, inscriptions, sites, and excavations that help confirm the historical reliability of the Bible. Due to space limitations, we will discuss only ten of them.

THE SILVER SCROLLS (AMULETS)

The Dead Sea Scrolls pushed back the date for the oldest extant copies of Old Testament Scripture from A.D. 980 to about 150 B.C., but a more recent discovery has now pushed the date back even further. In 1979 archaeologists in the Hinnom Valley of Jerusalem discovered nine burial caves that had been carved in the rock over 2,600 years ago, during the days when the descendants of David still sat on Israel's throne. Inside these tombs were two silver scrolls, rolled up and very tiny, designed to be worn on a necklace. They were caked with dirt and so fragile that no one dared unroll them.

Finally, the Israel Museum rinsed the scrolls in a solution of salt and acid to remove the corrosion and sprayed them with a film-like substance. Researchers started unrolling the tiny scrolls millimeter by millimeter. Faint scratches on one of them were recognized as coming from Scripture, from Numbers 6: "The LORD bless you and keep you; the Lord make his face shine upon you and be gracious to you; the LORD turn his face toward you and give you peace" (vv. 24-26). This is the oldest fragment of Scripture known to man, dating back 2,600 years.

HEZEKIAH'S TUNNEL

Modern biblical archaeology had its beginnings with a man named Edward Robinson, born in Connecticut in 1793. His father was a Congregationalist minister, and Edward grew up studying the Bible. He excelled in theological studies in America and Europe and in 1838 visited Palestine in the company of a missionary named Eli Smith. Robinson and Smith walked across the Holy Land with a Bible in one hand and a compass in the other, searching for the ruins and sites of ancient towns.

Among Robinson's discoveries—perhaps the first great archaeological find in modern history—was one that confirmed 2 Kings 20:20: "As for the other events of Hezekiah's reign, all his achievements and how he made the pool and the tunnel by which he brought water into the city, are they not written in the book of the annals of the kings of Judah?"

As Robinson poked about Jerusalem, he went to the Pool of Siloam. The water level was lower than usual, and Robinson took off his shoes and examined the pool. He discovered an entrance to a tunnel and followed the passage about eight hundred feet under the city. He had discovered the very water system designed by King Hezekiah and referred to in 2 Kings 20:20. Robinson eventually made it all the way through the subterranean channel, sometimes having to lie flat and push himself along with his elbows. By studying the chisel marks, he determined that men had started on both ends, tunneling toward each other and meeting in the middle.

A few years later, a Jewish school child playing in the Pool of Siloam felt markings of some kind on the walls of the pool. Archaeologists lowered the water level again and found this inscription, dating from the days of Hezekiah himself, inscribed on the stone in purest biblical Hebrew: "While there were still three cubits to be cut through, there was heard the voice of a man calling to his fellow, for there was an overlap in the rock on the right and on the left. And when the tunnel was driven through, the quarrymen hewed the rock, each man toward his fellow, ax against ax; and the water flowed from the spring toward the reservoir for 1,200 cubits, and the height of the rock above the heads of the quarrymen was 100 cubits."[1]

This is generally considered the most famous inscription ever found in Jerusalem. Because it was discovered in the nineteenth century while Jerusalem was under Turkish rule, the inscription was cut from the tunnel and taken to Istanbul where it now resides in the Istanbul Archaeological Museum.

THE HOUSE OF DAVID

Amazingly, many scholars of the nineteenth and twentieth centuries doubted the existence of King David. Their objections centered on two things. First, the stories attributed to him are fantastic—maintaining that he was a young shepherd boy who killed a giant with his slingshot and later established a royal dynasty. Second, there had never been historical confirmation outside the Bible of a king named David.

But in 1993 a discovery among the ruins of the northern Israeli town of Dan changed that. We now have a monument from antiquity inscribed with references to the "House of David." The inscription refers to the fact that the king of the house of David was defeated by the king of Damascus in a battle like the one in 1 Kings 15:20: "Ben-Hadad [King of Syria] agreed with King Asa and sent the commanders of his forces against the towns of Israel. He conquered . . . Dan." This is the first reference to the personage of David outside the Bible, but it confirms his existence (and confounds the critics).

Hot on the heels of that discovery came a new edition of the text of the Moabite Stone by Andre Lemaire. The Moabite Stone (the Mesha Stela) was uncovered in 1868 and dates to just after the death of King Ahab. It gives the Moabite account of its wars with Israel. The content of the Moabite Stone describes the king of Moab, Mesha, who led his people to break away from bondage to Israel. Omri, a king of Israel, is mentioned by name, thus giving extra-biblical evidence to his existence. The Moabite rebellion is mentioned in 2 Kings 1:1 and 3:5. Some of the text is hard to translate, for the stone was broken in unfortunate places. But Lemaire, professor at the Institute of Semitic Studies of the College de France, has prepared a reconstruction of its text. He published his findings in *Biblical Archaeology Review*, and, comparing his discovery with the inscription from Dan, he said:

> The recent discovery at Tel Dan of a fragment of a stela containing a reference to the "House of David" (that is, the dynasty of David) is indeed sensational. The inscription easily establishes the importance of Israel and Judah on the international scene at this time—no doubt to the chagrin of those modern scholars who maintain that nothing in the Bible before the Babylonian exile can lay claim to any historical accuracy. This fragment from the Tel Dan stela has been hailed because it contains the name "David," supposedly for the first time in ancient Semitic epigraphy. But this claim is not true—or at least not quite true; I believe these same words—the "House of David"—

appear on the famous Moabite inscription known as the Mesha stela, also from the 9th century (B.C.). While for most scholars the reference to the "House of David" on the Tel Dan fragment was quite unexpected, I must confess I was not surprised at all. I have been working on the Mesha stela for the past seven years, and I am now preparing a detailed edition of the text. Nearly two years before the discovery of the Tel Dan fragment, I concluded that the Mesha stela contains a reference to the "house of David." Now the Tel Dan fragment tends to support this conclusion.[2]

CAIAPHAS

A similar story involves Caiaphas, Israel's high priest during the time of Jesus. Critics charged that no such man ever existed. His name had never been found in ancient documentation apart from the Bible. But in 1990 a burial cave excavated in Jerusalem contained a tomb marked with the family name of Caiaphas. Coins in the tombs proved they were from the first part of the first century. *U. S. News and World Report* began their cover story on biblical archaeology by saying:

> From the fertile valley of the Euphrates to the desolate sands of the Sinai, it is a land of ancient civilizations whose material history lies buried in the rocky hills and deserts but whose stories of patriarchs and prophets have survived the centuries in sacred Scriptures. Now the sands of the Middle East are yielding secrets hidden for thousands of years that shed surprising new light on the historical veracity of those sacred writings. In this decade alone, archaeologists in Israel have unearthed amazing artifacts pertaining to two important figures from the Bible: a 9th century B.C. stone inscription bearing the name of David, the ancient Israelite warrior-king who killed the giant Goliath, and a first century A.D. tomb believed to be that of Caiaphas, the Jerusalem high priest who presided over the trial of Jesus. In both cases, it was the first archaeological evidence ever discovered suggesting that the two existed beyond the pages of the Bible. "These finds are tremendously important finds," says James K. Hoffmeier, chairman of archaeology and biblical studies at Wheaton College in Illinois. "They will certainly cause anxiety for the skeptics."[3]

THE PATRIARCHS

One of the frustrating areas of archaeological studies for biblical scholars has been the period of the patriarchs. Abraham, Isaac, and Jacob lived in tents as desert nomads. They left few archaeological traces. For years skeptics have questioned the historicity of the book of Genesis and the biblical story of Israel's beginnings. But consider these factors:

1. *The ruins of many of the cities of Genesis have been found, and those ruins are consistent with the biblical story.* For example, we have excavations at Ur, city of Abraham, showing it to be a huge, thriving city with an advanced civilization during the days of Abraham. The citizens lived in comfortable homes, and the children attended school to learn reading, writing, arithmetic, and religion. The cities of Shechem, Ai, Bethel, and Hebron have also been found. The book of Genesis says that when Abraham left Ur, he traveled toward the Promised Land, stopping in the city of Haran in upper Mesopotamia where his father died. Excavations now underway by archaeologists from the University of Chicago have shown Haran to be a thriving city during the days of the patriarchs. Shortly after, it was abandoned and remained uninhabited until the seventh century B.C. One archaeologist said, "It's highly improbable that someone inventing the story later would have chosen Haran as a key location when the town hadn't existed for hundreds of years."[4]

2. *The very name Abraham has been discovered in ancient clay tablets dating from the sixteenth century B.C.*

3. *In the ruins of ancient Nuzi (near modern Baghdad), a library of clay tablets was uncovered that demonstrates many of the customs we read about in the patriarchal stories.* For example, in Genesis 15 a childless Abraham laments that his servant Eliezer would inherit all his property. The Nuzi tablets shed light on this passage. In those days if a couple was childless, a trusted friend or servant would become that couple's heir, almost like an adopted son. But if the couple later conceived and gave birth to a son, the agreement with the servant was nullified, and the natural son became the heir. There are also several incidents described in the Nuzi tablets in which a barren woman asked her husband to take her slave as a sort of surrogate wife to produce an heir, much as Abraham did with Hagar.

The critics who asserted that the Genesis stories were late-dated fables have had to abandon many of their beliefs because it is not reasonable that so much authentic local color and customs could be injected into stories written centuries after the fact. Tablets at Nuzi (as well as those found at Ebla and Mari) confirm the cultural climate and customs of the Genesis accounts.

THE EXODUS

Another frustrating area for evangelical archaeologists has been the Exodus, for most scholars have consistently asserted that archaeological evidence for the Exodus of Israel from Egypt is lacking. After all, nomads wandering through the desert do not leave many ruins.

But recently some skeptics have been questioning their assumptions. For example, Charles Krahmalkov, Professor of Ancient Near East Languages at the University of Michigan, had always believed that the Exodus account was a fabrication. But while studying the inscriptions on the Temple of Amon at Karnak, dating from the reign of Thutmose III (c. 1504-1450 B.C.), he was astonished to find a listing of cities that corresponds remarkably to the cities listed in Numbers 33. Based on that and other evidence, Krahmalkov has changed his mind.[5] He said, "In short, the Biblical story of the invasion of Transjordan that set the stage for the conquest of all Palestine is told against a background that is historically accurate." He added, "I am not a conservative believer. I am a scholar of the old school who believes we try to let our data speak to us. We don't force it into a preconceived idea. I find myself astonished at the results. [The ancient historians of Israel] preserved in the Bible true historical sources of a very early age. They cannot possibly have invented them."[6]

THE CONQUEST OF HAZOR

Joshua 11 says that the king of Hazor mobilized the northern kings to fight against the Israelites during the conquest of the Promised Land. Verses 10 and 11 say, "At that time Joshua turned back and captured Hazor and put its king to the sword. (Hazor had been the head of all these kingdoms.) . . . he burned up Hazor itself." The next book, Judges, says that Hazor, having rebuilt itself to an extent, was again destroyed, this time by Deborah and Barak (Judges 4).

In 1955 Israeli archaeologist Yigael Yadin was excavating this bottle-shaped site ten miles north of the Sea of Galilee. He found a Canaanite worship site that had been deliberately defiled. He found a tiny statue, a false god whose head had been cut off. Yadin immediately thought of Deuteronomy 12, the passage in which the Israelites were instructed to defile and destroy pagan worship sites. Further studies showed that Hazor had been a teeming city, population of about 20,000, that had been suddenly destroyed by fire during the days of Joshua and the Judges. Yadin's discovery corresponded exactly to the Old Testament accounts.

THE CLAY SEAL OF GEMARIAH

Ever heard of Gemariah? He was an obscure figure in Scripture who lived in Jerusalem during the days of Jeremiah, an official in Solomon's temple with his office on an upper level of the temple itself. According to Jeremiah 36, the prophet Jeremiah wrote a sermon condemning the corruption of the national leaders. His servant read the scroll to the people in the office chamber of Gemariah. When King Jehoiakim heard of it, he sent for the scroll and hacked it to pieces. Among those who warned the king of his foolishness and begged him not to destroy the scroll was Gemariah. Shortly afterward, the Babylonians burned down the city of Jerusalem.

In 1980 the Jewish archaeologist Yagil Shiloh, excavating in Jerusalem near the temple mount, found a room containing fifty-one clay seals (bullae) that had originally been affixed to important documents. These seals bore the names of various officials during the days of the monarchy. Most remarkable of all of them was one bearing the name of a scribe named Gemariah, the son of Shaphan, who was employed in the royal court of King Jehoiakim toward the end of the seventh century B.C.—the very Gemariah mentioned in Jeremiah 36. The condition of the seal told its story. It had originally been affixed to a papyrus document, but a terrible fire had burned out of control, destroying the document and baking the clay seal as hard as brick, thus preserving it.

CAPERNAUM

Of all the ruins and sites in the Holy Land, perhaps the most interesting is Capernaum, where Jesus Himself lived. When Christ left Nazareth, he settled down in this lakeside village, home of Peter and Andrew. In the centuries that followed, the village disappeared from notice, and scholars had no idea where it had been. But archaeologists have been excavating Capernaum for the past one hundred years, and we have a village along the Roman Road, the Via Maris, with lined streets, the foundations of houses and shops, and the ruins of a magnificent synagogue.

Of particular interest is a house, evidently the home of a fisherman, which became a meeting place for early Christians and was later expanded into a church. Here archaeology and tradition merge to give us reasonable certainty that this is the very house of Peter himself, the house in which Jesus stayed, the house in which the invalid was lowered through the roof. Archaeologists have confirmed that this house was a single-story dwelling dating from the first century. Fishhooks were even found among the ruins. But toward the middle of the first century, it started receiving special treatment, becoming a house-church and then being enlarged as a gathering place for Christians.

Nearby are the ruins of a synagogue. Excavations have shown it to have been built on a first-century foundation, the foundation of the very synagogue commissioned, built, and paid for by the Roman centurion of Luke 7. This is the foundation of the same synagogue in which Jesus began His ministry. Visitors can go there today, walk down the street from Peter's house to the synagogue, and stand at the very spot where Jesus stood and taught the people near Galilee's shore.

THE "JESUS BOAT"

Almost as interesting as Capernaum is the ancient boat buried in the mud, discovered in 1986. A terrific drought had befallen Galilee that year, and the water level of the Sea of Galilee dropped dramatically. Local inhabitants noticed the oval outline of a boat buried deep in the mud, and Israeli archaeologists immediately began excavating it. The boat dates from the time of Jesus. Today the fragile remains of the "Jesus Boat" are housed in a museum and submerged in preserving solutions. The vessel measures twenty-six feet long and seven feet wide and would have carried about fifteen men. It could be, in fact, the very boat Jesus used when sailing across the Sea of Galilee. It was likely sailing the Sea of Galilee when Jesus was there, exactly as described in the Gospels.

SUMMARY

Admittedly, the jury of archaeological evidence is still out, especially as it relates to the world of the patriarchs, the nature of the Exodus under Moses, and the extent of the conquest under Joshua. But the eminent American archaeologist William Dever said that a century and a half of exploration "has for all time demolished the notion that the Bible is pure mythology. The Bible is about real, flesh-and-blood people, in a particular time and place, whose actual historical experience led them irrevocably to a vision of the human condition and promise that transcended anything yet conceived in antiquity."[7]

Nelson Glueck, the Jewish archaeologist, stated it even more plainly: "It may be stated categorically that no archaeological discovery has ever controverted a biblical reference."[8] On the contrary, archaeology has debunked the charges of one skeptic after another and has confirmed to a large extent the historical reliability of the Bible.

The critics, it seems, keep trying to bury the Bible. But the archaeologists bury the critics and keep digging the Bible back up.

FOR FURTHER DISCUSSION

1. Can archaeology "prove" the Bible? If not, what role can a study of archaeology play in the believer's faith and knowledge of Scripture?
2. Is making a pilgrimage to the Holy Land worth the time and money?

FOR APPLICATION

1. Perhaps a member of your group has visited the Middle East or even participated in an archaeological dig. Ask him or her to share impressions. Locate a travel video of Israel and view it together.
2. Visit your church or school library and examine copies of the magazine *Biblical Archaeological Review*. You might not agree with every article or interpretation in the magazine, but become familiar with the general field of archaeology and study the pictures carefully. Share some of the best pictures with the group.
3. Consider going on an archaeological dig. You will have to pay your own way, and the work is hard. But the costs are less than most other overseas trips, and the experience is invaluable. *Biblical Archaeological Review* provides a listing of digs each year.

Chapter Eleven

EXHIBIT F: THE EXPERIENCE OF CHRISTIANITY

The Witness of Changed Lives

DOES IT WORK? If Christianity is true, we would expect it to make a difference in the experience of its adherents. We would expect it to change their lives in a positive and profound way. Pragmatism is an inadequate philosophy for life, but it is not totally without merit. Christianity "must not only provide us with the materials of a great philosophy, a great theology," notes Bernard Ramm. "It must have a relevancy or tangency to human experience."[1]

In this chapter, I have selected a handful of witnesses from a pool of millions, allowing their stories to serve as collaborating evidence for the truth of the power of the Gospel.

WITNESS 1: SAUL OF TARSUS

Our first witness was the first century's greatest opponent of the Christian faith. Saul of Tarsus spearheaded the persecution against the early church, determined to extinguish the flame of Christianity before it could spread. He later told King Agrippa his story:

> The Jews all know the way I have lived ever since I was a child, from the beginning of my life in my own country, and also in Jerusalem. They have known me for a long time and can testify, if they are willing, that according to the strictest sect of our religion, I lived as a Pharisee. . . . I too was convinced that I ought to do all that was possible to oppose the name of Jesus of Nazareth. And that is just what I did in Jerusalem. On the authority of the chief priests I put many of the saints in prison, and when they were put to death, I cast my vote against them. Many a time I went from one synagogue to another to have them punished, and I tried to force them

to blaspheme. In my obsession against them, I even went to foreign cities to persecute them. On one of these journeys I was going to Damascus with the authority and commission of the chief priests. About noon, O king, as I was on the road, I saw a light from heaven, brighter than the sun, blazing around me and my companions. We all fell to the ground, and I heard a voice saying to me in Aramaic, "Saul, Saul, why do you persecute me? It is hard for you to kick against the goads. . . . Now get up and stand on your feet. I have appeared to you to appoint you as a servant and as a witness of what you have seen of me and what I will show you. I will rescue you from your own people and from the Gentiles. I am sending you to open their eyes and turn them from darkness to light, and from the power of Satan to God, so that they may receive forgiveness of sins and a place among those who are sanctified by faith in me." (Acts 26:4-18)

How could the greatest destroyer of Christianity become its greatest defender? How can you explain his metamorphosis, as he gladly endured a lifetime of shame, suffering, and the executioner's sword to spread the faith he had once labored to ruin?

The mind of Saul of Tarsus was brilliant. His training was superb. His passion was unquenchable. His background and heritage flowed with the Jewish blood of a hundred generations. Yet in one moment he was transformed from the greatest enemy the early church ever faced into the greatest missionary the world has ever known.

What power could so change a life? The Gospel! The Gospel's chain of witnesses from the days of Saul of Tarsus to our own is unbroken, and it grows stronger still.

WITNESS 2: JOHN NICHOLSON

There are stories from each generation of the Christian era. But I would like to skip from Paul's day to our own times, looking at stories of people whose lives have been transformed by the sheer force of Jesus Christ through nothing more than their eyes falling upon the powerful pages of Scripture. Perhaps the purest testimonies are of those who are changed—not by persuasive personalities or spellbinding oratory or magnetic appeals—but by merely reading the Word of God itself, finding in it the power and truth necessary to meet the deepest needs of their lives.

Such testimonies are heard constantly by an organization based in Nashville, Tennessee, which had its beginnings a hundred years ago.

John Nicholson checked into the Central Hotel at Boscobel, Wisconsin, on September 14, 1898. Because the hotel was full, he was asked to share a room with Samuel Hill. The two discovered they both were Christians, and that night they read Scripture and prayed together before retiring.

Some time later they met again and, remembering their previous refreshing fellowship, decided to establish an organization for Christian businessmen. These men, many of them sales representatives on the road, eventually determined to provide a witness for Christ by placing Bibles in the hotels they frequented. Thus was born the ministry of the Gideons.

What results have come from such a distribution of God's Word? The testimonies are legion, but among them is Gary Fossen's.

WITNESS 3: GARY FOSSEN

Gary had an outwardly happy childhood, playing Little League ball, camping, and fishing with his family. They lived in the suburbs and had everything money could buy. But under Gary's skin, the blood ran dark and devious. During his college years, he took a shotgun and killed the only three people who had ever loved him—his parents and sister.

He was arrested, convicted, and sent to prison. He felt no remorse and described himself as an animal. One day a clergyman came to his prison and started talking about Jesus Christ. Gary cursed him and told him that if he got any closer to the bars that separated them, he would kill him. To his surprise, the preacher kept returning. But Gary continued to curse him at every opportunity. One day the minister gave Gary a small Gideon New Testament. Gary took the book, spat on it, threw it on the floor, and kicked it across the room and under his bunk.

Sometime later Gary Fossen grew unbelievably lonely and decided to kill himself. A former paramedic in a nearby cell told him how to cut himself with razor blades so that he would bleed freely and die quickly. They smuggled in a razor, and Gary waited for the lights to go out. He thought about writing a suicide note, but he realized no one would be interested. He had no one to mourn his death.

Then he remembered the little book under his bunk. He thought perhaps he should at least read a verse of Scripture before killing himself. He turned to Romans and started reading chapter 6. He went on to Romans 7 and 8. He said, "I had never read the Bible before, and the words started burning inside of me." He knelt by his bunk and began trying to pray. He asked God to show him how to be sorry because he still had no remorse. "That night I saw a slow-motion movie of my life," he later said. "I saw every wicked thing I had ever done, and I began to write them all down. The list went on for page after page, and I wept over each one. I had not cried at all after the murders, but here I was in my cell crying."

That night forever changed Gary Fossen. "I was still in prison, but it didn't matter. That was the end of the pain and loneliness. I would never be alone again. I am still in prison, but I thank God for His Word that is so powerful that it cut into the deep calluses of my heart and seared through all the layers of hate."[2]

Now ask yourself—can Shakespeare have such an effect? Can Homer or Milton? Or, for that matter, can the writings of Darwin? No. Charles Darwin once wrote a letter to a Christian minister named J. W. Fegan, who had conducted a preaching crusade in a village in England. As a result of Fegan's campaign, the alcoholics were converted and the bars closed down. Darwin wrote to Fegan saying, "We [the evolutionists] have never been able to reclaim a drunkard, but through your services I do not know that there is a drunkard left in the village."[3]

WITNESS 4: BOTEMBO ISAKO

The message of Christ not only transforms alcoholics in England and prisoners in America but soldiers in Africa. Botembo Isako abandoned his profession as an educator to become a soldier in Zaire. After basic training, he was assigned to a military police unit in Muanda. He lived an evil and immoral life, doing drugs and misusing his authority over civilians.

One day he was assigned to security detail at a soccer game. Being in charge of his unit, he sent his men inside the stadium while he remained outside, bullying people and forcing them to give him their watches, jewelry, and money. He approached a seventeen-year-old youth and searched him. The youth had nothing but a little book. In a rage, Botembo beat the boy until the lad finally managed to get free and run away, badly hurt and drenched in his own blood. But as he fled, he shouted back, "God bless you. May the Lord forgive you."

Botembo laughed. After the game he went home and surveyed his loot. He saw the little book and discovered it was a New Testament. He began to read it, and for the first time in his life, he started feeling guilty for his evil ways. He could hear the young man's voice, saying over and over, "God bless you. May the Lord forgive you."

The more he read the little book, the more he began to change. His family noticed, unsure what to make of it. Shortly afterward Botembo fell ill and was rushed to the hospital. There he continued to read his stolen New Testament until he finally crawled out of his hospital bed, knelt on the floor, and begged God for forgiveness. When he asked Jesus Christ to be his Savior, he said, "A truckload of guilt fell off my heart, and I turned my life over to God." That day he decided to leave the army, and today he is serving the Lord as a pastor in the Democratic Republic of Congo (Zaire), always on the lookout for a young man with a missing New Testament.[4]

What book had such an effect on this soldier? Was it written by a philosopher like Jean-Jacques Rousseau? By a skeptic like Voltaire? Was it written by an educator like John Dewey? Or by a psychoanalyst like Sigmund Freud? Or by an existentialist like Sören Kierkegaard?

WITNESS 5: JIM TUCKER

Only one message has been able to perpetually and profoundly transform human life for the good—and that is the Gospel. It has the power to revolutionize even the most incorrigible. Jim Tucker at age seven saw his beautiful red-haired mother brutally beaten and disfigured by a man who broke into their house and tried to kill her. When she was taken to the hospital, Jim was placed in a foster home. From there he went to juvenile halls, reform schools, and jails. He turned to drugs, alcohol, and crime, making it onto the FBI's most-wanted list. In 1956 at age twenty-two, he was sentenced to ninety years in prison, to no one's surprise. He was facing over six hundred counts of robbery and lawbreaking. When the prison's steel door slammed behind him, his heart nearly stopped; but he swallowed hard, resolving to be tougher and meaner than ever. Wherever he was placed, he staged one-man riots—taking on five or six guards at a time, destroying cells, starting fires, attacking and maiming other inmates. His chest was fifty-four inches, his waist was thirty-two inches, and he could press four hundred pounds. They called him "The Animal."

He was beaten, counseled, and often injected with powerful doses of mind-bending drugs administered by four combat-equipped guards wearing special boots, who would charge into his cell carrying a mattress in front of them to pin him to the wall. He received electroshock therapy, and time after time he was thrown into the "hole"—a solitary, sound-proof five-by-eight-foot steel-doored box with no bed, no mattress, no bathroom facilities, nothing but a drain in the floor. No one was supposed to be there more than twenty-nine days, but they kept Jim Tucker there for as long as three years straight.

In all, Tucker spent twenty-seven years in confinement, never receiving one letter except a telegram handed to him by a taunting guard telling him of his brother's death.

He was finally released from prison, but he immediately started getting into trouble again, and the nightmare began repeating itself. He went to the top of a tall building, but could not bring himself to jump. He went back to his room and pulled a Bible from the dresser drawer. He opened it and started reading about the love of God. He began to cry. In all his years of confinement and prison, he had never cried, but now like a little child, he fell asleep crying and clutching the Bible.

Through the message of that book, his life was changed. Then he went to prison again—this time not as a prisoner, but as a preacher. With a burden for those behind bars, he now visits the jails telling the inmates, "No one wanted me . . . but God!"[5]

No one is beyond the power and influence of the Gospel, and no one is hopeless in God's sight. The Lord is in the business of transforming the heartless and giving hope to the hopeless.

WITNESS 6: JACOB KOSHY

We started this chapter with Paul's conversion, and we will also end there, in a manner of speaking. Jacob Koshy grew up in Singapore with one driving ambition: to be a success in life, to gain all the money and possessions he could. That led him into the world of drugs and gambling, and eventually he became a one-man international smuggling network. In 1980 he was arrested and placed in a government drug rehabilitation prison in Singapore.

He was frustrated beyond endurance. All his goals, purposes, dreams, and ambitions were locked up with him in a tiny cell, and in his heart was a cold emptiness. He was a smoker, and cigarettes were not allowed in the center. So he smuggled in tobacco and rolled it in the pages of a Gideon Bible. One day he fell asleep while smoking. He awoke to find that the cigarette had burned out, and all that remained was a scrap of charred paper. He unrolled it and read what was written there: "Saul, Saul, why do you persecute me?"

Jacob asked for another Bible and read the entire story of the conversion of Saul of Tarsus. He suddenly realized that if God could help someone like Saul, God could help him, too. There in his cell he knelt and prayed, asking Christ to come into his life and change him. He began crying and could not stop. The tears of a wasted life washed away his pain, and God redeemed him. He started sharing his story with the other prisoners, and as soon as he was released, he became involved in a church. He met a Christian woman, married, and is now a missionary in the Far East where he tells people far and wide, "Who would have believed that I could find the truth by smoking the Word of God?"[6]

What other book possesses such power?

SUMMARY

These people are but representatives of millions upon millions, many of whom have freely laid down their lives for Christ and His kingdom.

> No other religion, no other philosophy, gives a man so much to live for as Christianity. For this reason Christianity has a record of martyrology absolutely without comparison in the history of religions. Every religion has produced a Socrates here and there willing to drink poison hemlock, or a Buddha willing to forsake wealth and fortune for religious ideals. But where is the stream of martyrs like unto Christianity? What other devotees have been burned, tortured, torn asunder, and in many other diabolical ways have had their flesh baptized by excruciating pain, and yet have suffered it with words of forgiveness on their lips, with hymns of glory sung up to the last minute, with faces beaming and glowing amid smoke and torture, amid bleeding flesh and scorched limbs? And why do they so die? Because Christ has given them so much to live for that they choose to live for Christ and die, rather than deny Christ and live.[7]

Other religions and philosophies may modify behavior, but only Christianity transforms a person's character from the inside out. Only Christianity makes old sinners into new creatures by renewing their minds (Rom. 12:2). Only Christianity offers a never-ending parade of witnesses, millions upon millions, from every tongue and tribe, spanning every era since the cross, covering every age and race, who gladly say, "Come and see! Come and meet the Master. Come and let me tell you how He changed my life."

I should know. I am one among the untold millions whose lives have been touched by the Master's hand. I hope you, too, are among those who have learned that, yes . . .

. . . it works.

FOR FURTHER DISCUSSION

1. What is the value of one's personal testimony in apologetics? Discuss how you would answer someone who countered, "But all religions have people with testimonials. That isn't unique to Christianity. Personal testimonies don't prove anything."
2. The stories in this chapter are those of dramatic conversions. What if your story is not as "exciting" as someone else's. Is it less miraculous? Less valuable? Or more so?

FOR APPLICATION

1. In your group ask the participants to share their own stories of how Christ changed their lives.
2. Write out your own personal testimony and practice sharing it. Become comfortable enough to relate it casually and easily to a friend or stranger when the opportunity presents itself.
3. Collect conversion stories. Notice the variety of ways in which people have found Christ as their Savior.

Chapter Twelve

EXHIBIT F: THE EXPERIENCE OF CHRISTIANITY

The Absence of Alternatives

COLUMBA, SIXTH-CENTURY Irish missionary, harbored a passion and vision for the world. He established a missionary training school on the bleak island of Iona off the coast of Scotland, and he kept the burden of missions alive at the onset of the medieval age. One of Columba's missionaries, according to an ancient story, took the Gospel to Northumbria, and there the local tribal king called together his wise men and chiefs to consider the matter. "Should we hear the Gospel or not?" he asked. There was great debate, but one of the wise men finally brought the discussion around to this: "Our life is like the flight of a bird through our lighted hall," he said. "In comes the bird out of the dark, flies about a little while in the light of our torches, then flies out again into the dark. So with us. We come out of the dark and go into the dark. If these strangers can tell us anything better, let us listen."[1]

That pagan chieftain of 1,400 years ago put his finger on a great apologetic for Christianity. How do we know Christianity is true? Because if it is not, we are nothing more than frightened birds who come out of the dark and flutter around frantically before returning to a cold, black void. The well-known Calvinist apologist Cornelius Van Til bases his defense of Christianity on this very thing—all other theologies and philosophies lead inexorably to darkness and despair. All other philosophies, followed to their logical ends, lead to chaos and irrationality. Only Christianity gives meaning to life. One can be both consistent in mind and happy in spirit only with theism in general and Christianity in particular.

This is a great argument for truth. A truth-claim must be subjected to the test of experiential relevance. Does it work? Does it satisfy? Does it relate meaningfully to life? With other philosophies, you can be either consistent or happy, but not both. Christianity is the only belief system that allows a person to be both logically consistent and spiritually happy.

ECCLESIASTES

The Bible's case for this truth-claim is made in the book of Ecclesiastes, written by Solomon during a time of doubt and disbelief. The great king-philosopher turned from God, searching for meaning and significance in other pursuits. But he was disappointed and disillusioned at every point: "The words of the Teacher, son of David, king in Jerusalem: 'Meaningless! Meaningless!' says the Teacher. 'Utterly meaningless! Everything is meaningless!'" (Eccl. 1:1-2).

The philosopher experimented with various virtues and vices, seeking satisfaction. He tried education, but he described godless education as "a chasing after the wind" (Eccl. 1:17). He tried pleasure, "but that also proved to be meaningless" (2:1). He turned to alcohol. He gave himself to materialism, building a palatial home for himself. He instituted great public works, achieving fame and renown. But nothing filled his heart, and he instinctively knew why. He admitted in Ecclesiastes 3:11 that God has set "eternity in the hearts of men." God has made us for Himself and for eternity. He has created us in His own image to enjoy Him forever. All other pursuits end in that famous refrain of the Rolling Stones: "I Can't Get No Satisfaction."

Several years ago I had lunch with a businessman on Nashville's West End. He personified success, an entrepreneur whose neatly-trimmed beard matched his well-tailored clothes. But his aching eyes betrayed him. He spoke of his failed marriages and thriving career, admitting, "I've gone through women like water, and through money like sand. What can fill the gaps in my heart?"

The French physicist Blaise Pascal said, "There is a God-shaped vacuum in the heart of every man which cannot be filled by any created thing, but only by God the Creator made known through Jesus Christ."[2]

THE LINE OF DESPAIR

One of the great Christian minds of the twentieth century was Francis Schaeffer. As a young man, he grew up in a liberal church that believed nothing of substance in the Bible. He decided on the basis of what he was hearing that the only logical philosophy in life was agnosticism or perhaps atheism. As an agnostic, he started reading the Bible to compare it to the Greek philosophers. He had no thought of becoming a Christian, but as he read the Bible, he saw its logical consistency and the way Scripture alone answered the problems of life. He became a Christian and years later wrote a book titled *He Is There and He Is Not Silent*. In that book, he said:

> There is no other sufficient philosophical answer. You can search through university philosophy, underground philosophy, filling station philosophy—it does not matter which—there is no other sufficient philosophical answer to existence. There is only one philosophy, one religion, that fills this need in all the world's thought, whether the East, the West, the ancient, the modern, the new, the old. Only one fills the philosophical need of existence, of being, and it is the Judeo-Christian God—not just an abstract concept, but rather that this God is really there. He really exists. It is not that this is the best answer to existence; it is the only answer. That is why we may hold our Christianity with intellectual integrity.[3]

Schaeffer goes on to say that when you abandon God and Jesus Christ, you cross a frightening and ultimate line of despair. That, he says, is where our postmodern world is now living—below the line of despair.

Several years ago while traveling in Brazil, I saw graffiti scrawled across a building, written in Portuguese. I asked my guide what it said, and these were the words: "We are beautiful drunkards, comets wandering alone, looking at the stars, waiting for a future that doesn't come."

NIETZSCHE

No philosopher has a sadder life story than the German thinker Friedrich W. Nietzsche. He grew up in a Christian home. Both his grandfathers had been Christian ministers, and his father was a Lutheran pastor. But Nietzsche rejected Christianity and went on to formulate his famous "Death of God" philosophy.

When Nietzsche said God is dead, he did not mean that a literal God had literally died. He meant that in Western civilization belief in God was dead. Western philosophers no longer accepted God or sought to obey Him. He was saying that as far as Western philosophy is concerned, God just does not exist anymore. Christianity has been replaced by humanism as the cornerstone of Western thought. Nietzsche's famous parable about this is called *The Madman*.

Nietzsche said that a madman appeared in the marketplace one morning, holding a lighted lantern in the bright daylight. He startled everyone by crying, "I'm looking for God! I'm looking for God!"

The people made fun of him. They said, "Do you think God got lost? Do you think He's hiding?"

But the madman ran into the midst of the people, his eyes wild with alarm. He said, "Where is God? I'll tell you where he is. We have killed Him—you and I. All of us are His murderers. We have cut ourselves off from God as though we had unchained the earth from the sun, and we are wobbling out of control, plunging backward, sideward, forward, in all directions. We're becoming cold and dark and empty. Don't you feel it?"

And then Nietzsche asked a profound question: "How shall we, the murderers of all murderers, comfort ourselves?" Nietzsche understood the implication of what he was advocating. He was saying that in removing God from our civilization, our life, and our philosophy, we were removing our source of comfort. We were stripping ourselves of hope and peace. We were crossing the line of despair.

Nietzsche understood that when you abandon Christianity, you lose all basis for moral absolutes. You lose all basis for eternal life. You lose all basis for inner peace. But he thought that after an initial time of chaos and despair, his God-is-dead philosophy would pave the way for a great superman to come and take charge of the human race, someone who could lead humanity to its zenith.

What happened to Nietzsche? The insanity he predicted for the world came upon himself. He could not live with his own beliefs, and he became increasingly irrational. One day he collapsed on a street in Turin and was taken to an asylum. For the last twelve years of his life, he was insane, becoming himself a madman. Ironically, he was cared for by a devoted Christian—his mother.[4]

But there is more to the story. Nietzsche's philosophy not only led to his personal insanity; it led to the insanity of the Nazi Holocaust, and the superman he predicted for the world was personified in the person of one of his greatest disciples—Adolf Hitler.

Ravi Zacharias in his book *Can Man Live Without God?* wrote, "There is nothing in history to match the dire ends to which humanity can be led by following a political and social philosophy that consciously and absolutely excludes God."[5] He says, "I, for one, see Nietzsche's life and death as a blueprint for where we are headed inexorably as a nation."[6]

THE DEATH OF PHILOSOPHY

William Lane Craig, a brilliant Christian philosopher and apologist, put it this way: "Modern man thought that when he had gotten rid of

God, he had freed himself from all that repressed and stifled him. Instead, he discovered that in killing God, he had also killed himself."[7]

Why? Because only Christianity provides a comprehensive explanation for the reality of death and a satisfying answer for the problem of death. Only Christianity has authenticated its message about death by providing a leader who actually rose from the tomb. The world has never found another answer to death, and therefore death is the death of philosophy. All non-Christian belief systems crash and burn when they come to the subject of death.

I have never read a better summation of this idea than Craig's. He states with terrible eloquence the logical implications of rejecting Christianity:

> I realize I am going to die, and forever cease to exist. My life is just a momentary transition out of oblivion into oblivion [like the pagan's fluttering bird, out of the darkness, into the darkness]. And the universe, too, faces death. Scientists tell us that the universe is expanding, and everything in it is growing farther and farther apart. As it does so, it grows colder and colder, and its energy is used up. Eventually all the stars will burn out, and all matter will collapse into dead stars and black holes. There will be no light at all; there will be no heat; there will be no life; only the corpses of dead stars and galaxies, ever expanding into the endless darkness and the cold recesses of space—a universe in ruins. The entire universe marches irreversibly toward its grave. So not only is the life of each individual person doomed; the entire human race is doomed. The universe is plunging toward inevitable extinction—death is written throughout its structure. There is no escape. There is no hope.
>
> Look at it from another perspective: Scientists say that the universe originated in an explosion called the "Big Bang" about fifteen billion years ago. Suppose the Big Bang had never occurred. Suppose the universe had never existed. What ultimate difference would it make? The universe is doomed to die anyway. In the end it makes no difference whether the universe ever existed or not. Therefore, it is without ultimate significance.
>
> The same is true for the human race. Mankind is a doomed race in a dying universe. Because the human race will eventually cease to exist, it makes no ultimate difference whether it ever did exist. Mankind is thus no more significant than a swarm of mosquitoes or a barnyard of pigs, for their end is all the same. The same blind cosmic process that coughed them up in the first place will eventually swallow them all again.

And the same is true for each individual person. The contributions of the scientist to the advance of human knowledge, the researches of the doctor to alleviate pain and suffering, the efforts of the diplomat to secure peace in the world, the sacrifices of good men everywhere to better the lot of the human race—all these come to nothing. In the end they don't make one bit of difference, not one bit. Each person's life is therefore without ultimate significance. And because our lives are ultimately meaningless, the activities we fill our lives with are also meaningless. The long hours spent in study at the university, our jobs, our interests, our friendships—all these are, in the final analysis, utterly meaningless. This is the horror of modern man; because he ends in nothing, he is nothing.[8]

HOPE

If there is no God, there is nothing but despair. If there is no Christ, we are of all people most miserable. Perhaps that is why there is so much alcoholism in our society today and such rampant drug dependence. That is why we are flooded by sexual images and why the entertainment industry is such a global phenomenon. That is why the movie box office is such a symbol of our weekends and why we want five hundred channels on our television cable. Modern humanity can live with neither itself nor its despair, so it drowns itself in diversions.

But the diversions do not provide real spiritual satisfaction, and that is why non-Christian worldviews make it impossible to live both consistently and happily. Bertrand Russell, for example, admitted that life without God is absurd; but he said we have no choice but to put a good face to it. He claimed we must build our lives on the firm foundation of unyielding despair. We must recognize life's absurdity and then love one another.

If you really live a life consistent with that philosophy, happiness is impossible. If you live happily, it is because you are inconsistent. The antitheistic worldview has built-in logical contradictions and existential inadequacies that ultimately make it philosophically unlivable. Without Christ, "a philosophy of meaninglessness is an unavoidable consequence."[9] The apostle Paul said that if Christ has not risen from the dead, we are to be pitied; we are of all people most miserable.

"But," Paul continued, "Christ *has* indeed been raised from the dead, the firstfruits of those who have fallen asleep" (1 Cor. 15:20, emphasis mine). There is a philosophy that satisfies the soul. There is a theology that strengthens the heart. There is a Gospel! There is Good News!

Solomon ended Ecclesiastes by declaring that there is an answer to meaninglessness and despair. After searching all the philosophies, spec-ulations, and pursuits of mankind, he came to this conclusion: "Fear God and keep his commandments, for this is the whole duty of man" (Eccl. 12:13).

SUMMARY

Why do we believe Christianity is true? Not only because of the reality of the Resurrection. Not only because of the complexity of creation. Not only because of fulfilled prophecy, the wonder of Scripture, and the uniqueness of Christ. Not only because of the reliability of the biblical documents and the evidence of archaeology. Not only because of Christianity's remarkable ability to transform lives. But because, in the final analysis, all other philosophies, if followed to their logical ends, lead to chaos and irrationality. Only Christianity gives meaning to life. Only with theism in general and Christianity in particular can one be both consistent and happy. As the psalmist said three thousand years ago, "My soul finds rest in God alone" (Ps. 62:1).

Jesus said, "I am the way and the truth and the life. No one comes to the Father except through me" (John 14:6). He also said, "The thief comes only to steal and kill and destroy; I have come that they may have life, and have it to the full" (John 10:10).

Jesus said, "I am the resurrection and the life. He who believes in me will live, even though he dies; and whoever lives and believes in me will never die" (John 11:25-26). Also He said, "Because I live, you also will live" (John 14:19).

If you have never had a personal experience with Jesus Christ, why not follow the evidence where it leads—to the foot of Calvary's cross. Commit your life to Jesus Christ. Place your faith in His shed blood and glorious resurrection. For these things are written, said John, "that you may believe that Jesus is the Christ, the Son of God, and that by believing you may have life in his name" (John 20:31).

FOR FURTHER DISCUSSION

1. Explain the phrase "death is the death of philosophy." From your own experience, give examples of people who have faced death with Christ compared to those who have been without Christ.
2. Late at night when thoughts and fear trouble your heart, what verses of Scripture come to mind? Can you give a specific example of the power of Scripture to comfort the soul?

FOR APPLICATION

1. From an encyclopedia or biography, prepare a sketch of Nietzsche. Some say his insanity was caused by venereal disease. If true, in what ways did his personal values and philosophy contribute to his mental illness?

2. Prepare a report on the life of Francis Schaeffer or C. S. Lewis. Compare with Nietzsche.

3. Memorize 1 Peter 3:15. In what ways does the content of this chapter relate to the content of that verse?

THE STEP OF FAITH

CHRISTIAN EVIDENCES (including those discussed in this book) demonstrate Christianity to be true beyond reasonable doubt. Yet there remains a step of faith. We conclude our studies with three observations about the nature of this faith.

First, the step of faith is a reasonable one. Blaise Pascal, a brilliant French mathematician and physicist, was one of the finest apologists to articulate the reasonableness of Christianity. Pascal became a Christian and set to work on a book on apologetics. He died at age thirty-nine before writing the volume, but his notes were published under the title *Pensées.*

In the *Pensées,* Pascal formulated his "wager." He said that even if the probability of God's existence was no more than fifty-fifty, a logical person will "bet" in favor of God. For if he is wrong, he has lost nothing. He has, in fact, gained peace at least in this life. But if he is right, he has gained eternal peace and everlasting life. On the other hand, the man who "bets" against God runs the risk of despair in both this life and the life to come. Considering that the evidence for God's existence is far greater than fifty-fifty, faith in Christ is both reasonable and logical.

Second, faith in Christ involves personal commitment to Him. I have had the joy of leading many people to a saving knowledge of Christ. In almost every case, the seeker expressed his decision in prayer, praying something like this: "Dear God, I know I'm a sinner. I believe that You loved me enough to send Jesus Christ to die for my sin. I ask Him to become my Savior and Lord. Come into my life and help me to live as You want me to." It was not just intellectual assent but life commitment to Jesus Christ as Lord and Master.

Third, when a person takes such a step of faith, trusting Christ as Savior, the Holy Spirit comes into his or her heart, giving full assurance of salvation. The new Christian then knows that Christianity is true, not just because of a 99 percent degree of probability, but because of a 100 percent degree of inner assurance. Romans 8:16 says, "The Spirit himself testifies with our spirit that we are God's children." John wrote, "This is how we know that he lives in us: We know it by the Spirit he gave us" (1 John 3:24).

Christian evidences can never argue anyone into God's kingdom. It can answer questions and reinforce faith. But the decision to follow Christ is personal and spiritual and is a matter of both mind and heart.

If you have not trusted Christ as Savior, why not today?

If you have, why not pass it on?

NOTES

CHAPTER 1: THE EMPTY TOMB

1 Henry M. Morris, *Many Infallible Proofs* (San Diego: CLP Publishers, 1974; used by permission from Master Books, P. O. Box 727, Green Forest, AR 72638), 88.

2 William M. Ramsay, *St. Paul the Traveller and the Roman Citizen* (Grand Rapids: Baker Book House, 1982), xiii.

3 Ibid., 419.

4 Ibid., 420.

5 Wilbur M. Smith, *Therefore, Stand* (Chicago: Moody Press, 1945; Grand Rapids: Kregel Publications, 1981, used by permission), 400.

6 Morris, *Many Infallible Proofs*, 94.

7 Albert L. Roper, *Did Jesus Rise from the Dead?* (Grand Rapids: Zondervan Publishing House, 1965), Foreword.

8 Frank Morison, *Who Moved the Stone?* (London: Faber and Faber Ltd., 1958), 5.

CHAPTER 2: THE EYEWITNESSES

1 Josh McDowell, *The Resurrection Factor* (San Bernardino: Here's Life Publishers, Inc.), 2-7.

2 See also John 2:19; Matthew 12:38-42; Matthew 16:21; Matthew 17:22-23; Matthew 20:17-19; John 10:17-18.

3 Wilbur M. Smith, *Therefore, Stand* (Chicago: Moody Press, 1945; Grand Rapids: Kregel Publications, 1981, used by permission), 389-390.

4 John R. W. Stott, *Basic Christianity* (Grand Rapids: Eerdmans Publishing Co., 1969, used by permission), 57-59.

5 Mireille Hadas-Lebel, *Flavius Josephus* (New York: Macmillan, 1993), 225-227.

6 Stott, *Basic Christianity*, 45.

CHAPTER 3: THE EXISTENCE OF CREATION

1 Henry M. Morris and Gary E. Parker, *What Is Creation Science?* (San Diego: Creation-Life Publishers, Inc., 1982), Foreword.

2 Erik Larson, "Darwinian Struggle: Instead of Evolution, a Textbook Proposes 'Intelligent Design,'" *The Wall Street Journal*, November 14, 1994, A-1.

3 R. C. Sproul, *Not a Chance* (Grand Rapids: Baker Book House, 1994; used by permission), 12.

4 Quoted by Bill Durbin in "A Scientist Caught Between Two Faiths," *Christianity Today*, August 6, 1982, 14.

5 David Briggs, "Big Bang Findings Create Calm for Religion, Science," *The Nashville Banner*, April 24, 1992, A-7.

6 Henry M. Morris, *Many Infallible Proofs* (San Diego: CLP Publishers, 1974; used by permission from Master Books, P.O. Box 727, Green Forest, AR 72638), 101.

7 Ibid., 101-104.

8 Robert Wright, "Science, God and Man," *Time*, December 28, 1992, 40.

9 Hugh Ross, *Creation and Time* (Colorado Springs: NavPress, 1994; used by permission; for copies call 1-800-366-7788), 132-133.

10 Owen Gingerich, "Dare a Scientist Believe in Design?" in *Evidence of Purpose*, ed. John Marks Templeton (New York: The Continuum Publishing Group, 1994; copyright by Templeton Foundation, Inc. and Robert L. Herrmann; reprinted with permission), 24-26.

CHAPTER 4: THE COMPLEXITY OF CREATION

1 Quoted by Mark Hartwig in "Challenging Darwin's Myths," *Moody* Magazine, May 1995, 15.

2 Quoted in Phillip E. Johnson, *Darwin on Trial* (Downers Grove, Ill.: InterVarsity Press, 1993; reprinted by special permission of Regnery Publishing, Inc., Washington, D.C.), 10.

3 Garret Vanderkooi, "A Theistic Approach to Science" in *Evidence for Faith*, ed. John Warwick Montgomery (Dallas: Probe Books, 1991), 57.

4 William J. Cairney, "Biomedical Prescience 1" in *Evidence for Faith*, ed. Montgomery, 128.

5 For a more detailed study of this subject, see S. I. McMillen, *None of These Diseases* (Old Tappan, N.J.: Fleming H. Revell, 1984).

6 For a more detailed study of this subject, see David Breese, *Seven Men Who Rule the World from the Grave* (Chicago: Moody Press, 1990).

7 Ravi Zacharias, *Can Man Live Without God?* (Dallas: Word Publishing Co., 1994), xvii.

8 Hugh Ross, *The Creator and the Cosmos* (Colorado Springs: NavPress, 1993; used by permission; for copies call 1-800-366-7788), 13-17.

CHAPTER 5: HISTORICAL PROPHECY

1 George Park Fisher, *Manual of Christian Evidence* (New York: Charles Scribner's Sons, 1900), 95.

2 Moshe Davis, ed., *Israel: Its Role in Civilization*, (New York: Harper Brothers), 31, quoted in James and Marti Hefley, *Where in the World Are the Jews Today?* (Wheaton, Ill.: Victor, 1974), 7.

3 For further study, refer to the books for chapter 5 in the Bibliography at the end of this book.

CHAPTER 6: MESSIANIC PROPHECY

1 A. T. Pierson, *Many Infallible Proofs*, Vol. 2 (Grand Rapids: Zondervan Publishing House, n.d.), 15.

2 Peter Stoner and Robert C. Newman, *Science Speaks* (Chicago: Moody Press, 1976), 102-109.

3 Pierson, *Many Infallible Proofs*, Vol. 1, 33.

CHAPTER 7: THE UNEQUALED CHRIST

1 A. T. Pierson, *Many Infallible Proofs*, Vol. 2 (Grand Rapids: Zondervan Publishing House, n.d.), 48.

2 Will Durant, The Story of Civilization, Vol. 3, *Caesar and Christ* (New York: Simon and Schuster, 1972), 557.

3 Quoted by Paul E. Little in *Know Why You Believe* (Wheaton: Victor Books, 1978; used by permission of Chariot Victor Publishing), 39-40.

4 Pierson, *Many Infallible Proofs*, Vol. 2, 83, 88.

5 C. S. Lewis, *Mere Christianity* (New York: Macmillan, 1958; used by permission of HarperCollins, London), 41.

CHAPTER 8: THE SOLIDARITY OF SCRIPTURE

1 J. Sidlow Baxter, *The Master Theme of the Bible—Part 1: The Doctrine of the Lamb* (Wheaton, Ill.: Tyndale House Publishers, 1985), 19.
2 A. T. Pierson, *Many Infallible Proofs*, Vol. 1 (Grand Rapids: Zondervan Publishing House, n.d.), 90.
3 Jill Morgan, *A Man of the Word: Life of G. Campbell Morgan* (Grand Rapids: Baker Book House, 1972), 38-41.
4 Pierson, *Many Infallible Proofs*, Vol. 1, 124.
5 For a thorough study of this subject, see Baxter, *The Master Theme of the Bible— Part 1: The Doctrine of the Lamb.*

CHAPTER 9: THE RELIABILITY OF THE BIBLICAL DOCUMENTS

1 Gleason Archer, *A Survey of Old Testament Introduction* (Chicago: Moody Press, 1974), 25.
2 R. Laird Harris, "How Reliable Is the Old Testament Text?" in *Can I Trust the Bible?* ed. Howard F. Vos (Chicago: Moody Press, 1963), 124.
3 Two scholars, Carsten Peter Thiede and Matthew D'Ancona, have recently advanced the theory that three fragments of papyrus currently housed at Magdalen College, Oxford, can be dated even earlier. But their conclusions have been questioned. Their book *Eyewitness to Jesus* is published by Doubleday (New York, 1996) and is subjected to a critical review, "Indiana Jones and the Gospel Parchments," in *Christianity Today*, October 28, 1996, 26-27.
4 For a chart showing the manuscript evidence of the New Testament compared with other authors and works of antiquity, see Josh McDowell's *Evidence That Demands a Verdict* (San Bernardino: Here's Life Publishers, 1986).
5 A. Berkeley Mickelsen, "Is the Text of the New Testament Reliable?" in *Can I Trust the Bible?* ed. Vos, 176.

CHAPTER 10: THE EVIDENCE OF ARCHAEOLOGY

1 *Lost Civilizations: The Holy Land*, ed. Time-Life Books (Alexandria, Va.: Time-Life Books, 1992), 24.
2 Andre Lemaire, "'House of David' Restored in Moabite Inscription," *Biblical Archaeology Review*, May/June 1994, 31-32.
3 Jeffery L. Sheler, "The Mysteries of the Bible," *U.S. News and World Report*, April 17, 1995, 60-61. Also see the article "'David' Found at Dan," in *Biblical Archaeology Review*, March/April 1994.
4 Ibid., 63.
5 Charles R. Krahmalkov, "Exodus Itinerary Confirmed by Egyptian Evidence," *Biblical Archaeology Review*, September/October 1994, 58.
6 Gordon Grovier, "New Evidence for Israeli Exodus," *Christianity Today*, April 3, 1995, 87.
7 *Lost Civilizations: The Holy Land*, ed. Time-Life Books, 37.
8 Quoted in Josh McDowell, *Evidence That Demands a Verdict* (San Bernardino: Here's Life Publishers, 1986), 65.

CHAPTER 11: THE WITNESS OF CHANGED LIVES

1   Bernard Ramm, *Protestant Christian Evidences* (Chicago: Moody Press, 1953), 208.

2   Gary Fossen, "I Was a Cold-Blooded Murderer When Jesus Saved Me," *The Gideon*, June 1994, 25-26.

3   Ramm, *Protestant Christian Evidences*, 220.

4   Botembo Isako, "I Beat Him Up, but He Blessed Me," *Gideon Testimonies from International Extension Countries* (Nashville: The Gideons International, 1994), 75-77.

5   Jim Tucker, "No One Wanted Me . . . but God!" *The Gideon*, October 1993, 6-8.

6   Jacob Koshy, "From Smoking the Word to Speaking the Word," *Gideon Testimonies*, 59-60.

7   Ramm, *Protestant Christian Evidences*, 216.

CHAPTER 12: THE ABSENCE OF ALTERNATIVES

1   Julia H. Johnston, *Fifty Missionary Heroes Every Boy and Girl Should Know* (New York: Fleming H. Revell, 1913), 20-23.

2   Quoted in Bill Bright, *Jesus and the Intellectual* (San Bernardino: Campus Crusade for Christ, 1968), 14.

3   Francis A. Schaeffer, *He Is There and He Is Not Silent* (Wheaton, Ill.: Tyndale House Publishers, 1972; used by permission; all rights reserved), 13, 15.

4   *The Portable Nietzsche*, trans. Walter Kaufmann (New York: Viking Press, 1964), 95-96.

5   Ravi Zacharias, *Can Man Live Without God?* (Dallas: Word Publishing Co., 1994), xvii.

6   Ibid., 33.

7   William Lane Craig, *Reasonable Faith: Christian Truth and Apologetics* (Wheaton, Ill.: Crossway Books, 1994; used by permission), 57.

8   Ibid., 58-59.

9   Zacharias, *Can Man Live Without God?*, xvii.

BIBLIOGRAPHY

CHAPTER 1

Chapman, Colin. *The Case for Christianity.* Grand Rapids: Eerdmans Publishing Co., 1981.

McDowell, Josh. *Evidence That Demands a Verdict.* San Bernardino: Here's Life Publishers, 1986.

_____. *The Resurrection Factor.* San Bernardino: Here's Life Publishers, 1981.

Montgomery, John Warwick, ed. *Evidence for Faith.* Dallas: Probe Books, 1991.

Morison, Frank. *Who Moved the Stone?* London: Faber and Faber, Ltd., 1958.

Morris, Henry M. *Many Infallible Proofs.* San Diego: CLP Publishing Co., 1974.

Roper, Albert L. *Did Jesus Rise from the Dead?* Grand Rapids: Zondervan, 1965.

Smith, Wilbur M. *Therefore, Stand.* Chicago: Moody Press, 1945.

CHAPTER 2

Mullins, Edgar Y. *Why Is Christianity True?* Philadelphia: American Baptist Publication Society, 1905.

Stott, John R. W. *Basic Christianity.* Grand Rapids: Eerdmans Publishing Co., 1969.

CHAPTER 3

Ankerberg, John, and Weldon, John. *The Facts on Creation Vs. Evolution.* Eugene, Ore.: Harvest House Publishers, 1993.

Gish, Duane T. *The Amazing Story of Creation.* El Cajon, Calif.: Institute for Creation Research, 1990.

Johnson, Phillip E. *Darwin on Trial.* Downers Grove, Ill.: InterVarsity Press, 1993.

Kenyon, Dean, and Davis, Percival. *Of Pandas and People.* Mesquite, Texas: Haughton Publishing, 1993.

Lubenow, Marvin. *Bones of Contention: A Creationist Assessment of Human Fossils.* Grand Rapids: Baker Book House, 1992.

Morris, Henry M. *Biblical Creationism.* Grand Rapids: Baker Book House, 1993.

_____. *The Bible, Science, and Creation.* Lincoln, Neb.: Back to the Bible, 1991.

Morris, Henry M., and Parker, Gary. *What Is Creation Science?* San Diego: CLP Publishing Co., 1982.

Ross, Hugh. *Creation and Time.* Colorado Springs: NavPress, 1994.

_____. *The Creator and the Cosmos.* Colorado Springs: NavPress, 1993.

Stoner, Peter W., and Newman, Robert C. *Science Speaks.* Chicago: Moody Press, 1976.

Templeton, John Marks, ed. *Evidence of Purpose.* New York: Continuum, 1994.

CHAPTER 4

Breese, David. *Seven Men Who Rule the World from the Grave.* Chicago: Moody Press, 1990.

Ham, Ken. *The Lie: Evolution.* El Cajon, Calif.: Creation-Life Publishers, Master Books Division, 1987.

McMillen, S. I. *None of These Diseases.* Old Tappan, N.J.: Fleming H. Revell, 1984.

CHAPTER 5

McDowell, Josh. *Prophecy: Fact or Fiction.* San Bernardino: Here's Life Publishers, 1981.

Walvoord, John F. *Daniel: The Key to Prophetic Revelation.* Chicago: Moody Press, 1971.

_____. *Israel in Prophecy.* Grand Rapids: Zondervan, 1962.

_____. *The Nations in Prophecy.* Grand Rapids: Zondervan, 1967.

CHAPTER 6

Hengstenberg, E. W. *Christology of the Old Testament.* Grand Rapids: Kregel Publications, 1970.

Lockyer, Herbert. *All the Messianic Prophecies of the Bible.* Grand Rapids: Zondervan, 1973.

CHAPTER 7

Geisler, Norman. *Christian Apologetics.* Grand Rapids: Baker Book House, 1976.

Groothuis, Douglas. *Jesus in an Age of Controversy.* Eugene, Ore.: Harvest House Publishers, 1996.

Habermas, Gary R. *Ancient Evidence for the Life of Jesus.* Nashville: Thomas Nelson, 1984.

Lewis, C. S. *Mere Christianity.* New York: Macmillan, 1958.

McDowell, Josh. *More Than a Carpenter.* Wheaton, Ill.: Tyndale House Publishers, 1979.

Pierson, Arthur T. *Many Infallible Proofs,* Vol. 2. Grand Rapids: Zondervan, n.d.

Sanders, J. Oswald. *The Incomparable Christ.* Chicago: Moody Press, 1952.

CHAPTER 8

Baxter, J. Sidlow. *The Master Theme of the Bible*—Part 1: The Doctrine of the Lamb. Wheaton, Ill.: Tyndale House Publishers, 1985.

Pierson, Arthur T. *Many Infallible Proofs,* Vol. 1. Grand Rapids: Zondervan, n.d.

CHAPTER 9

Bruce, F. F. *The Books and the Parchments.* Westwood, N.J.: Fleming H. Revell, 1963.

Criswell, W. A. *Why I Preach That the Bible Is Literally True.* Nashville: Broadman Press, 1969.

Ryrie, Charles C. *Basic Theology.* Wheaton, Ill.: Victor Books, 1987.

Thiede, Carsten Peter, and D'Ancona, Matthew. *Eyewitness to Jesus.* New York: Doubleday, 1996.

CHAPTER 10

Archer, Gleason L. *A Survey of Old Testament Introduction.* Chicago: Moody Press, 1974.

Biblical Archaeological Review, a bi-monthly magazine published by the Biblical Archaeology Society, 3000 Connecticut Ave., NW, Suite 300, Washington, DC 20008. (Be aware that not every article in this magazine is written by an evangelical.)

Price, Randall. *Stones Cry Out.* Eugene, Ore.: Harvest House Publishers, 1997.

Vos, Howard F. *Archaeology in Bible Lands.* Chicago: Moody Press, 1977.

CHAPTER 11

Boyd, Gregory A., and Boyd, Edward K. *Letters from a Skeptic.* Wheaton, Ill.: Victor Books, 1994.

Lewis, Gordon R. *Testing Christianity's Truth Claims.* Chicago: Moody Press, 1974.

Ramm, Bernard. *Varieties of Christian Apologetics.* Grand Rapids: Baker Book House, 1961.

CHAPTER 12

Craig, William Lane. *Reasonable Faith*. Wheaton, Ill.: Crossway Books, 1994.

Schaeffer, Francis A. *Escape from Reason*. Downers Grove, Ill.: InterVarsity Press, 1968.

_____. *How Should We Then Live?* Old Tappan, N.J.: Fleming H. Revell, 1976.

_____. *The God Who Is There*. Downers Grove, Ill.: InterVarsity Press, 1968.

Zacharias, Ravi. *Can Man Live Without God?* Dallas: Word Publishing, 1994.

CONCLUSION

Pascal, Blaise. *Pensées*. Trans. Alban J. Krailsheimer. New York: Viking-Penguin, 1995.

Since 1930

Evangelical Training Association

THE MINISTRIES OF EVANGELICAL TRAINING ASSOCIATION (ETA)

Experienced – Founded in 1930.
Doctrinally Dependable – Conservative and evangelical theology.
Educationally Sound – Engaging all adult learning styles.
Thoroughly Field-Tested – Used by a global constituency.
Recommended – Officially endorsed by denominations and schools.
Ministry Driven – Committed to quality training resources for equipping lay volunteers to serve Christ more effectively in the church.
Affordable – Attractive and reasonably priced.

For many local ministries, the most important step to an effective lay leadership training program is locating and implementing an inspiring, motivational system of instruction. ETA curriculum is available as traditional classroom courses, audio and video seminars, audio and video CD-ROM packages, and other resources for your classroom teaching or personal study.

Contact ETA today for free information and a 20-minute video presentation. Request Information Packet: Crossway Partner.

EVANGELICAL TRAINING ASSOCIATION
110 Bridge Street • PO Box 327 • Wheaton, IL 60189
800-369-8291 • FAX 630-668-8437 • www.etaworld.org